Football in Northern Ireland

a statistical record

1881 to 2005

Alexander Graham

INTRODUCTION

This book features a statistical history of football in Ireland from 1881 to 1920 and of Northern Ireland from 1920 to 2005. More precisely, this follows the clubs who were members of the Irish Football Association and Irish League formed initially to cover the whole of Ireland but which continued to oversee football in Northern Ireland after the partition of the country in 1921.

The Irish Football Association was founded on the 18th November, 1880 at a meeting in the Queen's Hotel in Belfast presided over by Mr John Sinclair. The original idea had come from Mr John McAlery (founder of Cliftonville FC, Ireland's first football club in 1879), who was intrigued after seeing football being played while on his honeymoon in Edinburgh in 1878. Mr McAlery arranged for a challenge match between local players from Belfast and a selection of players from Scottish clubs Queen's Park FC and Caledonian FC. This match was played on 24th October, 1878 at Ulster Cricket Ground, Ballynafeigh and was won 3-1 by the Scots.

The meeting of 18th November, 1880 was attended by representatives of Belfast clubs Avoniel FC, Cliftonville FC, Distillery FC, Knock FC, Oldpark FC and also Alexander FC (Limavady) and Moyola Park FC (Castledawson). Major Spencer Chichester was appointed as the first president of the Association and Mr McAlery as the first secretary. Having formed an official association the next step was to introduce an official tournament and the draw for the inaugural Irish F.A. Cup was made on 10th January, 1881 with the above named clubs as entrants. The entrance fee for the IFA Cup was 1/- (one shilling = 5 pence in today's currency) which was the same as the annual fee for membership of the IFA.

Following the success of the Irish Cup, the Irish League was formed in 1890 with Mr W. McNeice as the first president. The founding members of this league were: Clarence FC, Cliftonville FC, Distillery FC, Glentoran FC, Linfield FC, Milford FC (Armagh), Oldpark FC, Ulster FC. All the clubs were based in the city of Belfast except for Milford FC whose home town was Armagh. Football in Ireland remained strictly an amateur affair until 1894 when a vote in favour of professionalism was passed with a 64–30 majority at the IFA annual meeting, a similar motion having been previously defeated since first proposed in 1882.

In 1920 all clubs from the south of Ireland resigned from the Irish League and the Irish FA to join the newly formed Irish Free State FA and Irish Free State League, today's Football Association of Ireland (Republic of Ireland). As the majority of the members of the Irish League were located in Northern Ireland, this did not prove to be a problem and the League continued much the same as before with the number of members increasing in subsequent years. The first major change to the League structure occurred in 1995 when the League was split into two divisions – the "Irish Premier League" and the "First Division" – both are covered in this book. In 1999, a "Second Division" was also added to the League structure and promotion/relegation occurs as standard between these three divisions.

In addition to the results of Irish League matches, Final League tables and Irish Cup results, this book also lists the top goal-scorers for each season, where known.

Most of the information in this book is taken from the now defunct "Statistical History of Football" series which were published by Skye Soccer Books. As in the original series, the full names of clubs are used whenever possible with name-changes, mergers etc. shown as and when they occur. The club names are listed in the following format: Club Name (Home Town/City/Village).

The information contained in this book has been gathered over a number of years and has come from myriad sources although most was collected through personal contacts. Other sources of information include newspapers, magazines, books etc. and in more recent times the internet. I would like to extend my thanks to all those who helped with the collection of this information, particularly Marshall Gillespie who was able to provide some missing information.

In an attempt to ensure accuracy, the information has been checked and collated. However, if any errors are found, readers are invited to notify the author care of the address below and if possible provide the corrected information.

Alex Graham

British Library Cataloguing in Publication Data

A catalogue record for this book is available from the British Library

ISBN 1-86223-136-2

Copyright © 2005, SOCCER BOOKS LIMITED. (01472 696226)   www.soccer-books.co.uk
72 St. Peter's Avenue, Cleethorpes, N.E. Lincolnshire, DN35 8HU, England

All rights are reserved. No part of this publication may be reproduced, stored in a retrieval system or transmitted, in any form or by any means, electronic, mechanical, photocopying, recording, or otherwise, without the prior written permission of Soccer Books Limited.

Printed by 4Edge Limited.

1881

IRISH CUP FINAL   (Cliftonville Ground, Belfast – 09/04/1881 – 1,500)
MOYOLA PARK FC (CASTLEDAWSON)   1-0   Cliftonville FC (Belfast)
Morrow   *(H.T. 0-0)*

Moyola: Mackrell, Hewison, Dowd, McLernon, McSwiggan, R.Redmond, McKenna, W.J. Houston, T. Houston, M. Redmond, Morrow.

Cliftonville: Kennedy, Howell, McAlery, Martin, Baird, R.M.C. Potts, Davidson, Beyer, Williams, McKeague, Hannay.

Semi-finals
Knock FC (Belfast)	2-2, 1-2	Cliftonville FC (Belfast)
Moyola Park FC (Castledawson)	3-0	Alexander FC (Limavady)

Round 1
Knock FC (Belfast)	11-0	Distillery FC (Belfast)
Moyola Park FC (Castledawson)	2-0	Avoniel FC (Belfast)
Oldpark FC (Belfast)	0-2	Cliftonville FC (Belfast)

Alexander FC (Limavady) received a bye

1881-82

IRISH CUP FINAL   (Ulster Ground, Ballynafeigh, Belfast – 13/05/1882 – 2,000)
QUEEN'S ISLAND FC (BELFAST)   1-0   Cliftonville FC (Belfast)
Bell

Queen's Island: W. Gilmour, Gouk, Cunningham, Orr, J. Gilmour, Kerr, Stewart, Bell, Drummond, McMillan, Monroe.

Cliftonville: Parlane, Hull, McAlery, Martin, Baird, Hannay, R.M.C. Potts, Davidson, Jackson, Spiller, Waring.

Semi-finals
Cliftonville FC (Belfast)	1-1, 0-0, 2-0	Avoniel FC (Belfast)
Queen's Island FC (Belfast)	w/o	Castlederg FC (Castlederg)

Round 1
Avoniel FC (Belfast)	1-1, 3-1, 1-0	Distillery FC (Belfast)
(A replay was ordered after a protest that the 2nd match was ended 4 minutes early)		
Castlederg FC (Castlederg)	2-1	Banbridge FC (Banbridge)
Knock FC (Belfast)	0-2	Cliftonville FC (Belfast)
Moyola Park FC (Castledawson)	1-1, 1-2	Queen's Island FC (Belfast)

1882-83

IRISH CUP FINAL (Bloomfield Ground, Belfast – 05/05/1883 – 2,000)
CLIFTONVILLE FC (BELFAST) 5-0 Ulster FC (Belfast)
J. Potts 1, McWha 2, Davison (H.T. 3-0)
Cliftonville: Houston, McAlery, Browne, Hannay, Martin, Davidson, McWha, R.M.C. Potts, J.T. Potts, Dill, Spiller.
Ulster: McCracken, Watson, Hamilton, Hastings, Elliott, Williams, J. Reid, J. Johnston, Jackson, Waring, Andrews.

Semi-finals

Cliftonville FC (Belfast)	7-0	Alexander FC (Limavady)
Ulster FC (Belfast)	4-1	Queen's Island FC (Belfast)

Quarter-finals

Alexander FC (Limavady) 1-0, 1-0 Strabane FC (Strabane)
(The result of the 1st match was changed to 0-0 after a protest)
Distillery FC (Belfast) 1-2, 0-1 Queen's Island FC (Belfast)
(The result of the 1st match changed to 1-1 after a protest)
Moyola Park FC (Castledawson) 0-1 (aet) Cliftonville FC (Belfast)
Ulster FC (Belfast) received a bye

1883-84

IRISH CUP FINAL (Ulster Ground, Ballynafeigh, Belfast – 19/04/1884 – 2,000)
DISTILLERY FC (BELFAST) 5-0 Wellington Park FC (Belfast)
Hogg 2, Stewart 2, S. Johnston (H.T. 3-0)
Distillery: Millar, M. Wilson, R. Wilson, Baxter, W. Crone, McClatchey, Hogg, S. Johnston, J. Johnston, Condy, Stewart.
Wellington: McCarroll, Gibb, King, Elliott, Hazlett, Herd, Totton, Dodds, Gibb, McCoull, McCashin.

Semi-finals

Distillery FC (Belfast)	3-0	Ulster FC (Belfast)
Wellington Park FC (Belfast)	4-2	Moyola Park FC (Castledawson)

Quarter-finals

Distillery FC (Belfast)	1-0	Cliftonville FC (Belfast)
Moyola Park FC (Castledawson)	2-0	Alexander FC (Limavady)
Wellington Park FC (Belfast)	w/o	Dublin Association (Dublin)
Ulster FC (Belfast) received a bye		

1884-85

IRISH CUP FINAL   (Ulster Ground, Ballynafeigh, Belfast – 21/03/1885 – 2,000)

DISTILLERY FC (BELFAST)	3-0	Limavady FC (Limavady)
(Johnston 2, Rankine)	*(H.T. 2-0)*	

Distillery: Millar, Cunningham, Wilson, W. Crone, Baxter, McClatchey, Hogg, S. Johnston, Beattie, Sinclair, Stewart.

Limerick: Rankin, Jack Sherrard, Devine, Douglas, Allen, Ferguson, Joe Sherrard, McLean, Magennis, Connell, Doyle.

Semi-finals

Limavady FC (Limavady)	2-1	Cliftonville FC (Belfast)

Distillery FC (Belfast) received a bye

Quarter-finals

Distillery FC (Belfast)	1-0	Oldpark FC (Belfast)
Hertford FC (Lisburn)	0-1	Limavady FC (Limavady)

Cliftonville FC (Belfast) received a bye

1885-86

IRISH CUP FINAL   (Ulster Ground, Ballynafeigh, Belfast – 27/03/1886 – 1,000)

DISTILLERY FC (BELFAST)	1-0	Limavady FC (Limavady)
J. Johnston	*(H.T. 0-0)*	

Distillery: Page, M. Wilson, R. Wilson, Baxter, W. Crone, McClatchey, McArthur, S. Johnston, J. Johnston, Bell, Condy.

Limerick: Fleming, Jack Sherrard, Devine, M. Douglas, Allen, Phillips, Joe Sherrard, Fleming, R. Douglas, Ferguson, McLean.

Semi-finals

Distillery FC (Belfast)	4-0	Dublin University AFC (Dublin)
Limavady FC (Limavady)	1-0	Belfast Y.M.C.A. (Belfast)

Quarter-finals

Dublin University FC (Dublin)	6-0	Banbridge FC (Banbridge)
Limavady FC (Limavady)	6-0	Moyola Park FC (Castledawson)

Belfast Y.M.C.A. (Belfast) and Distillery FC (Belfast) both received byes

1886-87

IRISH CUP FINAL   (Distillery Ground, Broadway, Belfast – 12/02/1887 – 4,000)

ULSTER FC (BELFAST)	3-1	Cliftonville FC (Belfast)
Mears, Jack Reid, Watson	*(H.T. 3-1)*	*Turner*

Ulster: Barclay, Fox, Watson, Moore, Hastings, Campbell, Miller, E. Reid, Jack Reid, John Reid, Mears.

Cliftonville: Phillips, Browne, Stewart, Molyneux, Rosbotham, Baxter, Turner, Dobbin, Barry, Ferguson, Elleman.

Semi-finals

Cliftonville FC (Belfast)	2-0	Limavady FC (Limavady)
Ulster FC (Belfast)	2-1	Glentoran FC (Belfast)

Quarter-finals

Cliftonville FC (Belfast)	10-1	St. Malachy's College FC (Belfast)
Glentoran FC (Belfast)	2-1	Distillery FC (Belfast)
Millmount FC (Banbridge)	0-5	Limavady FC (Limavady)
Ulster FC (Belfast)	2-2, 3-2	Belfast Y.M.C.A. (Belfast)

1887-88

IRISH CUP FINAL   (Ulster Ground, Ballynafeigh, Belfast – 17/03/1888 – 3,000)

CLIFTONVILLE FC (BELFAST)	2-1	Distillery FC (Belfast)
Barry, Gibb	*(H.T. 1-1)*	*Stanfield*

Cliftonville: Clugston, Browne, Wilson, Williamson, Rosbotham, Molyneux, Elleman, Gibb, Barry, McPherson, Turner.

Distillery: Irwin, R. Crone, Ritchie, W. Crone, Spencer, Crawford, McClatchey, Stanfield, McManus, Stewart, Johnston.

Semi-finals

Cliftonville FC (Belfast)	5-0	Linfield Athletic FC (Belfast)
Distillery FC (Belfast)	3-1	Oldpark FC (Belfast)

Quarter-finals

Limavady FC (Limavady	3-3, 5-3	Cliftonville FC (Belfast)
Oldpark FC (Belfast)	1-1, 3-2	Mount Collyer FC (Belfast)
Ulster FC (Belfast)	0-2	Distillery FC (Belfast)

Linfield Athletic FC (Belfast) received a bye

1888-89

IRISH CUP FINAL   (Ulster Ground, Ballynafeigh, Belfast – 16/03/1889 – 3,500)

DISTILLERY FC (BELFAST)   5-4   Belfast Y.M.C.A. (Belfast)
R.Stewart 2, McClatchey 2, Stanfield   *Lemon 2, Millar, Small*

Distillery: Galbraith, R. Crone, Ritchie, W. Crone, Spencer, Crawford, McClatchey, Stanfield, R. Stewart, W. Stewart, McIlvenny.

Belfast: Pinkerton, Ervine, Watson, E. Reid, Leslie, Cooke, Dalton, Small, Miller, Lemon, Percy.

Semi-finals

Belfast Y.M.C.A. (Belfast)	3-1	Glentoran FC (Belfast)
Distillery FC (Belfast)	13-0	Hilden FC (Lisburn)

Quarter-finals

Distillery FC (Belfast)	10-0	Oldpark FC (Belfast)
Glentoran FC (Belfast)	8-0	Limavady FC (Limavady)
St. Columb's Court FC (Londonderry)	1-3	Belfast Y.M.C.A. (Belfast)

Hilden FC (Lisburn) received a bye

1889-90

IRISH CUP FINAL   (Ulster Ground, Ballynafeigh, Belfast – 08/03/1890 – 4,500)

GORDON HIGHLANDERS REGIMENT   2-2   Cliftonville FC (Belfast)
Swan, Archibald   *Wilton, Small*

Gordon Highlanders: Grant, Thompson, Buchanan, Maguire, Milne, Johnston, Swan, Hall, Archibald, McCormack, Beveridge.

Cliftonville: Clugston, Nelson, Ervine, Willianson, Crawford, Cooke, Elleman, Small, Barry, Lemon, Wilton.

IRISH CUP FINAL REPLAY   (Ulsterville, Belfast – 12/03/1890 – 3,500)

GORDON HIGHLANDERS REGIMENT   3-0   Cliftonville FC (Belfast)
Swan 2, Beveridge

Cliftonville: Clugston, Nelson, Gibb, Williamson, Crawford, Cooke, Stewart, Small, Barry, Wilton, Turner.

Gordon Highlanders: Grant, Thompson, Buchanan, Maguire, Milne, Johnston, Swan, Reid, Hall, McCormack, Beveridge,

Semi-finals

Cliftonville FC (Belfast)	3-2, 4-2	Dublin Association (Dublin)
	(The replay was ordered after a protest)	
Gordon Highlanders Regiment	2-1	Linfield FC (Belfast)

Quarter-finals

Dublin Association (Dublin)	6-2	Limavady FC (Limavady)

Cliftonville FC (Belfast), Gordon Highlanders Regiment and Linfield FC (Belfast) all received byes

1890-91

Irish League 1890-91 Season	Clarence	Cliftonville	Distillery	Glentoran	Linfield	Milford	Oldpark	Ulster
Clarence FC	■	2-5	0-4	5-4	1-3	-:+	1-3	2-6
Cliftonville FC	2-2	■	7-3	0-0	0-8	3-2	2-2	4-1
Distillery FC	4-3	1-6	■	5-2	2-1	-:+	2-0	3-5
Glentoran FC	9-1	4-3	0-3	■	0-7	4-2	3-2	-:+
Linfield FC	5-2	10-2	6-2	6-0	■	9-1	14-0	9-5
Milford FC	-:+	-:+	1-9	0-8	1-6	■	-:+	2-5
Oldpark FC	+:-	2-3	2-4	0-2	0-3	5-0	■	2-10
Ulster FC	4-2	9-0	4-4	5-3	2-2	10-1	4-4	■

	Irish League	**Pd**	**Wn**	**Dw**	**Ls**	**GF**	**GA**	**Pts**	
1.	LINFIELD FC (BELFAST)	14	12	1	1	89	18	25	
2.	Ulster FC (Belfast)	14	9	3	2	70	38	21	
3.	Distillery FC (Belfast)	14	9	1	4	46	37	19	
4.	Cliftonville FC (Belfast)	14	7	3	4	37	46	17	
5.	Glentoran FC (Belfast)	14	6	1	7	39	39	13	
6.	Oldpark FC (Belfast)	14	4	2	8	22	48	10	
7.	Clarence FC (Belfast)	14	3	1	10	21	49	7	#
8.	Milford FC (Armagh)	14	-	-	14	10	59	-	#
		112	50	12	50	334	334	112	

Top goalscorers 1890-91

1) Robert HILL   (Linfield FC)   20
2) John PEDEN   (Linfield FC)   19
3) Sam TORRANS   (Linfield FC)   18

\# Milford FC (Armagh) resigned from the league on 20/01/1891 with 5 games still to play. These remaining games were awarded to their opponents (-:+) and a 0-0 scoreline was registered.

Other matches shown as +:- or -:+ were awarded to (+) with a 0-0 score-line being recorded.

Clarence FC (Belfast) withdrew from the league on 01/09/1891 and disbanded later in the same year. Their place was given to the Lancashire Fusiliers Regiment (Belfast) who were unable to play their opening game due to the short notice being given.

Elected: Belfast Y.M.C.A. (Belfast), Ligoniel FC (Belfast), Milltown FC (Belfast)

The league was extended to 10 clubs for the next season

IRISH CUP FINAL   (Solitude, Belfast – 14/03/1891 – 5,000)

LINFIELD FC (BELFAST)	4-2	Ulster FC (Belfast)
Hill, Torrans, Gaffiken, Flanelly o.g.	*(H.T. 4-2)*	*Tierney, McIlvenny*

Linfield: T. Gordon, W. Gordon, Morrison, McKeown, Milne, Moore, Dalton, Gaffiken, Hill, S. Torrans, Peden.
Ulster: Johnstone, Purvis, Campbell, Flanelly, Reynolds, Cunningham, McIlvenny, Tierney, McCabe, McAuley, Haig.

Semi-finals

Linfield FC (Belfast)	9-0	St. Columb's Court FC (Londonderry)
Ulster FC (Belfast)	6-2	Clarence FC (Belfast)

Quarter-finals

Omagh Wanderers FC (Omagh)	0-6	St. Columb's Court FC (Londonderry)
St. Columb's Hall FC (Londonderry)	0-7	Ulster FC (Belfast)

Clarence FC (Belfast) and Linfield FC (Belfast) both received byes

1891-92

Irish League 1891-92 Season	Cliftonville	Distillery	Glentoran	Lancs. Fus.	Ligonel	Linfield	Milltown	Oldpark	Ulster	Y.M.C.A.
Cliftonville FC	■	---	1-1	2-3	4-1	0-5	8-0	7-1	0-3	3-3
Distillery FC	3-1	■	---	-:+	5-0	2-1	---	7-0	5-3	---
Glentoran FC	4-4	4-3	■	2-3	3-1	1-7	11-0	15-1	6-5	---
Lancashire Fusiliers Regiment	1-0	(a)	1-1	■	13-2	0-0	4-0	+:-	2-5	---
Ligoniel FC	(b)	---	0-9	1-5	■	3-8	4-0	+:-	2-4	---
Linfield FC	8-0	6-1	8-0	6-2	7-1	■	14-0	9-0	8-1	---
Milltown FC	-:+	0-4	0-9	0-8	7-3	1-3	■	+:-	0-4	3-2
Oldpark FC	-:+	1-5	0-7	3-10	3-0	1-7	-:+	■	0-2	+:-
Ulster FC	4-0	---	7-1	5-0	+:-	1-5	3-1	9-2	■	5-2
Y.M.C.A. Belfast	---	2-10	0-7	3-4	2-4	0-4	---	---	---	■

	Irish League	**Pd**	**Wn**	**Dw**	**Ls**	**GF**	**GA**	**Pts**	
1.	LINFIELD FC (BELFAST)	17	15	1	1	106	14	31	
2.	Lancashire Fusiliers Regiment (Belfast)	17	11	3	3	56	30	25	#
3.	Ulster FC (Belfast)	16	12	-	4	61	34	24	
4.	Glentoran FC (Belfast)	16	9	3	4	80	41	21	
5.	Distillery FC (Belfast)	12	8	1	3	45	18	15	-2
6.	Cliftonville FC (Belfast)	16	5	4	7	30	37	14	
7.	Milltown FC (Belfast)	16	4	-	12	12	77	8	#
8.	Ligoniel FC (Belfast)	16	3	1	12	22	70	7	#
9.	Oldpark FC (Belfast)	17	2	-	15	12	78	4	#
10.	Belfast Y.M.C.A. (Belfast)	9	-	1	8	14	40	1	
		152	69	14	69	439	439	150	

On 02/02/1892 Distillery FC were fined £10.00 and had 2 points deducted for fielding an ineligible player versus Linfield FC but the result 2-1 was allowed to stand. They were later expelled from the league on 10/02/1892 for failing to pay the fine but were reinstated on 24/02/1892 after paying a reduced amount. However, some teams refused to accept this decision.

On 12/04/1892 Glentoran FC were fined £15.00 for refusing to play against Distillery FC

(a) On 18/04/1892, the Lancashire Fusiliers were awarded 2 points for the opening match of the season which they had been unable to play due to late acceptance to league status. They were also awarded 1 point for their unplayed match against Distillery FC, but they then resigned from the league prior to the start of the 1892-93 season. (All matches had been played on their opponents grounds).

Unplayed Distillery matches against Glentoran, Milltown, Ulster, Cliftonville and Ligoniel were declared void (---).

The Cliftonville FC vs Glentoran FC match was not played but was registered as a 1-1 draw by the Irish League.

(b) The Ligoniel FC vs Cliftonville FC match was not played but both teams were awarded 1 point by the Irish League.

Belfast Y.M.C.A. (Belfast) resigned from the league on 19/12/1891, their remaining fixtures were declared void (---).

Oldpark FC (Belfast) resigned from the league on 20/04/1892 after hostility had been shown towards them for playing against Distillery FC. Their remaining fixtures were awarded to their opponents (+:- or -:+)

Top goalscorers 1891-92

1) Tom MORRISON   (Glentoran FC)   21
2) Robert HILL   (Linfield FC)   15
3) Robert McILVENNY   (Ulster FC)   14
(not fully recorded)

Ligoniel FC (Belfast) and Milltown FC (Belfast) were excluded from the league from the next season.

Elected: Derry Olympic FC (Londonderry)

IRISH CUP FINAL   (Solitude, Belfast – 12/03/1892)

LINFIELD FC (BELFAST)   7-0   Black Watch Regiment (Limerick)
Hill 4, S. Torrans, R. Torrans, Dalton   *(H.T. 4-0)*

Linfield: T. Gordon, W. Gordon, Arnott, McKeown, Milne, S. Johnston, Dalton, Gaffiken, Hill, S. Torrans, R. Torrans.
Black Watch: Mann, Cassels, Barr, McGee, Porter, Clarke, McAuley, Connor, Reynolds, Malcolm, Thom.

Semi-finals

Black Watch Regiment (Limerick)	4-1	St. Columb's Court FC (Londonderry)
Linfield FC (Belfast)	3-0	Ulster FC (Belfast)

Quarter-finals

Black Watch Regiment (Limerick)	8-2	Lancashire Fusiliers Regiment (Belfast)
Linfield FC (Belfast)	6-0	Glentoran FC (Belfast)
Ulster FC (Belfast)	4-2	Cliftonville FC (Belfast)

St. Columb's Court FC (Londonderry) received a bye

1892-93

Irish League 1892-93 Season	Cliftonville	Derry Olympic	Distillery	Glentoran	Linfield	Ulster
Cliftonville FC		8-1	3-2	2-1	0-3	3-1
Derry Olympic FC	1-2		0-9	1-2	-:+	2-3
Distillery FC	5-3	2-2		0-4	1-1	7-0
Glentoran FC	1-3	+:-	3-3		1-2	3-0
Linfield FC	3-3	+:-	3-0	5-0		3-1
Ulster FC	0-1	+:-	2-3	0-1	1-7	

	Irish League	Pd	Wn	Dw	Ls	GF	GA	Pts	
1.	LINFIELD FC (BELFAST)	10	8	2	-	27	7	18	
2.	Cliftonville FC (Belfast)	10	7	1	2	28	18	15	
3.	Distillery FC (Belfast)	10	4	3	3	32	21	11	
4.	Glentoran FC (Belfast)	10	5	1	4	16	16	11	
5.	Ulster FC (Belfast)	10	2	-	8	8	30	4	
6.	Derry Olympic FC (Londonderry)	10	-	1	9	7	26	1	#
		60	26	8	26	118	118	60	

Top goalscorers 1892-93

1) Robert HILL   (Linfield FC)   9
   James PERCY   (Cliftonville FC)   9

Derry Olympic FC (Londonderry) resigned from the league after only 6 games. The remaining games were awarded to their opponents with a 0-0 scoreline being registered.

Elected: Ligoniel FC (Belfast)

IRISH CUP FINAL   (Ulsterville, Belfast – 11/03/1893)

LINFIELD FC (BELFAST)	5-1	Cliftonville FC (Belfast)
T. Torrans, Milne 2, McKeown, Turley	*(H.T. 5-0)*	*J. Williamson*

Linfield: T. Gordon, W. Gordon, S. Torrans, McKeown, S. Johnston, R. Torrans, T. Torrans, Peden, Gaffiken, Milne, Turley.

Cliftonville: Clugston, R. Stewart, Thompson, Crawford, McKee, Anderson, Small, G. Williamson, J. Williamson, Turner, Blayney.

Semi-finals

Cliftonville FC (Belfast)	10-1	Ulster FC (Belfast)
Linfield FC (Belfast)	4-1, 4-0	Distillery FC (Belfast)
	(The replay was ordered after a protest)	

Quarter-finals

Distillery FC (Belfast)	6-0	Leinster Nomads FC (Dublin)
Ivy FC (Londonderry)	0-8	Linfield FC (Belfast)

Cliftonville FC (Belfast) and Ulster FC (Belfast) both received byes

1893-94

Irish League 1893-94 Season	Cliftonville	Distillery	Glentoran	Ligoniel	Linfield	Ulster
Cliftonville FC	■	3-2	0-1	2-2	3-1	1-3
Distillery FC	2-1	■	1-0	1-2	4-4	2-0
Glentoran FC	8-0	4-2	■	5-1	1-3	5-1
Ligoniel FC	1-5	0-6	0-2	■	0-5	3-4
Linfield FC	3-3	6-0	0-1	4-0	■	5-2
Ulster FC	2-4	4-3	2-4	5-1	1-5	■

	Irish League	Pd	Wn	Dw	Ls	GF	GA	Pts	
1.	GLENTORAN FC (BELFAST)	10	8	-	2	31	10	16	
2.	Linfield FC (Belfast)	10	6	2	2	36	15	14	
3.	Cliftonville FC (Belfast)	10	4	2	4	22	25	10	
4.	Distillery FC (Belfast)	10	4	1	5	23	24	9	
5.	Ulster FC (Belfast)	10	4	-	6	24	33	8	#
6.	Ligoniel FC (Belfast)	10	1	1	8	10	39	3	#
		60	27	6	27	146	146	60	

Top goalscorer 1893-94

1) Michael McERLEAN   (Linfield FC)   9

Ligoniel FC (Belfast) and Ulster FC (Belfast) were not in the league for next season. As no new teams were elected the league was reduced to 4 clubs.

IRISH CUP FINAL   (Solitude, Belfast – 17/03/1894 – 5,500)

DISTILLERY FC (BELFAST)   2-2   Linfield FC (Belfast)
Stanfield 2   *Milne, McAllen*

Distillery: Thompson, Brown, Ponsonby, Myles, J. Stilges, Burnett, Stanfield, Shannon, Emerson, W. Stilges, McClatchey.

Linfield: T. Gordon, H. Gordon, W. Gordon, McKeown, S. Johnston, J. Jordan, Dalton, Gaffiken, Milne. T. Jordan, McAllen.

IRISH CUP FINAL REPLAY   (Solitude, Belfast – 18/04/1894)

DISTILLERY FC (BELFAST)   3-2   Linfield FC (Belfast)
Emerson 2, Stanfield   *Jordan, McErlean*

Linfield: T. Gordon, S. Torrans, W. Gordon, McKeown, Milne, H. Gordon, Dalton, Gaffiken, McErlean, T. Jordan, McAllen.

Distillery: Thompson, J. Stilges, Mawhinney, Ponsonby, McClatchey, Myles, Thompson, Stanfield, Burnett, W. Stilges, Emerson.

Semi-finals

Distillery FC (Belfast)	8-3	St. Columb's Court FC (Londonderry)
Linfield FC (Belfast)	3-2	Cliftonville FC (Belfast)

Quarter-finals

Ligoniel FC (Belfast)	2-4	Cliftonville FC (Belfast)
St. Columb's Court FC (Londonderry)	3-4, w/o	Bohemian FC (Dublin)

(A replay was ordered after a protest but Bohemian refused to play)

Distillery FC (Belfast) and Linfield FC (Belfast) both received byes.

1894-95

Irish League 1894-95 Season	Cliftonville	Distillery	Glentoran	Linfield
Cliftonville FC		1-2	2-2	0-5
Distillery FC	4-3		3-1	2-2
Glentoran FC	1-3	3-1		2-2
Linfield FC	3-1	3-1	3-0	

	Irish League	Pd	Wn	Dw	Ls	GF	GA	Pts
1.	LINFIELD FC (BELFAST)	6	4	2	-	18	6	10
2.	Distillery FC (Belfast)	6	3	1	2	13	13	7
3.	Glentoran FC (Belfast)	6	1	2	3	9	14	4
4.	Cliftonville FC (Belfast)	6	1	1	4	10	17	3
		24	9	6	9	50	50	24

No clubs were promoted or relegated

Top goalscorers 1894-95

1)	George GAUKRODGER	(Linfield FC)	4
	Joe McALLEN	(Linfield FC)	4
	William SHERRARD	(Glentoran FC)	4
	Oliver STANFIELD	(Glentoran FC)	4
	J.H. TORRANS	(Cliftonville FC)	4

IRISH CUP FINAL (Solitude, Belfast – 23/03/1895 – 2,000)

LINFIELD FC (BELFAST)   10-1 (H.T. 3-1)   Bohemian FC (Dublin)

Milne 3, McAllen 3, H. Gordon, Williamson, Gaffiken, Gaukrodger   *Blayney*

Linfield: T. Gordon, H. Gordon, S. Torrans, S. Johnston, Milne, R. Torrans, G. Williamson, Gaffiken, Gaukrodger, T. Jordan, McAllen.

Bohemian: Morrogh, Murray, Whelan, McCaughey, Fitzpatrick, O'Sullivan, Farrell, Wilson, Sheehan, Murray, Blayney.

Semi-finals

Bohemian FC (Dublin)	4-1	St. Columb's Hall Celtic FC (Londonderry)
Linfield FC (Belfast)	6-1	Belfast Celtic FC (Belfast)

Quarter-finals

Bohemian FC (Dublin)	6-4	Glentoran FC (Belfast)
Dublin University FC (Dublin)	1-3	Belfast Celtic FC (Belfast)
Linfield FC (Belfast)	0-0, 4-1	Distillery FC (Belfast)
St. Columb's Hall Celtic FC (Londonderry)	3-1	St. Columb's Court FC (Londonderry)

1895-96

Irish League 1895-96 Season	Cliftonville	Distillery	Glentoran	Linfield
Cliftonville FC	■	2-2	2-1	2-3
Distillery FC	2-2	■	6-1	2-1
Glentoran FC	1-3	6-2	■	2-3
Linfield FC	1-3	0-3	2-2	■

Play-off (Solitude, Belfast – 11/01/1896)

DISTILLERY FC (BELFAST)   2-1   Cliftonville FC (Belfast)

	Irish League	Pd	Wn	Dw	Ls	GF	GA	Pts
1.	Distillery FC (Belfast)	6	3	2	1	17	12	8
1.	Cliftonville FC (Belfast)	6	3	2	1	14	10	8
3.	Linfield FC (Belfast)	6	2	1	3	10	14	5
4.	Glentoran FC (Belfast)	6	1	1	4	13	18	3
		24	9	6	9	54	54	24

Elected: Belfast Celtic FC (Belfast), North Staffordshire Regiment (Belfast)

The league was extended to 6 clubs for next season

IRISH CUP FINAL (Solitude, Belfast – 14/03/1896 – 6,000)

DISTILLERY FC (BELFAST)   3-1   Glentoran FC (Belfast)
Riley, Baird, Campbell   *Carmichael*

Distillery: Thompson, Brown, Ponsonby, McCoy, Farrell, McClatchey, Baird, Rylie, Stanfield, Campbell, Peden.
Glentoran: E. Johnston, Purvis, McFall, Hatty, Shannon, Burnett, Carmichael, Hall, P. Johnston, Kelly, Somerset.

Semi-finals

| Distillery FC (Belfast) | 4-1 | Cliftonville FC (Belfast) |
| Glentoran FC (Belfast) | 8-2 | Derry North End FC (Londonderry) |

Quarter-finals

Cliftonville FC (Belfast)	1-0	Linfield FC (Belfast)
Derry North End FC (Londonderry)	0-0, 1-1, 4-1	St. Columb's Court FC (Londonderry)
Distillery FC (Belfast)	3-1	Bohemian FC (Dublin)
2nd Battalion Scots Guard Regiment (Dublin)	2-2, 0-3	Glentoran FC (Belfast)

1896-97

Irish League 1896-97 Season	Belfast Celtic	Cliftonville	Distillery	Glentoran	Linfield	North Staffs.
Belfast Celtic FC	■	1-3	2-1	1-3	3-3	1-1
Cliftonville FC	3-1	■	2-3	1-3	1-1	2-2
Distillery FC	2-0	2-2	■	2-0	0-6	1-1
Glentoran FC	2-0	3-2	2-1	■	1-0	6-0
Linfield FC	4-2	3-4	7-4	2-2	■	7-1
North Staffordshire Regiment	3-0	1-2	1-1	1-2	6-1	■

	Irish League	Pd	Wn	Dw	Ls	GF	GA	Pts
1.	GLENTORAN FC (BELFAST)	10	8	1	1	24	10	17
2.	Cliftonville FC (Belfast)	10	4	3	3	22	20	11
3.	Linfield FC (Belfast)	10	4	3	3	34	24	11
4.	Distillery FC (Belfast)	10	3	3	4	17	23	9
5.	North Staffordshire Regiment (Belfast)	10	2	4	4	17	23	8
6.	Belfast Celtic FC (Belfast)	10	1	2	7	11	25	4
		60	22	16	22	125	125	60

2nd/3rd Place Play-Off (Solitude, Belfast)

Cliftonville FC (Belfast)　　　　　　　3-2　　　　　　　Linfield FC (Belfast)

No clubs were promoted or relegated

Top goalscorers 1896-97

1)	John DARLING	(Linfield FC)	6
	Richard PEDEN	(Linfield FC)	6
3)	George HALL	(Distillery FC)	5
	HIGERTY	(North Staffordshire Regiment)	5
	Tom JORDAN	(Linfield FC)	5
	Sam MARTIN	(Cliftonville FC)	5
	James PYPER	(Cliftonville FC)	5

IRISH CUP FINAL (Grosvenor Park, Belfast – 20/03/1897 – 5,000)

CLIFTONVILLE FC (BELFAST)　　　　　3-1　　　　　Sherwood Foresters FC (Curragh)
Jas. Campbell, Martin, Pyper　　　　　　　　　　　　　　　　　　　　　　　　　*Bedford*

Cliftonville: Scott, Gibson, Foreman, Jack Campbell, Polland, Jack Pyper, James Campbell, McCashin, Barron, James Pyper, Martin.
Shelbourne: Lewis, Pykett, Vernon, Locker, Cleland, Murphy, Thorpe, Porter, Roberts, Hoare, Bedford.

Semi-finals

Cliftonville FC (Belfast)	2-1	Distillery FC (Belfast)
Sherwood Foresters FC (Curragh)	3-2	St. Columb's Hall Celtic FC (Londonderry)

Quarter-finals

Bohemian FC (Dublin)	0-1	Sherwood Foresters FC (Curragh)
Cliftonville FC (Belfast)	2-1	Linfield FC (Belfast)
Derry North End FC (Londonderry)	2-2, 3-4	St. Columb's Hall Celtic FC (Londonderry)

Distillery FC (Belfast) received a bye

1897-98

Irish League 1897-98 Season	Belfast Celtic	Cliftonville	Distillery	Glentoran	Linfield	North Staffs.
Belfast Celtic FC	■	1-2	5-1	1-5	0-3	2-1
Cliftonville FC	1-0	■	4-3	1-1	0-1	3-1
Distillery FC	0-2	5-0	■	0-6	1-1	2-0
Glentoran FC	1-0	3-0	6-0	■	2-4	1-2
Linfield FC	2-1	2-4	1-0	2-1	■	3-0
North Staffordshire Regiment	3-3	0-8	3-1	2-5	1-3	■

	Irish League	Pd	Wn	Dw	Ls	GF	GA	Pts
1.	LINFIELD FC (BELFAST)	10	8	1	1	22	10	17
2.	Cliftonville FC (Belfast)	10	6	1	3	23	17	13
3.	Glentoran FC (Belfast)	10	6	1	3	31	12	13
4.	Belfast Celtic FC (Belfast)	10	3	1	6	15	19	7
5.	Distillery FC (Belfast)	10	2	1	7	13	28	5
6.	North Staffordshire Regiment (Belfast)	10	2	1	7	13	31	5
		60	27	6	27	117	117	60

No clubs promoted or relegated

IRISH CUP FINAL (The Oval, Belfast – 19/03/1898 – 3,000)

LINFIELD FC (BELFAST)   2-0   St. Columb's Hall Celtic FC (Londonderry)

Darling, Jordan

Linfield: White, Howard, S. Torrans, Anderson, Milne, Maginnis, Stevenson, Darling, T. Jordan, R. Rea, S. Rea.
St. Columb's: P. Boyle, Hassan, Gallagher, McComb, McNulty, Phillips, Gallagher, Maginnis, McIntyre, Lynch, G. Boyle.

Semi-finals

Linfield FC (Belfast)	1-1, 2-1	Belfast Celtic FC (Belfast)
St. Columb's Hall Celtic FC (Londonderry)	1-0	Bohemian FC (Dublin)

Quarter-finals

Bohemian FC (Dublin)	0-0, 1-2, w/o	Yorkshire Regiment

Belfast Celtic FC (Belfast), Linfield FC (Belfast) and St. Columb's Hall Celtic FC (Londonderry) all received byes

1898-99

Irish League 1898-99 Season	Belfast Celtic	Cliftonville	Distillery	Glentoran	Linfield	North Staffs.
Belfast Celtic FC	■	1-2	1-2	2-3	1-6	2-0
Cliftonville FC	4-0	■	1-3	3-0	1-2	3-0
Distillery FC	0-2	2-1	■	0-2	2-1	5-2
Glentoran FC	2-1	1-2	1-2	■	1-2	3-0
Linfield FC	0-0	2-0	2-0	0-1	■	2-0
North Staffordshire Regiment	3-4	1-2	3-4	0-3	2-4	■

Play-off

DISTILLERY FC (BELFAST)　　　　　　　2-0　　　　　　　　　　Linfield FC (Belfast)

	Irish League	Pd	Wn	Dw	Ls	GF	GA	Pts
1.	Distillery FC (Belfast)	10	7	1	2	23	17	15
1.	Linfield FC (Belfast)	10	7	1	2	21	8	15
3.	Cliftonville FC (Belfast)	10	6	-	4	19	12	12
4.	Glentoran FC (Belfast)	10	6	-	4	17	12	12
5.	Belfast Celtic FC (Belfast)	10	2	2	6	15	25	6
6.	North Staffordshire Regiment (Belfast)	10	-	-	10	11	32	- #
		60	28	4	28	106	106	60

\# The North Staffordshire Regiment (Belfast) resigned from the league due to the regiment being posted to serve in South Africa.

Elected: Royal Scots Regiment (Belfast)

IRISH CUP FINAL   (Solitude, Belfast – 18/03/1899 – 7,000)

LINFIELD FC (BELFAST)　　　　　　　1-0　　　　　　　　　Glentoran FC (Belfast)
Peden
(The match ended early after Glentoran players refused to continue claiming that a Linfield player had punched a shot clear from the goal-line and no penalty had been awarded).
Linfield: Murray, Swan. S. Torrans, Maginnis, Milne, Wilson, John Peden, Darling, T. Jordan, Doherty, McAllen.
Glentoran: J. Lewis, Purvis, Kerr, Lyttle, McCann, McMaster, Gill, Smith, P. Johnston, Seaton, Duncan.

Semi-finals

Glentoran FC (Belfast)　　　　　　2-2, 2-1, 2-0　　　　　　　Belfast Celtic FC (Belfast)
　　　　　　　　　(The 2nd replay was ordered after a protest)
Linfield FC (Belfast)　　　　　　　　　4-2　　　　　　　　　　Bohemian FC (Dublin)

Quarter-finals

Glentoran FC (Belfast)　　　　　　　8-0　　　　　　King's Own Rifles Regiment (Cork)
Belfast Celtic FC (Belfast), Bohemian FC (Dublin) and Linfield FC (Belfast) all received byes

1899-1900

Irish League 1899-1900 Season	Belfast Celtic	Cliftonville	Distillery	Glentoran	Linfield	Royal Scots
Belfast Celtic FC	■	5-1	3-1	2-1	2-0	1-0
Cliftonville FC	0-0	■	3-1	4-1	0-4	2-2
Distillery FC	4-3	3-3	■	0-0	1-1	4-0
Glentoran FC	0-1	1-4	0-1	■	4-4	2-4
Linfield FC	4-2	1-1	0-0	2-0	■	5-0
Royal Scots Regiment	---	4-1	0-2	---	---	■

	Irish League	Pd	Wn	Dw	Ls	GF	GA	Pts	
1.	BELFAST CELTIC FC (BELFAST)	9	6	1	2	19	11	13	
2.	Linfield FC (Belfast)	9	4	4	1	21	10	12	
3.	Distillery FC (Belfast)	10	4	4	2	17	13	12	
4.	Cliftonville FC (Belfast)	10	3	4	3	19	22	10	
5.	Royal Scots Regiment (Belfast)	7	2	1	4	10	17	5	#
6.	Glentoran FC (Belfast)	9	-	2	7	9	22	2	
		54	19	16	19	95	95	54	

\# The Royal Scots Regiment (Belfast) resigned from the league after only 7 games due to the regiment being posted to serve in South Africa because of the "Boer War".

Elected: Derry Celtic FC (Londonderry)

Note: Some publications show the following final table which excludes the record of the Royal Scots Regiment:

	Irish League	Pd	Wn	Dw	Ls	GF	GA	Pts
1.	Belfast Celtic FC (Belfast)	8	5	1	2	18	11	11
2.	Linfield FC (Belfast)	8	3	4	1	16	10	10
3.	Cliftonville FC (Belfast)	8	3	3	2	16	16	9
4.	Distillery FC (Belfast)	8	2	4	2	11	13	8
5.	Glentoran FC (Belfast)	8	-	2	6	7	18	2
		40	13	14	13	68	68	40

IRISH CUP FINAL   (Grosvenor Park, Belfast – 24/03/1900 – 5,500)

CLIFTONVILLE FC (BELFAST)   2-1   Bohemian FC (Dublin)
Campbell, Martin   *Sheehan*

Cliftonville: McAlpine, John Pyper, Jack Sheppard, Cochrane, McCoull, McShane, James Campbell, Wheeler, James Pyper, Martin, Thompson.
Bohemian: Farrell, McCausland, Whelan, Fulton, H. Barry, Crozier, Sheehan, Hooper, Pratt, Curtis, A. Barry.

Semi-finals

Bohemian FC (Dublin)	2-1	Belfast Celtic FC (Belfast)
Cliftonville FC (Belfast)	w/o	King's Own Scottish Borderers Regiment

Quarter-finals

Belfast Celtic FC (Belfast)	3-1	St. Columb's Court FC (Londonderry)
Cliftonville FC (Belfast)	5-1	Derry Celtic FC (Londonderry)
Distillery FC (Belfast)	1-5	Bohemian FC (Dublin)
King's Own Scottish Borderers Regiment	1-1, 5-2	Richmond Rovers FC (Dublin)

1900-01

Irish League 1900-01 Season	Belfast Celtic	Cliftonville	Derry Celtic	Distillery	Glentoran	Linfield
Belfast Celtic FC	■	1-1	6-2	1-1	1-0	1-0
Cliftonville FC	1-0	■	3-3	3-4	2-4	0-0
Derry Celtic FC	0-1	2-3	■	0-6	2-4	1-4
Distillery FC	4-1	1-1	9-0	■	3-1	3-0
Glentoran FC	3-1	3-1	3-1	3-1	■	0-0
Linfield FC	1-0	0-2	4-1	0-1	1-3	■

	Irish League	**Pd**	**Wn**	**Dw**	**Ls**	**GF**	**GA**	**Pts**
1.	DISTILLERY FC (BELFAST)	10	7	2	1	33	10	16
2.	Glentoran FC (Belfast)	10	7	1	2	24	13	15
3.	Belfast Celtic FC (Belfast)	10	4	2	4	13	13	10
4.	Cliftonville FC (Belfast)	10	3	4	3	17	18	10
5.	Linfield FC (Belfast)	10	3	2	5	10	12	8
6.	Derry Celtic FC (Londonderry)	10	-	1	9	12	43	1
		60	24	12	24	109	109	60

Elected: St. Columb's Court FC (Londonderry) and Ulster FC (Belfast)

The league was extended to 8 clubs for the next season

IRISH CUP FINAL   (Grosvenor Park, Belfast – 13/04/1901)

CLIFTONVILLE FC (BELFAST)	1-0	Freebooters FC (Dublin)

Scott

Cliftonville: McAlpine, Gibson, Sheppard, Cochrane, McKee, Anderson, Scott, Wheeler, James Pyper, Kirkwood, James Campbell.

Freebooters: Nolan-Whelan, Finney, Ryan, Fottrell, Crozier, H. Thomas, McCann, T. Thomas, B. O'Reilly, H. O'Reilly, J. O'Reilly.

Semi-finals

Cliftonville FC (Belfast)	3-1	Derry Celtic FC (Londonderry)
Freebooters FC (Dublin)	2-1	Linfield FC (Belfast)

Quarter-finals

Cliftonville FC (Belfast)	2-0, 4-2	Belfast Celtic FC (Belfast)

Derry Celtic FC (Londonderry), Freebooters FC (Dublin) and Linfield FC (Belfast) all received byes

1901-02

Irish League 1901-02 Season	Belfast Celtic	Cliftonville	Derry Celtic	Distillery	Glentoran	Linfield	St. Columb's	Ulster
Belfast Celtic FC	■	0-0	2-1	0-0	1-3	0-3	4-0	6-1
Cliftonville FC	2-0	■	1-0	1-2	1-2	3-0	3-0	1-0
Derry Celtic FC	3-2	2-0	■	1-1	2-1	0-1	2-0	1-2
Distillery FC	1-1	2-1	5-1	■	1-2	2-1	4-1	5-1
Glentoran FC	4-0	3-3	4-1	3-1	■	0-2	7-1	5-2
Linfield FC	4-0	2-0	4-0	2-0	5-1	■	3-0	4-2
St. Columb's Court FC	2-5	1-5	1-7	2-10	0-4	1-3	■	3-4
Ulster FC	1-1	0-3	2-2	3-4	2-4	1-4	1-1	■

	Irish League	Pd	Wn	Dw	Ls	GF	GA	Pts	
1.	LINFIELD FC (BELFAST)	14	12	-	2	38	10	24	
2.	Glentoran FC (Belfast)	14	10	1	3	43	22	21	
3.	Distillery FC (Belfast)	14	8	3	3	38	20	19	
4.	Cliftonville FC (Belfast)	14	7	2	5	24	14	16	
5.	Belfast Celtic FC (Belfast)	14	4	4	6	22	25	12	
6.	Derry Celtic FC (Londonderry)	14	5	2	7	23	26	12	
7.	Ulster FC (Belfast)	14	2	3	9	22	44	7	
8.	St. Columb's Court FC (Londonderry)	14	-	1	13	13	62	1	#
		112	48	16	48	223	223	112	

St. Columb's Court FC (Londonderry) did not compete in the Irish League for the next season.

Elected: Bohemian FC (Dublin)

IRISH CUP FINAL   (Solitude, Belfast – 15/03/1902)

LINFIELD FC (BELFAST)	5-1	Distillery FC (Belfast)
Mercer 2, Milne, Peden 2		*Cairns*

Linfield: W. Scott, Darling, S. Torrans, Crothers, Milne, Maginnis, Mercer, Maxwell, Carnegie, John Peden, McAllen.

Distillery: Andrews, Ponsonby, McCracken, Cochrane, Parsons, McFarlane, Kearns, McArthur, Jones, Cairns, Kirkwood.

Semi-finals

Distillery FC (Belfast)	5-3	Richmond Rovers FC (Dublin)
Linfield FC (Belfast)	2-0	Bohemian FC (Dublin)

Quarter-finals

Derry Celtic FC (Londonderry)	1-4	Bohemian FC (Dublin)
Distillery FC (Belfast)	2-1, 2-0	Cliftonville FC (Belfast)
Freebooters FC (Dublin)	0-5	Linfield FC (Belfast)
Richmond Rovers FC (Dublin)	1-0	Shelbourne FC (Dublin)

1902-03

Irish League 1902-03 Season	Belfast Celtic	Bohemian	Cliftonville	Derry Celtic	Distillery	Glentoran	Linfield	Ulster
Belfast Celtic FC	■	2-1	1-1	2-0	1-2	3-1	4-2	4-0
Bohemian FC	1-4	■	1-1	3-3	2-1	1-3	0-3	5-1
Cliftonville FC	2-1	2-3	■	2-0	1-3	1-0	0-2	1-0
Derry Celtic FC	3-3	2-1	2-2	■	3-1	4-1	1-1	6-0
Distillery FC	2-1	5-0	1-3	3-1	■	1-1	2-1	2-1
Glentoran FC	2-1	4-0	2-1	6-0	2-2	■	0-1	4-1
Linfield FC	6-1	2-2	4-0	3-0	2-4	1-1	■	5-1
Ulster FC	0-7	3-2	1-0	3-2	1-5	1-3	0-5	■

	Irish League	Pd	Wn	Dw	Ls	GF	GA	Pts	
1.	DISTILLERY FC (BELFAST)	14	9	2	3	34	20	20	
2.	Linfield FC (Belfast)	14	8	3	3	38	16	19	
3.	Glentoran FC (Belfast)	14	7	3	4	30	18	17	
4.	Belfast Celtic FC (Belfast)	14	7	2	5	35	23	16	
5.	Derry Celtic FC (Londonderry)	14	4	4	6	27	31	12	
6.	Cliftonville FC (Belfast)	14	5	3	6	17	21	11	-2
7.	Bohemian FC (Dublin)	14	3	3	8	22	36	9	
8.	Ulster FC (Belfast)	14	3	-	11	13	51	6	#
		112	46	20	46	216	216	110	

Note: Cliftonville FC (Belfast) had 2 points deducted for fielding an ineligible player.

Ulster FC (Belfast) did not compete in the league for the next season.

Elected: K.O.S.B. Regiment (Belfast) (K.O.S.B. = King's Own Scottish Borderers)

IRISH CUP FINAL (Dalymount Park, Dublin – 14/03/1903)

DISTILLERY FC (BELFAST)	3-1	Bohemian FC (Dublin)
Kearns, Hunter, Hamilton		*Pratt*

Distillery: J. Andrews, W. McCracken, G. McMillan, J. Hunter, W. Morton, Jos. Burnison, J.T. Mercer, Aitken, A. Kearns, David McDougall, W.J. Hamilton.

Bohemian: Monson, Meadows, Crane, Caldwell, D.B. Fulton, Bastow, H.A. Sloan, H. Pratt, W.F. Hooper, Callinan, Greene.

Semi-finals

Bohemian FC (Dublin)	6-1	Derry Celtic FC (Londonderry)
Distillery FC (Belfast)	2-1	Linfield FC (Belfast)

Quarter-finals

Bohemian FC (Dublin)	4-1	Shelbourne FC (Dublin)
Glentoran FC (Belfast)	1-2	Linfield FC (Belfast)

Derry Celtic FC (Londonderry) and Distillery FC (Belfast) both received byes

1903-04

Irish League 1903-04 Season	Belfast Celtic	Bohemian	Cliftonville	Derry Celtic	Distillery	Glentoran	K.O.S.B.	Linfield
Belfast Celtic FC	■	6-0	3-0	1-0	1-2	1-0	5-1	0-2
Bohemian FC	2-2	■	3-1	2-1	0-2	0-0	8-0	2-4
Cliftonville FC	2-1	1-2	■	1-0	3-3	1-1	5-1	1-8
Derry Celtic FC	0-0	4-1	0-2	■	1-1	2-3	2-0	2-3
Distillery FC	2-1	5-1	3-1	2-1	■	1-1	7-0	0-1
Glentoran FC	2-1	2-0	4-2	1-0	0-0	■	3-0	1-1
K.O.S.B. Regiment	3-2	2-2	1-2	2-3	0-6	1-2	■	0-7
Linfield FC	1-0	3-1	1-0	7-1	2-1	0-0	7-0	■

	Irish League	Pd	Wn	Dw	Ls	GF	GA	Pts	
1.	LINFIELD FC (BELFAST)	14	12	2	-	47	9	26	
2.	Distillery FC (Belfast)	14	8	4	2	35	13	20	
3.	Glentoran FC (Belfast)	14	7	6	1	20	10	20	
4.	Belfast Celtic FC (Belfast)	14	5	2	7	24	17	12	
5.	Cliftonville FC (Belfast)	14	5	2	7	22	31	12	
6.	Bohemian FC (Dublin)	14	4	3	7	24	33	11	
7.	Derry Celtic FC (Londonderry)	14	3	2	9	17	26	8	
8.	K.O.S.B. Regiment (Belfast)	14	1	1	12	11	61	3	#
		112	45	22	45	200	200	112	

K.O.S.B. Regiment (Belfast) did not compete in the league the for the next season.

Elected: Shelbourne FC (Dublin)

IRISH CUP FINAL   (Grosvenor Park, Belfast – 17/03/1904)

LINFIELD FC (BELFAST)   5-0   Derry Celtic FC (Londonderry)
Hagan 3, Milne, Darling
Linfield: Scott, McCartney, Sheppard, Anderson, Milne, Maginnis, Darling, Hagan, Carnegie, Stewart, Whaites.
Derry: McGonagle, Sheeran, McCourt, N. Blayney, Gallaher, Taylor, McGinnis, E. Blayney, Ward, Lynch, McClure.

Semi-finals
Derry Celtic FC (Londonderry)	9-3	Derry Hibernians FC (Londonderry)
Linfield FC (Belfast)	1-0	Cliftonville FC (Belfast)

Quarter-finals
Bohemian FC (Dublin)	0-2	Derry Celtic FC (Londonderry)
Cliftonville FC (Belfast)	1-0, +:-	Belfast Celtic FC (Belfast)
Linfield FC (Belfast)	3-3, 2-0	Freebooters FC (Dublin)

Derry Hibernians FC (Londonderry) received a bye

1904-05

Irish League 1904-05 Season	Belfast Celtic	Bohemian	Cliftonville	Derry Celtic	Distillery	Glentoran	Linfield	Shelbourne
Belfast Celtic FC		3-1	2-0	3-0	0-3	1-1	0-0	2-1
Bohemian FC	0-1		3-1	4-0	0-1	1-2	1-1	0-2
Cliftonville FC	0-1	5-0		2-1	2-1	1-2	3-0	0-2
Derry Celtic FC	2-4	3-3	0-0		0-3	0-2	0-0	3-1
Distillery FC	0-2	2-0	0-1	0-0		2-0	0-2	0-0
Glentoran FC	1-0	1-0	3-0	3-1	1-1		1-0	2-0
Linfield FC	0-1	3-2	2-0	4-0	1-2	2-2		2-0
Shelbourne FC	1-1	1-0	0-2	2-2	2-1	3-1	0-1	

Play-off

GLENTORAN FC (BELFAST)　　　3-1　　　Belfast Celtic FC (Belfast)

	Irish League	Pd	Wn	Dw	Ls	GF	GA	Pts
1.	Glentoran FC (Belfast)	14	9	3	2	22	12	21
1.	Belfast Celtic FC (Belfast)	14	9	3	2	21	10	21
3.	Linfield FC (Belfast)	14	6	4	4	18	12	16
4.	Distillery FC (Belfast)	14	6	3	5	16	11	15
5.	Cliftonville FC (Belfast)	14	6	1	7	17	17	13
6.	Shelbourne FC (Dublin)	14	5	3	6	15	17	13
7.	Derry Celtic FC (Londonderry)	14	1	5	8	12	31	7
8.	Bohemian FC (Dublin)	14	2	2	10	15	26	6
		112	44	24	44	136	136	112

No clubs promoted or relegated

IRISH CUP FINAL (Solitude, Belfast – 11/03/1905)

DISTILLERY FC (BELFAST)　　　3-0　　　Shelbourne FC (Dublin)

Magill 2, Soye

Distillery: Sloan, Watson, McMillan, Grieve, Johnston, Ferguson, Hunter, Andrews, Soye, Murray, Magill.
Shelbourne: Rowe, Heslin, Connor, Abbey, Doherty, Lawless, Owens, John, Byrne, Harris, Clery.

Semi-finals

Distillery FC (Belfast)	1-0	Derry Celtic FC (Londonderry)
Shelbourne FC (Dublin)	4-1	Glentoran FC (Belfast)

Quarter-finals

Derry Celtic FC (Londonderry)	3-1	Linfield FC (Belfast)
Distillery FC (Belfast)	1-0	Cameron Highlanders Regiment
Shelbourne FC (Dublin)	2-1	Bohemian FC (Dublin)

Glentoran FC (Belfast) received a bye

1905-06

Irish League 1905-06 Season	Belfast Celtic	Bohemian	Cliftonville	Derry Celtic	Distillery	Glentoran	Linfield	Shelbourne
Belfast Celtic FC	■	2-1	1-1	3-1	2-2	3-0	1-3	2-3
Bohemian FC	1-2	■	2-0	1-1	1-2	3-2	1-0	2-0
Cliftonville FC	1-0	3-0	■	2-0	0-1	5-1	2-2	1-0
Derry Celtic FC	0-1	0-4	0-0	■	1-0	3-1	3-1	3-0
Distillery FC	1-0	3-1	0-0	5-1	■	1-0	2-2	1-0
Glentoran FC	1-2	0-0	1-1	1-0	1-2	■	1-2	3-2
Linfield FC	0-0	3-0	0-1	3-0	2-0	1-0	■	1-0
Shelbourne FC	3-1	2-0	0-2	0-0	2-0	1-1	3-1	■

Play-off

CLIFTONVILLE FC (BELFAST)   0-0, 3-3   DISTILLERY FC (BELFAST)
(After 2 drawn matches it was decided that the clubs should share the championship)

	Irish League	Pd	Wn	Dw	Ls	GF	GA	Pts
1.	Cliftonville FC (Belfast)	14	7	5	2	19	8	19
1.	Distillery FC (Belfast)	14	8	3	3	20	13	19
3.	Linfield FC (Belfast)	14	7	3	4	21	14	17
4.	Belfast Celtic FC (Belfast)	14	6	3	5	20	18	15
5.	Bohemian FC (Dublin)	14	5	2	7	17	20	12
6.	Shelbourne FC (Dublin)	14	5	2	7	16	18	12
7.	Derry Celtic FC (Londonderry)	14	4	3	7	13	22	11
8.	Glentoran FC (Belfast)	14	2	3	9	13	26	7
		112	44	24	44	139	139	112

No clubs promoted or relegated

IRISH CUP FINAL   (Dalymount Park, Dublin – 28/04/1906)

SHELBOURNE FC (DUBLIN)   2-0   Belfast Celtic FC (Belfast)
James Owens 2 (1 pen.)

Shelbourne: Rowe, Heslin, Kelly, Abbey, Doherty, Ledwidge, John Owens, Byrne, James Owens, Harris, Clery.
Belfast: Haddock, McClelland, Pinkerton, McColl, Connor, Nicholl, Gall, Mulholland, Runnigan, Maguire, Maxwell.

Semi-finals

Belfast Celtic FC (Belfast)	2-0	Bohemian FC (Dublin)
Shelbourne FC (Dublin)	3-0	Derry Celtic FC (Londonderry)

Quarter-finals

Belfast Celtic FC (Belfast)	3-1	Cameron Highlanders Regiment
Cliftonville FC (Belfast)	0-1	Derry Celtic FC (Londonderry)
Glentoran FC (Belfast)	0-2	Shelbourne FC (Dublin)

Bohemian FC (Dublin) received a bye

1906-07

Irish League 1906-07 Season	Belfast Celtic	Bohemian	Cliftonville	Derry Celtic	Distillery	Glentoran	Linfield	Shelbourne
Belfast Celtic FC		0-2	0-1	1-0	3-1	4-2	0-1	1-2
Bohemian FC	2-3		1-0	1-1	1-1	1-1	2-4	1-3
Cliftonville FC	0-0	2-2		5-1	2-1	2-1	0-1	1-1
Derry Celtic FC	1-1	0-4	1-1		1-2	3-1	2-3	1-0
Distillery FC	6-3	0-0	3-1	2-0		3-2	2-1	2-2
Glentoran FC	3-0	1-2	1-1	2-0	1-1		0-2	2-2
Linfield FC	1-1	3-0	1-1	3-0	1-0	1-1		7-0
Shelbourne FC	3-1	3-0	2-1	2-0	4-3	3-0	0-1	

	Irish League	**Pd**	**Wn**	**Dw**	**Ls**	**GF**	**GA**	**Pts**
1.	LINFIELD FC (BELFAST)	14	10	3	1	30	9	23
2.	Shelbourne FC (Dublin)	14	8	3	3	27	21	19
3.	Distillery FC (Belfast)	14	6	4	4	27	22	16
4.	Cliftonville FC (Belfast)	14	4	6	4	18	16	14
5.	Bohemian FC (Dublin)	14	4	5	5	19	22	13
6.	Belfast Celtic FC (Belfast)	14	4	3	7	18	25	11
7.	Glentoran FC (Belfast)	14	2	5	7	18	25	9
8.	Derry Celtic FC (Londonderry)	14	2	3	9	11	28	7
		112	40	32	40	168	168	112

No clubs promoted or relegated

IRISH CUP FINAL   (Celtic Park, Belfast – 23/03/1907)

CLIFTONVILLE FC (BELFAST)   0-0   Shelbourne FC (Dublin)

Cliftonville: McKee, Seymour, McIlroy, Wright, Martin, McClure, Blair, Robertson, Beattie, Hull, Shanks.
Shelbourne: Rowe, Heslin, Kelly, Abbey, Doherty, Moran, Harris, Murphy, James Owens, John Owens, Clery.

IRISH CUP FINAL REPLAY   (Dalymount Park, Dublin – 20/04/1907)

CLIFTONVILLE FC (BELFAST)   1-0   Shelbourne FC (Dublin)
Beattie

Shelbourne: Rowe, Heslin, Moran, Abbey, Doherty, Ledwidge, Harris, Murphy, John Owens, James Owens, Clery.
Cliftonville: McKee, Seymour, McIlroy, Spence, Martin, McClure, Blair, Robertson, Campbell, Beattie, Shanks.

Semi-finals

Cliftonville FC (Belfast)	2-2, 3-2	Linfield FC (Belfast)
Shelbourne FC (Dublin)	1-0	Belfast Celtic FC (Belfast)

Quarter-finals

Belfast Celtic FC (Belfast)	1-0	Derry Celtic FC (Londonderry)
Cliftonville FC (Belfast)	6-1	Reginald FC (Dublin)

Linfield FC (Belfast) and Shelbourne FC (Dublin) both received byes

1907-08

Irish League 1907-08 Season	Belfast Celtic	Bohemian	Cliftonville	Derry Celtic	Distillery	Glentoran	Linfield	Shelbourne
Belfast Celtic FC		7-0	0-0	1-2	5-2	2-1	1-2	0-3
Bohemian FC	0-1		0-3	3-0	3-1	1-3	2-4	1-2
Cliftonville FC	3-1	3-0		2-0	1-1	1-1	1-1	0-2
Derry Celtic FC	1-0	1-1	2-3		1-2	2-1	2-4	1-0
Distillery FC	0-1	1-0	1-2	2-1		3-1	0-1	4-1
Glentoran FC	0-2	3-1	2-0	4-3	1-1		2-2	3-2
Linfield FC	3-0	1-0	3-1	4-0	3-1	2-3		1-0
Shelbourne FC	3-0	1-1	2-2	3-0	0-2	1-2	2-0	

	Irish League	Pd	Wn	Dw	Ls	GF	GA	Pts	
1.	LINFIELD FC (BELFAST)	14	10	2	2	31	15	22	
2.	Cliftonville FC (Belfast)	14	6	5	3	22	16	17	PO
3.	Glentoran FC (Belfast)	14	7	3	4	27	23	17	PO
4.	Distillery FC (Belfast)	14	6	2	6	21	21	14	
5.	Shelbourne FC (Dublin)	14	6	2	6	22	17	14	
6.	Belfast Celtic FC (Belfast)	14	6	1	7	21	20	14	
7.	Derry Celtic FC (Londonderry)	14	4	1	9	16	30	9	
8.	Bohemian FC (Dublin)	14	2	2	10	13	31	6	
		112	47	18	47	173	173	112	

2nd/3rd Place Play-off

Cliftonville FC (Belfast)	3-2	Glentoran FC (Belfast)

No clubs promoted or relegated

IRISH CUP FINAL   (Dalymount Park, Dublin – 21/03/1908)

BOHEMIAN FC (DUBLIN)	1-1	Shelbourne FC (Dublin)
Sloane		*Lacey*

Bohemian: O'Hehir, Balfe, Thunder, Bastow, Healy, Curtis, R.M. Hooper, Hannon, W. Hooper, Sloan, Slemin.
Shelbourne: Reilly, Heslin, Kelly, Harris, Doherty, Moran, John Owens, Murphy, Merrigan, James Owens, Lacey.

IRISH CUP FINAL REPLAY   (Dalymount Park, Dublin – 28/03/1908)

BOHEMIAN FC (DUBLIN)	3-1	Shelbourne FC (Dublin)
R.M. Hooper 2, W. Hooper		*James Owens*

Shelbourne: Reilly, Heslin, Kelly, Abbey, Harris, Ledwidge, John Owens, Murphy, Merrigan, James Owens, Lacey.
Bohemian: O'Hehir, Balfe, Thunder, Bastow, Healy, McElhinny, W. Hooper, Hannon, R. Hooper, Sloan, Slemin.

Semi-finals

Bohemian FC (Dublin)	2-2, 2-0	Belfast Celtic FC (Belfast)
Shelbourne FC (Dublin)	0-0, 2-0	Distillery FC (Belfast)

Quarter-finals

Belfast Celtic FC (Belfast)	w/o	Reginald FC (Dublin)
Bohemian FC (Dublin)	2-2, 2-1	Linfield FC (Belfast)
Distillery FC (Belfast)	2-0	Derry Celtic FC (Londonderry)
Shelbourne FC (Dublin)	1-1, 2-0	Cliftonville FC (Belfast)

1908-09

Irish League 1908-09 Season	Belfast Celtic	Bohemian	Cliftonville	Derry Celtic	Distillery	Glentoran	Linfield	Shelbourne
Belfast Celtic FC	■	---	2-1	2-1	2-3	1-1	2-3	3-2
Bohemian FC	0-1	■	2-2	2-1	1-0	6-1	0-4	3-1
Cliftonville FC	0-2	---	■	5-0	0-1	1-1	2-1	1-3
Derry Celtic FC	2-1	2-1	1-0	■	3-2	0-1	0-2	0-1
Distillery FC	2-2	3-0	1-3	3-1	■	0-1	0-1	1-2
Glentoran FC	6-0	4-2	4-1	3-1	2-1	■	2-2	2-1
Linfield FC	3-2	2-1	0-1	2-0	0-2	4-1	■	1-0
Shelbourne FC	3-0	2-4	1-0	1-0	1-3	2-0	0-2	■

	Irish League	Pd	Wn	Dw	Ls	GF	GA	Pts
1.	LINFIELD FC (BELFAST)	14	10	1	3	27	13	21
2.	Glentoran FC (Belfast)	14	8	3	3	29	22	19
3.	Shelbourne FC (Dublin)	14	7	-	7	20	20	14
4.	Distillery FC (Belfast)	14	6	1	7	22	19	13
5.	Bohemian FC (Dublin)	12	6	1	5	27	24	13
6.	Cliftonville FC (Belfast)	13	4	2	7	17	19	10
7.	Belfast Celtic FC (Belfast)	13	4	2	7	21	32	10
8.	Derry Celtic FC (Londonderry)	14	4	-	10	12	26	8
		108	49	10	49	175	175	108

Note: Bohemian FC (Dublin) away matches versus Belfast Celtic FC (Belfast) and Cliftonville FC (Belfast) were not played.

IRISH CUP FINAL   (Windsor Park, Belfast – 03/04/1909)

CLIFTONVILLE FC (BELFAST)   0-0   Bohemian FC (Dublin)

Bohemian: O'Hehir, Curtis, Thunder, Doyle, Healy, Sloan, D. Hooper, Hannon, McDonnell, W. Hooper, Slemin.
Cliftonville: McKee, Seymour, Neilly, Wright, Martin, Palmer, McComb, Robertson, Houghton, McAuley, Thompson.

IRISH CUP FINAL REPLAY   (Dalymount Park, Dublin – 10/04/1909)

CLIFTONVILLE FC (BELFAST)   2-1   Bohemian FC (Dublin)
McAuley, McComb   *W. Hooper*

Bohemian: O'Hehir, Curtis, Thunder, Doyle, Healy, Sloan, W. Hooper, McDonnell, R.M. Hooper, Slemin.
Cliftonville: McKee, Neely, Seymour, Martin, Wright, Palmer, McComb, Robertson, Houghton, McAuley, Thompson.

Semi-finals

Bohemian FC (Dublin)	2-1	Glentoran FC (Belfast)
Cliftonville FC (Belfast)	2-0, 2-3, 3-2	Distillery FC (Belfast)

Quarter-finals

Bohemian FC (Dublin)	10-2	St. James's Gate AFC (Dublin)
Cliftonville FC (Belfast)	+:-	Dublin University AFC (Dublin)
Glentoran FC (Belfast)	1-1, 2-0	Belfast Celtic FC (Belfast)
Linfield FC (Belfast)	0-4	Distillery FC (Belfast)

1909-10

Irish League 1909-10 Season	Belfast Celtic	Bohemian	Cliftonville	Derry Celtic	Distillery	Glentoran	Linfield	Shelbourne
Belfast Celtic FC	■	1-0	2-0	2-1	0-1	2-0	1-2	5-0
Bohemian FC	1-3	■	4-3	1-2	1-0	2-1	1-1	2-2
Cliftonville FC	2-1	4-1	■	1-0	1-0	1-0	2-1	4-2
Derry Celtic FC	2-0	3-1	1-1	■	2-2	5-4	2-2	0-0
Distillery FC	0-1	0-1	1-1	2-0	■	0-1	1-0	3-0
Glentoran FC	1-4	6-1	1-4	1-0	1-2	■	4-0	2-0
Linfield FC	3-2	3-2	0-0	0-0	3-1	2-1	■	1-1
Shelbourne FC	0-1	2-2	1-1	4-1	1-1	0-0	2-1	■

	Irish League	Pd	Wn	Dw	Ls	GF	GA	Pts
1.	CLIFTONVILLE FC (BELFAST)	14	8	4	2	25	15	20
2.	Belfast Celtic FC (Belfast)	14	9	-	5	25	13	18
3.	Linfield FC (Belfast)	14	5	5	4	19	20	15
4.	Distillery FC (Belfast)	14	5	3	6	14	13	13
5.	Derry Celtic FC (Londonderry)	14	4	5	5	19	21	13
6.	Bohemian FC (Dublin)	14	4	3	7	20	31	11
7.	Glentoran FC (Belfast)	14	5	1	8	23	23	11
8.	Shelbourne FC (Dublin)	14	2	7	5	15	24	11
		112	42	28	42	160	160	112

No clubs promoted or relegated

IRISH CUP FINAL (The Oval, Belfast – 26/03/1910)

DISTILLERY FC (BELFAST)	1-0	Cliftonville FC (Belfast)

Johnston

Distillery: Sloan, Burnison, Creighton, Flannagan, Donnelly, Scott, Wright, Hamilton, Johnston, Uprichard, Heggarty.

Cliftonville: McKee, Sterling, Seymour, Wright, Martin, Palmer, McComb, Robertson, Neville, McAuley, Thompson.

Semi-finals

Cliftonville FC (Belfast)	3-0	Bohemian FC (Dublin)
Distillery FC (Belfast)	4-0	Glentoran FC (Belfast)

Quarter-finals

Belfast Celtic FC (Belfast)	0-2	Bohemian FC (Dublin)
Cliftonville FC (Belfast)	2-0, +:-	Shelbourne FC (Dublin)

Distillery FC (Belfast) and Glentoran FC (Belfast) both received byes

1910-11

Irish League 1910-11 Season	Belfast Celtic	Bohemian	Cliftonville	Derry Celtic	Distillery	Glentoran	Linfield	Shelbourne
Belfast Celtic FC	■	3-3	3-0	2-1	0-0	1-3	0-1	3-2
Bohemian FC	1-3	■	1-1	4-0	0-2	0-1	0-2	2-2
Cliftonville FC	1-1	1-0	■	1-0	2-0	1-4	0-1	4-1
Derry Celtic FC	2-1	2-1	3-3	■	1-0	3-1	2-2	5-2
Distillery FC	1-1	5-2	1-1	0-0	■	1-2	0-1	0-1
Glentoran FC	1-2	2-0	4-0	9-0	2-1	■	3-0	4-0
Linfield FC	1-1	1-0	3-0	2-2	4-0	2-2	■	6-1
Shelbourne FC	2-0	0-0	0-1	1-0	2-2	1-1	0-3	■

Play-off

LINFIELD FC (BELFAST)	3-2	Glentoran FC (Belfast)

	Irish League	**Pd**	**Wn**	**Dw**	**Ls**	**GF**	**GA**	**Pts**	
1.	Linfield FC (Belfast)	14	9	4	1	29	11	22	
1.	Glentoran FC (Belfast)	14	10	2	2	39	12	22	
3.	Belfast Celtic FC (Belfast)	14	5	5	4	21	19	15	
4.	Cliftonville FC (Belfast)	14	5	4	5	16	22	14	
5.	Derry Celtic FC (Londonderry)	14	5	4	5	21	29	14	
6.	Shelbourne FC (Dublin)	14	3	4	7	15	31	10	
7.	Distillery FC (Belfast)	14	2	5	7	13	19	9	
8.	Bohemian FC (Dublin)	14	1	4	9	14	25	6	#
		112	40	32	40	168	168	112	

\# Bohemian FC (Dublin) did not compete in the league for next season.

Elected: Glenavon FC (Lurgan)

IRISH CUP FINAL (Dalymount Park, Dublin – 25/03/1911)

SHELBOURNE FC (DUBLIN)	0-0	Bohemian FC (Dublin)

Shelbourne: Rowe, Dunne, Bennett, Watson, Doherty, Moran, Clarkin, Murphy, Merrigan, Halpin, Devlin.

Bohemian: O'Hehir, Bill McConnell, Thunder, Hannon, Brennan, Magwood, Johnston, W.Hooper, McDonnell, West, Willett.

IRISH CUP FINAL REPLAY   (Dalymount Park, Dublin – 15/04/1911)

SHELBOURNE FC (DUBLIN)   2-1   Bohemian FC (Dublin)
Moran pen., Devlin   *R.H. Hooper*

Bohemian: O'Hehir, McConnell, Thunder, Hannon, Brennan, Hagwood, Ryder, R.H. Hooper, McDonnell, West, Willets.

Shelbourne: Rowe, Dunne, Bennett, Watson, Doherty, Moran, Clarkin, Murphy, Merrigan, Halpin, Devlin.

Semi-finals

Bohemian FC (Dublin)	2-2, 2-2, 2-1	Cliftonville FC (Belfast)
Shelbourne FC (Dublin)	3-0	Derry Celtic FC (Londonderry)

Quarter-finals

Derry Celtic FC (Londonderry)	2-3, +:−	Linfield FC (Belfast)
Shelbourne FC (Dublin)	+:−	St. James's Gate AFC (Dublin)

Bohemian FC (Dublin) and Cliftonville FC (Belfast) both received byes

1911-12

Irish League 1911-12 Season	Belfast Celtic	Cliftonville	Derry Celtic	Distillery	Glenavon	Glentoran	Linfield	Shelbourne
Belfast Celtic FC	■	0-0	4-1	1-1	1-0	1-3	2-1	1-1
Cliftonville FC	0-2	■	0-1	4-5	2-1	0-1	1-2	1-0
Derry Celtic FC	0-2	4-2	■	1-3	4-3	1-1	1-0	1-0
Distillery FC	1-1	5-0	3-1	■	3-0	2-3	0-0	4-1
Glenavon FC	0-2	0-1	2-0	0-1	■	1-5	1-3	3-1
Glentoran FC	1-1	10-0	2-0	2-1	3-2	■	1-0	7-0
Linfield FC	2-2	3-2	2-2	0-1	2-2	2-1	■	5-1
Shelbourne FC	0-1	2-1	2-0	0-2	2-2	2-5	0-0	■

	Irish League	Pd	Wn	Dw	Ls	GF	GA	Pts
1.	GLENTORAN FC (BELFAST)	14	11	2	1	45	13	24
2.	Distillery FC (Belfast)	14	9	3	2	32	14	21
3.	Belfast Celtic FC (Belfast)	14	7	6	1	21	11	20
4.	Linfield FC (Belfast)	14	6	4	4	25	16	16
5.	Derry Celtic FC (Londonderry)	14	5	1	8	16	29	11
6.	Shelbourne FC (Dublin)	14	2	3	9	12	33	7
7.	Cliftonville FC (Belfast)	14	3	1	10	14	36	7
8.	Glenavon FC (Lurgan)	14	2	2	10	17	30	6
		112	45	22	45	182	182	112

Elected: Bohemian FC (Dublin), Tritonville FC (Dublin)

The league was extended to 10 clubs for next season

After a dispute between the Irish FA and the County Antrim FA, a new but unofficial Association was formed on 22/12/1912 with the following clubs as members: Belfast Celtic FC (Belfast), Cliftonville FC (Belfast), Derry Celtic FC (Londonderry), Distillery FC (Belfast), Glenavon FC (Lurgan), Glentoran FC (Belfast) and Shelbourne FC.

However, after a series of meetings and proposals, agreement was reached and the "rebel" clubs were re-admitted to the Irish FA and competed in the league/cup for the next season.

IRISH CUP

LINFIELD FC (BELFAST)

The competition was completed to the quarter-final stage on 17th February 1912. However, on 21st February 1912, Cliftonville, Glentoran and Shelbourne resigned from the Irish Football Association, leaving Linfield as the only remaining competitor. These three clubs were among the 7 who resigned from the IFA after a dispute between the Irish FA and the County Antrim FA over ground levies for international matches. These 7 clubs formed an "unofficial" association on 22/12/1912. Another team of mainly Linfield Swifts FC players (Linfield's reserve team) also joined the "new" IFA as Belfast Blues FC. The dispute was however settled in time for the start of the 1912-13 season.

On the 7th May 1912 Linfield were declared holders of the Irish Football Association Challenge Cup for season 1911/12. Winners medals were presented to the Linfield Team which had defeated Bohemians 3-2 in Dublin on 3rd February 1912.

1912-13

Irish League 1912-13 Season	Belfast Celtic	Bohemian	Cliftonville	Derry Celtic	Distillery	Glenavon	Glentoran	Linfield	Shelbourne	Tritonville
Belfast Celtic FC		1-0	3-1	3-0	1-1	0-0	2-3	0-0	2-0	5-3
Bohemian FC	4-0		1-1	3-0	1-4	1-0	4-1	1-2	3-0	4-2
Cliftonville FC	1-2	3-0		1-0	1-0	3-2	0-1	1-1	0-0	2-1
Derry Celtic FC	3-2	0-1	1-2		0-1	0-0	0-0	4-2	3-1	2-2
Distillery FC	0-2	5-1	1-0	3-0		3-0	1-0	1-2	1-1	4-1
Glenavon FC	1-0	3-0	2-0	3-0	2-1		2-3	0-1	3-1	2-0
Glentoran FC	2-0	2-1	0-2	5-0	0-1	2-0		0-0	2-0	8-0
Linfield FC	4-0	1-1	3-0	2-1	0-1	1-4	2-4		1-0	4-3
Shelbourne FC	1-1	2-0	3-0	4-2	2-1	1-0	0-2	1-1		1-0
Tritonville FC	2-0	1-5	2-5	4-1	3-5	0-1	1-2	1-2	1-2	

	Irish League	Pd	Wn	Dw	Ls	GF	GA	Pts	
1.	GLENTORAN FC (BELFAST)	18	12	2	4	37	16	26	
2.	Distillery FC (Belfast)	18	11	2	5	34	17	24	
3.	Linfield FC (Belfast)	18	9	5	4	29	23	23	
4.	Glenavon FC (Lurgan)	18	9	2	7	25	17	20	
5.	Cliftonville FC (Belfast)	18	8	3	7	23	23	19	
6.	Bohemian FC (Dublin)	18	8	2	8	31	28	18	
7.	Belfast Celtic FC (Belfast)	18	7	4	7	24	26	18	
8.	Shelbourne FC (Dublin)	18	7	4	7	20	23	18	
9.	Derry Celtic FC (Londonderry)	18	3	3	12	17	39	9	#
10.	Tritonville FC (Dublin)	18	2	1	15	27	55	5	#
		180	76	28	76	267	267	180	

\# Derry Celtic FC (Londonderry) and Tritonville FC (Dublin) did not compete in the league which was reduced to 8 clubs for next season.

IRISH CUP FINAL (Celtic Park, Belfast – 29/03/1913)

LINFIELD FC (BELFAST)   2-0   Glentoran FC (Belfast)

McNeill, McEwan

Linfield: Kelly, Darling, Sterling, Rollo, Clifford, Bartlett, Brown, Nixon, Smith, McNeill, McEwan.
Glentoran: Murphy, McAlpine, Waters, Ferrett, Ritchie, Reid, Lyner, J. Lunday, Napier, McKnight, Monroe.

Semi-finals

Glentoran FC (Belfast)	5-1	Belfast Celtic FC (Belfast)
Linfield FC (Belfast)	4-1	Tritonville FC (Dublin)

Quarter-finals

Linfield FC (Belfast)	4-0	Derry Guilds FC (Londonderry)
Shelbourne FC (Dublin)	0-0, 0-1	Glentoran FC (Belfast)
Tritonville FC (Dublin)	5-1	St. James's Gate AFC (Dublin)

Belfast Celtic FC (Belfast) received a bye

1913-14

Irish League 1913-14 Season	Belfast Celtic	Bohemian	Cliftonville	Distillery	Glenavon	Glentoran	Linfield	Shelbourne
Belfast Celtic FC	■	4-1	1-0	2-1	2-0	1-0	1-2	1-0
Bohemian FC	4-5	■	2-3	0-0	2-1	2-5	3-1	0-1
Cliftonville FC	0-1	4-2	■	0-1	6-2	0-3	0-3	0-3
Distillery FC	1-0	3-1	3-1	■	1-0	0-0	1-3	1-0
Glenavon FC	0-0	1-0	1-0	2-1	■	2-3	1-1	1-0
Glentoran FC	4-0	5-1	3-1	0-0	1-0	■	2-2	3-2
Linfield FC	2-1	3-1	2-0	2-0	5-1	4-2	■	1-0
Shelbourne FC	3-0	0-0	2-0	1-1	1-0	3-1	0-1	■

	Irish League	Pd	Wn	Dw	Ls	GF	GA	Pts
1.	LINFIELD FC (BELFAST)	14	11	2	1	32	13	24
2.	Glentoran FC (Belfast)	14	8	3	3	32	18	19
3.	Belfast Celtic FC (Belfast)	14	8	1	5	19	18	17
4.	Distillery FC (Belfast)	14	6	4	4	14	12	16
5.	Shelbourne FC (Dublin)	14	6	2	6	16	10	14
6.	Glenavon FC (Lurgan)	14	4	2	8	12	23	10
7.	Bohemian FC (Dublin)	14	2	2	10	19	36	6
8.	Cliftonville FC (Belfast)	14	3	-	11	15	29	6
		112	48	16	48	159	159	112

No clubs promoted or relegated

IRISH CUP FINAL (Grosvenor Park, Belfast – 28/03/1914)

GLENTORAN FC (BELFAST)   3-1   Linfield FC (Belfast)

W. Lindsay 2, Lyner   *McEwan*

Glentoran: Murphy, McCann, Annesley, Ferrett, Scraggs, Emerson, Lyner, J. Lindsay, Napier, Boyd, W. Lindsay.
Linfield: Kelly, Rollo, Foye, McConnell, Clifford, Wallace, Lyner, Nixon, Young, McNeill, McEwan.

Semi-finals

Glentoran FC (Belfast)	1-1, 1-1, 0-0, 3-1	Shelbourne FC (Dublin)
Linfield FC (Belfast)	4-2	Glenavon FC (Lurgan)

Quarter-finals

Shelbourne FC (Dublin)	1-1, +:-	Belfast Celtic FC (Belfast)

Glenavon FC (Lurgan), Glentoran FC (Belfast) and Linfield FC (Belfast) all received byes

1914-15

Irish League 1914-15 Season	Belfast Celtic	Bohemian	Cliftonville	Distillery	Glenavon	Glentoran	Linfield	Shelbourne
Belfast Celtic FC	■	1-1	5-0	1-0	3-0	1-0	2-1	1-0
Bohemian FC	0-3	■	1-2	2-3	2-4	0-3	2-5	0-3
Cliftonville FC	1-3	2-0	■	0-1	3-1	0-3	1-2	1-3
Distillery FC	0-1	3-0	4-0	■	4-2	1-2	0-0	0-1
Glenavon FC	2-2	6-0	1-1	0-3	■	0-0	5-1	0-0
Glentoran FC	2-0	3-0	2-0	4-3	5-0	■	1-1	1-0
Linfield FC	0-0	5-2	3-0	3-0	1-1	3-0	■	2-2
Shelbourne FC	0-1	2-0	0-2	0-1	3-2	1-1	2-0	■

	Irish League	**Pd**	**Wn**	**Dw**	**Ls**	**GF**	**GA**	**Pts**
1.	BELFAST CELTIC FC (BELFAST)	14	10	3	1	24	7	23
2.	Glentoran FC (Belfast)	14	9	3	2	27	10	21
3.	Linfield FC (Belfast)	14	6	5	3	27	18	17
4.	Distillery FC (Belfast)	14	7	1	6	23	16	15
5.	Shelbourne FC (Dublin)	14	6	3	5	17	12	15
6.	Glenavon FC (Lurgan)	14	3	5	6	24	28	11
7.	Cliftonville FC (Belfast)	14	4	1	9	13	29	9
8.	Bohemian FC (Dublin)	14	-	1	13	10	45	1
		112	45	22	45	165	165	112

The league was suspended due to World War 1 but the Irish Cup and some "unofficial" league competitions continued to be contested until the resumption of the "official" Irish League for the 1919-20 season.

IRISH CUP FINAL (Solitude, Belfast – 27/03/1915)

LINFIELD FC (BELFAST)   1-0   Belfast Celtic FC (Belfast)

Bovill

Linfield: McKee, Rollo, Foye, Wallace, Clifford, Bartlett, Young, Nixon, Hamilton, Bovill, McEwan.
Belfast: MeHaffey, Nelson, Barrett, Leatham, Hamill, Norwood, Kerr, McKnight, Williams, Cowell, Hegan.

Semi-finals

Belfast Celtic FC (Belfast)	0-0, 1-0	Shelbourne FC (Dublin)
Linfield FC (Belfast)	2-0	Distillery FC (Belfast)

Quarter-finals

Bohemian FC (Dublin)	0-4	Belfast Celtic FC (Belfast)
Distillery FC (Belfast)	4-1	Glenavon FC (Lurgan)
Glentoran FC (Belfast)	1-2	Shelbourne FC (Dublin)
Linfield FC (Belfast)	3-2	Cliftonville FC (Belfast)

1915-16

Belfast & District League 1915-16 Season	Belfast United	Cliftonville	Distillery	Glenavon	Glentoran	Linfield
Belfast United FC	■	0-0	0-2	3-1	2-2	1-0
Cliftonville FC	2-1	■	0-2	0-0	1-1	0-2
Distillery FC	1-1	1-1	■	7-0	1-0	0-1
Glenavon FC	0-4	2-3	0-1	■	1-2	1-6
Glentoran FC	2-1	4-0	4-2	5-2	■	0-0
Linfield FC	3-1	1-0	2-1	2-0	0-0	■

	Belfast & District League	Pd	Wn	Dw	Ls	GF	GA	Pts
1.	LINFIELD FC (BELFAST)	10	7	2	1	17	4	16
2.	Glentoran FC (Belfast)	10	5	4	1	20	10	14
3.	Distillery FC (Belfast)	10	5	2	3	18	9	12
4.	Belfast United FC (Belfast)	10	3	3	4	14	13	9
5.	Cliftonville FC (Belfast)	10	2	4	4	7	14	8
6.	Glenavon FC (Lurgan)	10	-	1	9	7	33	1
		60	22	16	22	83	83	60

No clubs promoted or relegated

IRISH CUP FINAL   (Celtic Park, Belfast – 25/03/1916)

LINFIELD FC (BELFAST)	1-1	Glentoran FC (Belfast)
Nixon		*Ferrett pen.*

Linfield: McKee, Rollo, Foye, McCandless, Clifford, Bartlett, Houston, Nixon, Bovill, Campbell, McEwan.
Glentoran: Steele, Stafford, Grainger, Ferrett, Scraggs, Emerson, Lyner, Seymour, Boyd, West, Bookman.

IRISH CUP FINAL REPLAY   (Grosvenor Park, Belfast – 01/04/1916)

LINFIELD FC (BELFAST)	1-0	Glentoran FC (Belfast)
Nixon		

Glentoran: Steele, Stafford, Frainger, Ferrett, Scraggs, Emerson, Lyner, Seymour, Boyd, West, Bookman.
Linfield: McKee, Rollo, Foye, McCandless, Clifford, Bartlett, Houston, Nixon, Bovill, Campbell, McEwan.

Semi-finals

Belfast Celtic FC (Belfast)	0-1	Linfield FC (Belfast)
Glentoran FC (Belfast)	4-2	Bohemian FC (Dublin)

Quarter-finals

Bohemian FC (Dublin)	0-0, 3-0, 1-0	Shelbourne FC (Dublin)
	(The 2nd match was abandoned)	
Distillery FC (Belfast)	0-3	Glentoran FC (Belfast)

Belfast Celtic FC (Belfast) and Linfield FC (Belfast) both received byes

1916-17

Belfast & District League 1916-17 Season	Belfast United	Cliftonville	Distillery	Glenavon	Glentoran	Linfield
Belfast United FC		0-1	1-1	1-1	1-3	0-3
Cliftonville FC	3-0		0-1	3-2	0-2	1-1
Distillery FC	1-1	1-0		5-3	3-3	1-1
Glenavon FC	1-0	0-0	1-5		2-3	0-5
Glentoran FC	2-1	1-1	4-3	4-3		4-0
Linfield FC	3-2	2-0	0-2	2-0	2-2	

	Belfast & District League	**Pd**	**Wn**	**Dw**	**Ls**	**GF**	**GA**	**Pts**
1.	GLENTORAN FC (BELFAST)	10	7	3	-	28	16	17
2.	Distillery FC (Belfast)	10	5	4	1	23	14	14
3.	Linfield FC (Belfast)	10	5	3	2	19	12	13
4.	Cliftonville FC (Belfast)	10	3	3	4	9	10	9
5.	Glenavon FC (Lurgan)	10	1	2	7	13	28	4
6.	Belfast United FC (Belfast)	10	-	3	7	7	19	3
		60	21	18	21	99	99	60

No clubs promoted or relegated

IRISH CUP FINAL   (Windsor Park, Belfast – 31/03/1917)

GLENTORAN FC (BELFAST)	2-0	Belfast Celtic FC (London)

Seymour 2

Glentoran: Steele, G.Moore, Grainger, Bennett, Scraggs, Ferrett, Lyner, Seymour, Boyd, Emerson, W.Moore.
Belfast: Scott, Kennedy, McIlroy, Norwood, Hamill, Stewart, McKinney, Kelly, Heaney, Johnston, Frazer.

Semi-finals

Belfast Celtic FC (Belfast)	4-0	Bohemian FC (Dublin)
Glentoran FC (Belfast)	1-1, 3-1	Distillery FC (Belfast)

Quarter-finals

Belfast Celtic FC (Belfast)	1-1, 2-0	Linfield FC (Belfast)
Bohemian FC (Dublin)	3-1	Strandville FC (Dublin)

Distillery FC (Belfast) and Glentoran FC (Belfast) both received byes

1917-18

Belfast & District League 1917-18 Season	Belfast United	Cliftonville	Distillery	Glenavon	Glentoran	Linfield
Belfast United FC		1-1	1-0	4-1	1-3	0-1
Cliftonville FC	1-1		0-0	3-0	0-4	1-3
Distillery FC	3-2	3-2		5-0	0-2	2-2
Glenavon FC	1-0	1-0	0-1		1-4	1-5
Glentoran FC	2-1	0-0	2-0	1-0		0-0
Linfield FC	4-0	3-1	3-0	7-0	2-0	

	Belfast & District League	**Pd**	**Wn**	**Dw**	**Ls**	**GF**	**GA**	**Pts**	
1.	LINFIELD FC (BELFAST)	10	8	2	-	30	5	18	
2.	Glentoran FC (Belfast)	10	7	2	1	18	5	16	
3.	Distillery FC (Belfast)	10	4	2	4	14	14	10	
4.	Cliftonville FC (Belfast)	10	1	4	5	9	16	6	
5.	Belfast United FC (Belfast)	10	2	2	6	11	17	6	
6.	Glenavon FC (Lurgan)	10	2	-	8	5	30	4	#
		60	24	12	24	87	87	60	

Glenavon FC (Lurgan) did not compete in this league for the next season.

Elected: Belfast Celtic FC (Belfast)

IRISH CUP FINAL   (The Oval, Belfast – 30/03/1918)

BELFAST CELTIC FC (BELFAST)   0-0   Linfield FC (Belfast)

Belfast: Scott, McStay, Barrett, Mulligan, Hamill, Stewart, McKinney, McIlroy, Ferris, Johnstone, Norwood.
Linfield: McKee, Rollo, Foye, Dunlop, Lacey, McCandless, Cochrane, Nixon, West, Rea, McEwan.

IRISH CUP FINAL REPLAY   (Solitude, Belfast – 13/04/1918)

BELFAST CELTIC FC (BELFAST)   0-0   Linfield FC (Belfast)

Belfast: Scott, McStay, Barrett, Mulligan, Hamill, Stewart, McKinney, McIlroy, Ferris, Johnstone, Frazer.
Linfield: McKee, Rollo, Foye, Dunlop, Lacey, McCandless, Campbell, Nixon, Cochrane, West, McEwan.

IRISH CUP FINAL 2ND REPLAY   (Grosvenor Park, Belfast – 24/04/1918)

BELFAST CELTIC FC (BELFAST)   2-0   Linfield FC (Belfast)

Foye o.g., Stewart

Belfast: Scott, McStay, Barrett, Mulligan, Hamill, Stewart, McKinney, McIlroy, Ferris, Johnston, Frazer.
Linfield: McKee, Rollo, Foye, Dunlop, Fulton, McCandless, Rea, Stitt, McLaughlin, Lacey, McEwan.

Semi-finals

| Belfast Celtic FC (Belfast) | 2-1 | Belfast United FC (Belfast) |
| Linfield FC (Belfast) | 2-1 | Distillery FC (Belfast) |

Quarter-finals

| Belfast Celtic FC (Belfast) | 0-0, 4-0 | Glentoran FC (Belfast) 2nd XI |
| Belfast United FC (Belfast) | 3-0 | Shelbourne FC (Dublin) |

Distillery FC (Belfast) and Linfield FC (Belfast) both received byes

1918-19

Belfast & District League 1918-19 Season	Belfast Celtic	Belfast United	Cliftonville	Distillery	Glentoran	Linfield
Belfast Celtic FC	■	2-1	2-0	1-0	2-1	0-1
Belfast United FC	2-2	■	2-2	2-4	2-1	1-2
Cliftonville FC	0-3	0-1	■	1-1	1-0	2-3
Distillery FC	0-1	2-0	1-1	■	0-0	0-2
Glentoran FC	0-2	1-0	2-0	3-2	■	1-0
Linfield FC	2-0	3-1	1-0	1-1	0-2	■

Play-off
BELFAST CELTIC FC (BELFAST)   1-0   Linfield FC (Belfast)

	Belfast & District League	Pd	Wn	Dw	Ls	GF	GA	Pts	
1.	Belfast Celtic FC (Belfast)	10	7	1	2	15	7	15	
1.	Linfield FC (Belfast)	10	7	1	2	15	8	15	
3.	Glentoran FC (Belfast)	10	5	1	4	11	9	11	
4.	Distillery FC (Belfast)	10	2	4	4	11	12	8	
5.	Belfast United FC (Belfast)	10	2	2	6	12	19	6	#
6.	Cliftonville FC (Belfast)	10	1	3	6	7	16	5	
		60	24	12	24	71	71	60	

Belfast United FC (Belfast) were not included in the "official" Irish League which started next season, 1919-20. Bohemian FC (Dublin), Glenavon FC (Lurgan) and Shelbourne FC (Dublin) were elected in addition to the other 5 clubs in the above Belfast & District League.

IRISH CUP FINAL   (Celtic Park, Belfast – 29/03/1919)
LINFIELD FC (BELFAST)   1-1   Glentoran FC (Belfast)
Featherstone   *Lyner*
Linfield: McKee, Rollo, B. McCandless, Seymour, Lacey, Pollins, J.McCandless, Lindsay, Featherstone, McDonald, McEwan.
Glentoran: Liddell, Spencer, Grainger, Bennett, Scraggs, Emerson, Lyner, Ferrett, Chambers, Mathieson, Moore.

IRISH CUP FINAL REPLAY   (Grosvenor Park, Belfast – 05/04/1919)
LINFIELD FC (BELFAST)   0-0   Glentoran FC (Belfast)
Linfield: McKee, Rollo, B.McCandless, Houston, Lacey, Pollins, Campbell, Lindsay, Featherstone, McDonald, McEwan.
Glentoran: Liddell; Spencer, Christie Grainger, Bennett, Scraggs, Emerson, Lyner, Chambers, Boyd, Mathieson, Moore.

IRISH CUP FINAL 2ND REPLAY (Solitude, Belfast – 07/04/1919)

LINFIELD FC (BELFAST)　　　　　2-1　　　　　Glentoran FC (Belfast)
McEwan 2　　　　　　　　　　　　　　　　　　　　　　　　　　　　　*Scraggs*

Linfield: McKee, Rollo, McCandless, Houston, Lacey, Pollins, Campbell, Lindsay, Featherstone, McDonald, McEwan.

Glentoran: Liddell, Spencer, Grainger, Bennett, Scraggs, Emerson, Lyner, Chambers, Boyd, Mathieson, Moore.

Semi-finals

Glentoran FC (Belfast)	2-0	Belfast Celtic FC (Belfast)
Linfield FC (Belfast)	2-0	Shelbourne FC (Dublin)

Quarter-finals

Linfield FC (Belfast)　　　　　4-0, 1-0　　　　　Distillery FC (Belfast)
Belfast Celtic FC (Belfast), Glentoran FC (Belfast) and Shelbourne FC (Dublin) all received byes

1919-20

Irish League 1919-20 Season	Belfast Celtic	Bohemian	Cliftonville	Distillery	Glenavon	Glentoran	Linfield	Shelbourne
Belfast Celtic FC	■	5-0	4-0	0-0	3-0	1-0	1-0	1-0
Bohemian FC	0-4	■	1-0	0-2	0-4	2-2	0-1	1-3
Cliftonville FC	1-2	2-0	■	0-1	0-4	0-0	0-0	2-2
Distillery FC	0-0	4-1	0-0	■	0-0	2-2	1-0	7-3
Glenavon FC	1-2	5-1	2-3	1-7	■	1-3	0-0	0-0
Glentoran FC	2-0	6-0	3-1	1-0	4-0	■	2-0	4-0
Linfield FC	1-3	0-1	1-1	1-2	2-0	1-0	■	1-0
Shelbourne FC	1-1	0-0	2-1	0-0	3-3	2-0	0-0	■

	Irish League	Pd	Wn	Dw	Ls	GF	GA	Pts	
1.	BELFAST CELTIC FC (BELFAST)	14	10	3	1	27	6	23	#
2.	Distillery FC (Belfast)	14	7	6	1	26	9	20	
3.	Glentoran FC (Belfast)	14	8	3	3	29	10	19	
4.	Shelbourne FC (Dublin)	14	3	7	4	16	21	13	#
5.	Linfield FC (Belfast)	14	4	4	6	8	11	12	
6.	Glenavon FC (Lurgan)	14	3	4	7	21	28	10	
7.	Cliftonville FC (Belfast)	14	2	5	7	11	22	9	
8.	Bohemian FC (Dublin)	14	2	2	10	7	38	6	#
		112	39	34	39	145	145	112	

\# Belfast Celtic FC (Belfast) resigned from the league after being expelled from the Irish Cup and did not compete in the league for the next season. Bohemian FC (Dublin) and Shelbourne FC (Dublin) resigned from the Irish League to join the newly-formed League of Ireland in the newly constituted Irish Free State (later to become the Republic of Ireland).

The Irish League was reduced to 5 clubs for next season

IRISH CUP

SHELBOURNE FC (DUBLIN)

Shelbourne were awarded the cup after both Belfast Celtic and Glentoran were expelled from the competition

Semi-finals

Glentoran FC (Belfast)   1-1, 0-0   Belfast Celtic FC (Belfast)

During the replay on 17th March 1920, Celtic left-back Fred Barrett was ordered off the field of play. This resulted in a spectator running on to the field firing a revolver at the Glentoran fans. This caused panic and rioting in the crowd and the match was abandoned after 70 minutes. A number of spectators were injured, Celtic were found guilty of "lack of control of fans" and were expelled from the cup on 20th March 1920. Belfast Celtic then protested that Glentoran had fielded H. McIlveen who was ineligible as his name was not included on the list submitted to the referee. Glentoran were duly expelled from the competition also. As a result of this double expulsion Shelbourne, the only remaining competitors, were awarded the cup.

Shelbourne FC (Dublin)   3-0   Glenavon FC (Lurgan)

Quarter-finals

Bohemian FC (Dublin)   0-2   Belfast Celtic FC (Belfast)
Glentoran FC (Belfast)   0-0, 2-0   Cliftonville FC (Belfast)

Glenavon FC (Lurgan) and Shelbourne FC (Dublin) both received byes

1920-21

Irish League 1920-21 Season	Cliftonville	Distillery	Glenavon	Glentoran	Linfield
Cliftonville FC	■	4-1	0-0	0-2	0-0
Distillery FC	2-0	■	0-1	0-3	0-1
Glenavon FC	3-0	4-3	■	3-1	0-0
Glentoran FC	2-0	5-1	3-0	■	1-0
Linfield FC	3-1	1-0	1-1	2-3	■

	Irish League	Pd	Wn	Dw	Ls	GF	GA	Pts
1.	GLENTORAN FC (BELFAST)	8	7	-	1	20	6	14
2.	Glenavon FC (Lurgan)	8	5	2	1	14	8	12
3.	Linfield FC (Belfast)	8	3	3	2	8	6	9
4.	Cliftonville FC (Belfast)	8	1	1	6	5	15	3
5.	Distillery FC (Belfast)	8	1	-	7	7	19	2
		40	17	6	17	54	54	40

Elected: Queen's Island FC (Belfast)

The league was extended to 6 clubs for the next season

Note: All "southern" clubs resigned from the Irish FA to join the newly formed Irish Free State FA.

IRISH CUP FINAL (Windsor Park, Belfast – 26/03/1921)

GLENTORAN FC (BELFAST) 2-0 Glenavon FC (Lurgan)

Crooks, Snape

Glentoran: McHaffey, McSeveney, Ferguson, Ferrett, Scraggs, Emerson, McGregor, Crooks, Davey, Meek, Snape.
Glenavon: Mehaffey, Curran, Burnison, Campbell, Barbour, Rollins, McMullan, W. Brown, J. Brown, Steele, Clarke.

Semi-finals

Glenavon FC (Lurgan) 0-0, w/o Shelbourne FC (Dublin)
(Glenavon were awarded a walk over after Shelbourne refused to replay in Belfast on St. Patrick's Day, claiming that the replay should be held in Dublin on a different day).
Glentoran FC (Belfast) 4-3 Brantwood FC (Belfast)

Quarter-finals

Glenavon FC (Lurgan) 1-0 Linfield FC (Belfast)
Glentoran FC (Belfast) 2-1 Forth River FC
St. James's Gate AFC (Dublin) 0-0, 1-2 Shelbourne FC (Dublin)
Brantwood FC (Belfast) received a bye

1921-22

Irish League 1921-22 Season	Cliftonville	Distillery	Glenavon	Glentoran	Linfield	Queen's Island
Cliftonville FC		0-2	2-1	0-2	0-1	0-1
Distillery FC	1-0		2-1	2-2	2-3	3-0
Glenavon FC	1-0	2-1		1-1	1-3	2-1
Glentoran FC	3-1	3-1	1-0		0-0	0-1
Linfield FC	1-0	4-0	1-1	1-0		1-1
Queen's Island FC	0-0	2-4	2-1	0-2	1-3	

	Irish League	Pd	Wn	Dw	Ls	GF	GA	Pts
1.	LINFIELD FC (BELFAST)	10	7	3	-	18	6	17
2.	Glentoran FC (Belfast)	10	5	3	2	14	7	13
3.	Distillery FC (Belfast)	10	5	1	4	18	17	11
4.	Glenavon FC (Lurgan)	10	3	2	5	11	14	8
5.	Queen's Island FC (Belfast)	10	3	2	5	9	16	8
6.	Cliftonville FC (Belfast)	10	1	1	8	3	13	3
		60	24	12	24	73	73	60

No clubs promoted or relegated

IRISH CUP FINAL (Solitude, Belfast – 25/03/1922)

LINFIELD FC (BELFAST) 2-1 Glenavon FC (Lurgan)

Savage, McCracken *Boyd*

Linfield: Harland, Gaw, Frame, Wallace, Morgan, McIlveen, Cowan, McCracken, Savage, McIlreavey, Scott.
Glenavon: Morrow, Brown, Curran, Barbour, Short, Killen, McMullan, Thompson, Rushe, Boyd, McMahon.

Semi-finals

Glenavon FC (Lurgan)	2-1	Linfield Rangers FC (Belfast)
Queen's Island FC (Belfast)	0-1	Linfield FC (Belfast)

Quarter-finals

Distillery FC (Belfast)	1-5	Linfield FC (Belfast)
Glenavon FC (Lurgan)	1-0	Glentoran FC (Belfast)
Linfield Rangers FC (Belfast)	3-1	Forth River FC
Queen's Island FC (Belfast)	1-1, 1-1, 2-0	Cliftonville FC (Belfast)

1922-23

Irish League 1922-23 Season	Cliftonville	Distillery	Glenavon	Glentoran	Linfield	Queen's Island
Cliftonville FC		2-2	1-0	1-1	1-2	1-2
Distillery FC	0-2		1-0	1-0	1-0	2-3
Glenavon FC	4-1	2-3		2-1	0-0	0-1
Glentoran FC	3-0	1-0	3-1		1-2	2-0
Linfield FC	1-0	1-0	4-1	1-1		3-0
Queen's Island FC	4-2	2-2	4-2	1-1	0-6	

	Irish League	**Pd**	**Wn**	**Dw**	**Ls**	**GF**	**GA**	**Pts**
1.	LINFIELD FC (BELFAST)	10	7	2	1	20	5	16
2.	Queen's Island FC (Belfast)	10	5	2	3	17	21	12
3.	Glentoran FC (Belfast)	10	4	3	3	14	9	11
4.	Distillery FC (Belfast)	10	4	2	4	12	13	10
5.	Cliftonville FC (Belfast)	10	2	2	6	11	19	6
6.	Glenavon FC (Lurgan)	10	2	1	7	12	19	5
		60	24	12	24	86	86	60

Elected: Ards FC (Newtownards), Barn FC (Carrickfergus), Larne FC (Larne), Newry Town FC (Newry)

The league was extended to 10 clubs for next season

IRISH CUP FINAL   (Solitude, Belfast – 31/03/1923)

LINFIELD FC (BELFAST)	2-0	Glentoran FC (Belfast)

McCracken, Savage

Linfield: Diffin, Maulstaid, Frame, Wallace, Moorhead, Robinson, Cowan, McCracken, Savage, McIlreavy, McGrillen.

Glentoran: McCormick, Peden, Ferrett, Reid, Burns, Evans, Swindell, Elwood, Keenan, McAnally, Topping.

Semi-finals

Glentoran FC (Belfast)	2-1	Glenavon FC (Lurgan)
Linfield FC (Belfast)	1-0	Distillery FC (Belfast)

Quarter-finals

Dunmurry Recreation FC (Dunmurry)	3-2	Distillery FC (Belfast)
	(Distillery were awarded the match after a protest)	
Glenavon FC (Lurgan)	1-1, 3-2	Queen's Island FC (Belfast)
Glentoran FC (Belfast)	0-0, 2-2, 2-2, 4-1	Brantwood FC (Belfast)
Linfield FC (Belfast)	2-0	Cliftonville FC (Belfast)

1923-24

Irish League 1923-24 Season	Ards	Barn	Cliftonville	Distillery	Glenavon	Glentoran	Larne	Linfield	Newry Town	Queen's Island
Ards FC		0-0	0-2	1-0	1-1	1-2	2-0	4-3	1-0	1-2
Barn FC	1-2		0-1	2-2	2-0	2-1	3-1	0-0	3-2	4-2
Cliftonville FC	1-1	4-1		1-2	3-3	0-1	3-2	1-0	0-0	1-1
Distillery FC	4-0	0-0	2-1		4-4	0-3	3-1	1-2	3-2	1-1
Glenavon FC	2-1	1-0	3-2	1-1		2-1	0-0	1-1	0-0	0-2
Glentoran FC	2-0	4-1	0-1	1-2	4-0		5-1	2-1	2-2	0-3
Larne FC	5-2	1-0	1-1	4-3	3-3	2-1		3-3	4-1	0-5
Linfield FC	2-0	2-1	2-0	1-1	1-2	1-2	4-1		3-1	3-2
Newry Town FC	1-1	2-3	5-2	1-2	2-2	1-0	1-3	1-2		3-4
Queen's Island FC	2-0	4-0	0-0	4-1	2-2	3-1	3-1	4-0	4-0	

	Irish League	**Pd**	**Wn**	**Dw**	**Ls**	**GF**	**GA**	**Pts**	
1.	QUEEN'S ISLAND FC (BELFAST)	18	12	4	2	48	18	26	-2
2.	Distillery FC (Belfast)	18	7	6	5	32	30	20	PO
3.	Linfield FC (Belfast)	18	8	4	6	31	27	20	PO
4.	Glenavon FC (Lurgan)	18	5	10	3	27	30	20	PO
5.	Glentoran FC (Belfast)	18	9	1	8	32	23	19	
6.	Cliftonville FC (Belfast)	18	6	6	6	24	24	18	
7.	Barn FC (Carrickfergus)	18	6	4	8	23	29	16	
8.	Larne FC (Larne)	18	6	4	8	33	43	16	
9.	Ards FC (Newtownards)	18	5	4	9	18	30	14	
10.	Newry Town FC (Newry)	18	2	5	11	25	39	9	
		180	66	48	66	293	293	178	

2nd Place 2nd Play-off

Distillery FC (Belfast)	2-1	Linfield FC (Belfast)

Irish League 2nd Place Play-off 1923-24 Season	Linfield	Distillery	Glenavon
Linfield FC	*	---	4-0
Distillery FC	2-2	*	---
Glenavon FC	---	1-3	*

Play-off (2nd Place)	Pd	Wn	Dw	Ls	GF	GA	Pts
1. Linfield FC (Belfast)	2	1	1	-	6	2	3
1. Distillery FC (Belfast)	2	1	1	-	5	3	3
3. Glenavon FC (Lurgan)	2	-	-	2	1	7	-
	6	2	2	2	12	12	6

Note: Queen's Island FC (Belfast) had 2 points deducted by the Irish League committee.

Elected: Belfast Celtic FC (Belfast), Portadown FC (Portadown)

The league was extended to 12 clubs for the next season

IRISH CUP FINAL (Windsor Park, Belfast – 29/03/1924)

QUEEN'S ISLAND FC (BELFAST)　　　1-0　　　Willowfield FC (Belfast)

Burns

Queen's Island: Gough, McKeown, Fergie, Kennedy, Gowdy, Murdough, Cowan, Croft, Burns, McCleery, Morton.
Willowfield: Jackson, Savage, Fulton, Ingram, Kirkwood, McClure, Bothwell, Clarke, Hewitt, Johnston, Snape.

Semi-finals

| Queen's Island FC (Belfast) | 1-1, 1-0 | Crusaders FC (Belfast) |
| Willowfield FC (Belfast) | 1-0 | Larne FC (Larne) |

Quarter-finals

| Crusaders FC (Belfast) | 5-4 | Distillery FC (Belfast) |
| Willowfield FC (Belfast) | 2-2, 1-1, 3-0 | Newry Town FC (Newry) |

Larne FC (Larne) and Queen's Island FC (Belfast) both received byes

1924-25

Irish League 1924-25 Season	Ards	Barn	Belfast Celtic	Cliftonville	Distillery	Glenavon	Glentoran	Larne	Linfield	Newry Town	Portadown	Queen's Island
Ards FC	■	4-0	7-0	2-1	3-2	2-0	0-3	0-3	0-2	4-0	1-0	1-4
Barn FC	1-0	■	2-1	1-2	1-1	0-2	1-1	2-0	2-3	5-1	3-2	0-0
Belfast Celtic FC	2-2	0-0	■	2-1	4-1	0-1	0-1	2-0	2-1	4-1	2-1	1-1
Cliftonville FC	3-0	4-0	2-2	■	1-0	3-1	0-1	1-0	0-3	1-1	0-0	0-3
Distillery FC	1-1	1-0	1-5	2-0	■	3-0	1-3	1-1	1-2	4-2	0-1	2-3
Glenavon FC	5-2	2-1	1-3	2-0	2-1	■	2-1	4-1	1-2	10-2	1-2	1-2
Glentoran FC	2-1	2-1	4-0	1-0	2-2	1-0	■	7-2	4-0	6-2	5-1	1-0
Larne FC	5-4	2-1	0-2	0-0	1-0	2-5	0-2	■	2-1	2-0	2-2	1-4
Linfield FC	0-1	1-2	0-0	4-1	1-2	0-2	2-1	0-0	■	3-0	2-1	2-3
Newry Town FC	4-3	4-2	1-2	3-0	3-2	2-2	1-2	1-3	1-0	■	1-2	1-1
Portadown FC	1-0	4-2	1-2	3-1	3-1	1-1	1-2	6-2	4-3	3-1	■	2-2
Queen's Island FC	2-1	3-2	2-0	1-0	1-2	5-0	1-1	2-1	1-2	6-1	1-1	■

	Irish League	Pd	Wn	Dw	Ls	GF	GA	Pts
1.	GLENTORAN FC (BELFAST)	22	17	3	2	53	18	37
2.	Queen's Island FC (Belfast)	22	13	6	3	48	23	32
3.	Belfast Celtic FC (Belfast)	22	11	5	6	36	31	27
4.	Portadown FC (Portadown)	22	10	5	7	42	35	25
5.	Glenavon FC (Lurgan)	22	11	2	9	45	36	24
6.	Linfield FC (Belfast)	22	10	2	10	34	31	22
7.	Ards FC (Newtownards)	22	8	2	12	39	41	18
8.	Larne FC (Larne)	22	7	4	11	30	47	18
9.	Barn FC Carrickfergus)	22	6	4	12	29	40	16
10.	Cliftonville FC (Belfast)	22	6	4	12	21	32	16
11.	Distillery FC (Belfast)	22	6	4	12	31	40	16
12.	Newry Town FC (Newry)	22	5	3	14	33	67	13
		264	110	44	110	441	441	264

No clubs were promoted or relegated

IRISH CUP FINAL   (Solitude, Belfast – 21/03/1925)

DISTILLERY FC (BELFAST)　　　　2-1　　　　　　　　　　Glentoran FC (Belfast)
McKenzie, Burnison pen.　　　　　　　　　　　　　　　　　　　　　　　　　　*Burns*

Distillery: Fitzroy, Thompson, Burnison, Garrett, Sloan, Anderson, McKenzie, Dalrymple, Rushe, Blair, McMullan.

Glentoran: Bowden, McSeveney, Reid, Inch, Burns, Emerson, McKeague, Rainey, Keenan, Meek, Allen.

Semi-finals

Distillery FC (Belfast)	2-0	Glenavon FC (Lurgan)
Glentoran FC (Belfast)	2-0	Crusaders FC (Belfast)

Quarter-finals

Crusaders FC (Belfast)	2-0	Belfast Celtic FC (Belfast)
Distillery FC (Belfast)	0-0, 1-0	Barn FC (Carrickfergus)
Glentoran FC (Belfast)	5-3	Newry Town FC (Newry)

Glenavon FC (Lurgan) received a bye

1925-26

Irish League 1925-26 Season	Ards	Barn	Belfast Celtic	Cliftonville	Distillery	Glenavon	Glentoran	Larne	Linfield	Newry Town	Portadown	Queen's Island
Ards FC	■	3-1	1-2	1-1	1-2	3-1	2-1	1-3	6-1	5-1	3-3	4-2
Barn FC	3-4	■	0-2	1-2	2-1	0-2	0-6	2-1	1-3	4-4	1-1	0-2
Belfast Celtic FC	2-0	5-1	■	3-2	2-1	0-1	2-1	5-2	5-3	4-3	1-3	2-1
Cliftonville FC	0-2	3-2	3-0	■	1-3	0-1	2-3	2-2	2-2	1-2	0-2	2-2
Distillery FC	2-5	2-1	0-0	1-1	■	1-1	2-1	1-0	4-1	3-2	3-2	2-0
Glenavon FC	0-2	3-1	0-2	1-4	2-1	■	2-1	2-2	2-3	1-2	4-1	3-1
Glentoran FC	4-2	4-1	2-3	2-1	2-1	4-1	■	2-1	3-2	5-1	2-2	2-2
Larne FC	4-1	2-0	3-1	3-0	4-1	3-3	1-1	■	3-0	1-0	4-1	2-0
Linfield FC	1-0	6-1	2-4	2-1	3-1	4-1	0-1	2-2	■	5-0	0-1	1-2
Newry Town FC	3-3	3-1	1-2	1-0	0-0	0-2	2-3	1-2	1-1	■	3-2	2-2
Portadown FC	2-2	4-2	2-3	0-0	2-2	1-3	0-2	4-0	3-3	4-1	■	1-2
Queen's Island FC	3-5	3-0	6-2	3-1	2-3	1-0	1-1	3-0	2-2	2-0	0-2	■

	Irish League	Pd	Wn	Dw	Ls	GF	GA	Pts
1.	BELFAST CELTIC FC (BELFAST)	22	16	1	5	52	38	33
2.	Glentoran FC (Belfast)	22	13	4	5	53	31	30
3.	Larne FC (Larne)	22	11	5	6	45	33	27
4.	Ards FC (Newtownards)	22	11	4	7	56	42	26
5.	Distillery FC (Belfast)	22	10	5	7	37	35	25
6.	Queen's Island FC (Belfast)	22	9	5	8	42	37	23
7.	Glenavon FC (Lurgan)	22	10	3	9	36	37	23
8.	Linfield FC (Belfast)	22	8	5	9	47	46	21
9.	Portadown FC (Portadown)	22	7	7	8	43	41	21
10.	Newry Town FC (Newry)	22	5	5	12	33	53	15
11.	Cliftonville FC (Belfast)	22	4	6	12	29	39	14
12.	Barn FC (Carrickfergus)	22	2	2	18	25	66	6
		264	106	52	106	498	498	264

IRISH CUP FINAL   (Solitude, Belfast – 27/03/1926)

BELFAST CELTIC FC (BELFAST)　　　　3-2　　　　　　　　　　Linfield FC (Belfast)
Curran 3　　　　　　　　　　　　　　　　　　　　　　　　　　*Andrews, Cooke*

Belfast: Fitzmaurice, Scott, Ferguson, Pollock, Moore, Perry, McGrillen, Ferris, Curran, S. Mahood, J. Mahood.
Linfield: McMeekin, Holmes, Frame, Stewart, Moorehead, Grant, Coates, Cooke, Andrews, McIlreavy, Morton.

Semi-finals

| Belfast Celtic FC (Belfast) | 3-0 | Newry Town FC (Newry) |
| Linfield FC (Belfast) | 2-2, 2-2, 3-2 | Glentoran FC (Belfast) |

Quarter-finals

Belfast Celtic FC (Belfast)	2-1	Glenavon FC (Lurgan)
Glentoran FC (Belfast)	2-1	Belfast United FC (Belfast)
Newry Town FC (Newry)	1-1, 3-1	Portadown FC (Portadown)
Linfield FC (Belfast) received a bye		

1926-27

Irish League 1926-27 Season	Ards	Barn	Belfast Celtic	Cliftonville	Distillery	Glenavon	Glentoran	Larne	Linfield	Newry Town	Portadown	Queen's Island
Ards FC		4-1	1-6	0-1	3-0	0-1	3-2	2-1	2-1	4-2	3-3	1-1
Barn FC	1-3		2-6	0-4	3-7	3-2	2-6	2-1	2-2	3-3	3-8	2-3
Belfast Celtic FC	1-1	4-1		1-0	3-0	3-1	4-1	3-1	4-2	7-2	0-0	1-0
Cliftonville FC	4-1	3-1	1-1		0-1	4-1	0-2	0-2	1-3	0-1	2-6	2-1
Distillery FC	2-2	4-0	1-2	5-3		5-1	3-2	4-0	1-0	2-1	5-1	1-2
Glenavon FC	2-2	5-0	2-4	3-2	1-4		2-3	3-1	0-1	1-4	0-4	1-1
Glentoran FC	2-2	3-2	3-3	3-2	1-1	3-1		2-4	3-1	3-2	3-2	1-3
Larne FC	5-1	4-1	3-3	1-1	6-6	3-0	2-6		3-1	2-1	4-2	3-3
Linfield FC	4-1	3-0	2-2	4-0	1-1	3-3	0-1	3-0		2-1	3-1	1-3
Newry Town FC	0-0	2-2	0-4	2-0	1-1	3-2	1-1	2-4	4-2		2-0	3-4
Portadown FC	0-3	5-1	1-1	1-2	0-1	1-0	5-2	3-5	2-2	2-1		0-1
Queen's Island FC	2-3	5-3	1-3	0-0	3-1	3-1	3-3	1-0	0-0	2-1	4-3	

	Irish League	Pd	Wn	Dw	Ls	GF	GA	Pts
1.	BELFAST CELTIC FC (BELFAST)	22	15	7	-	66	26	37
2.	Queen's Island FC (Belfast)	22	12	6	4	46	34	30
3.	Distillery FC (Belfast)	22	12	5	5	56	36	29
4.	Glentoran FC (Belfast)	22	11	5	6	56	48	27
5.	Ards FC (Newtownards)	22	9	7	6	42	42	25
6.	Larne FC (Larne)	22	10	4	8	55	50	24
7.	Linfield FC (Belfast)	22	8	6	8	41	35	22
8.	Portadown FC (Portadown)	22	7	4	11	50	48	18
9.	Cliftonville FC (Belfast)	22	7	3	12	32	40	17
10.	Newry Town FC (Newry)	22	6	5	11	39	48	17
11.	Glenavon FC (Lurgan)	22	4	3	15	33	57	11
12.	Barn FC (Carrickfergus)	22	2	3	17	35	87	7
		264	103	58	103	551	551	264

Elected: Bangor FC (Bangor), Coleraine FC (Coleraine)

The league was extended to 14 clubs for next season

IRISH CUP FINAL   (The Oval, Belfast – 26/03/1927)

ARDS FC (NEWTOWNARDS)	3-2	Cliftonville FC (Belfast)
Croft, McGee 2		*Mortished, Hughes*

Ards: McMullan, McKeown, Wilson, Smyth, Risk, Gamble, Bothwell, Patton, McGee, Croft, McIlreavy.
Cliftonville: Gardiner, Jones, McGuire, Simpson, Cooke, Addis, Davis, Gowdy, Hughes, Mortished, Ferguson.

Semi-finals

Belfast Celtic FC (Belfast)	1-3	Ards FC (Newtownards)
Crusaders FC (Belfast)	2-4	Cliftonville FC (Belfast)

Quarter-finals

Belfast Celtic FC (Belfast)	4-0		Linfield Rangers FC (Belfast)
Glenavon FC (Lurgan)	1-2		Ards FC (Newtownards)
Larne FC (Larne)	1-2		Crusaders FC (Belfast)
Cliftonville FC (Belfast) received a bye			

1927-28

Irish League 1927-28 Season	Ards	Bangor	Barn	Belfast Celtic	Cliftonville	Coleraine	Distillery	Glenavon	Glentoran	Larne	Linfield	Newry Town	Portadown	Queen's Island
Ards FC	■	1-1	3-1	1-4	3-1	0-1	3-3	4-3	5-2	1-2	1-1	0-0	3-1	7-1
Bangor FC	4-3	■	3-1	2-6	2-3	3-1	1-1	5-1	0-2	4-3	1-5	2-1	2-4	2-4
Barn FC	1-3	2-0	■	0-8	2-1	2-6	2-1	2-4	3-2	1-1	1-1	1-3	1-2	5-3
Belfast Celtic FC	8-3	5-3	6-0	■	5-1	2-1	2-2	4-0	6-2	7-0	1-1	3-2	1-1	3-3
Cliftonville FC	0-2	1-1	3-2	0-2	■	2-0	0-2	1-4	0-2	3-3	1-3	0-2	2-1	2-1
Coleraine FC	3-0	1-3	6-1	3-2	4-1	■	0-3	5-3	5-4	3-2	1-4	1-2	5-2	2-0
Distillery FC	2-0	3-0	6-1	0-3	3-2	4-0	■	1-3	1-1	2-2	3-2	1-1	1-2	2-3
Glenavon FC	2-0	2-4	3-3	3-4	7-1	2-2	2-1	■	2-2	4-3	3-5	0-0	1-1	0-2
Glentoran FC	0-0	5-4	4-0	0-2	5-2	3-1	4-1	3-2	■	2-1	1-5	1-1	3-1	3-2
Larne FC	5-2	3-2	7-1	1-3	2-0	0-2	3-0	4-2	3-2	■	1-3	2-0	4-3	2-1
Linfield FC	8-4	8-4	2-0	2-2	5-1	7-0	0-0	3-0	6-1	3-4	■	3-0	2-1	1-0
Newry Town FC	5-3	2-2	6-2	0-1	3-0	4-0	4-0	3-5	6-1	0-0	1-0	■	4-1	4-1
Portadown FC	7-2	0-1	5-1	4-5	5-0	1-1	2-0	3-2	2-4	3-2	1-4	0-1	■	2-4
Queen's Island FC	3-0	1-1	2-2	0-6	1-1	3-3	1-2	2-3	4-4	1-3	1-4	0-0	2-6	■

	Irish League	Pd	Wn	Dw	Ls	GF	GA	Pts	
1.	BELFAST CELTIC FC (BELFAST)	26	20	5	1	101	35	45	
2.	Linfield FC (Belfast)	26	18	5	3	88	34	41	
3.	Newry Town FC (Newry)	26	13	7	6	55	30	33	
4.	Larne FC (Larne)	26	13	4	9	63	55	30	
5.	Glentoran FC (Belfast)	26	12	5	9	63	65	29	
6.	Coleraine FC (Coleraine)	26	12	3	11	57	60	27	
7.	Distillery FC (Belfast)	26	9	7	10	45	44	25	
8.	Portadown FC (Portadown)	26	10	3	13	61	58	23	
9.	Glenavon FC (Lurgan)	26	9	5	12	63	68	23	
10.	Bangor FC (Bangor)	26	9	5	12	57	69	23	
11.	Ards FC (Newtownards)	26	8	5	13	54	69	21	
12.	Queen's Island FC (Belfast)	26	5	7	14	46	70	17	
13.	Barn FC (Carrickfergus)	26	5	4	17	38	91	14	#
14.	Cliftonville FC (Belfast)	26	5	3	18	29	72	13	
		364	148	68	148	820	820	364	

\# Barn FC (Carrickfergus) were not re-elected to the league for the next season.

Elected: Ballymena FC (Ballymena)

IRISH CUP FINAL   (Windsor Park, Belfast – 31/03/1928)

WILLOWFIELD FC (BELFAST)　　　　　　　1-1　　　　　　　　　　Larne FC (Larne)
Kimlin　　　　　　　　　　　　　　　　　　　　　　　　　　　　　　　　*Crooks*

Willowfield: McFarlane, Mallon, Vance, Conway, Kirkwood, McClure, Aiken, Young, Hume, Kimlin, Shaw.
Larne: Irvine, McCambridge, Fulton, Horner, Fergie, Rodgers, White, Crooks, Houston, Snodden, Gunning.

IRISH CUP FINAL REPLAY   (Windsor Park, Belfast – 25/04/1928)

WILLOWFIELD FC (BELFAST)　　　　　　　1-0　　　　　　　　　　Larne FC (Larne)
Aiken

Willowfield: McFarlane, Mallon, Vance, Conway, Kirkwood, McClure, Aiken, Young, Hume, Kimlin, Shaw.
Larne: Irvine, Fergie, Fulton, Horner, Gamble, Rodgers, McLean, Crooks, Houston, McCambridge, Gunning.

Semi-finals

Larne FC (Larne)	2-1	Portadown FC (Portadown)
Willowfield FC (Belfast)	1-1, 2-1	Belfast Celtic FC (Belfast)

Quarter-finals

Belfast Celtic FC (Belfast)	2-1	Cliftonville FC (Belfast)
Larne FC (Larne)	2-0	Distillery FC (Belfast)
Portadown FC (Portadown)	2-1	Coleraine FC (Coleraine)
Willowfield FC (Belfast)	4-2	Barn FC (Carrickfergus)

1928-29

Irish League 1928-29 Season	Ards	Ballymena	Bangor	Belfast Celtic	Cliftonville	Coleraine	Distillery	Glenavon	Glentoran	Larne	Linfield	Newry Town	Portadown	Queen's Island
Ards FC	■	1-2	2-1	2-6	4-1	5-1	0-1	1-1	4-3	4-0	2-4	1-1	1-2	3-2
Ballymena FC	4-2	■	1-2	0-3	4-0	3-3	5-3	2-2	3-0	2-0	4-2	0-1	1-3	7-3
Bangor FC	3-0	2-2	■	0-0	2-1	2-2	3-1	3-3	1-3	2-1	1-3	4-2	4-2	2-0
Belfast Celtic FC	3-0	3-2	7-2	■	4-0	3-2	6-1	1-1	6-0	7-1	5-0	7-1	6-0	5-0
Cliftonville FC	1-1	3-2	0-1	0-5	■	1-3	0-1	0-1	2-4	3-4	1-5	2-2	1-2	4-2
Coleraine FC	2-2	0-0	2-1	1-4	4-2	■	5-3	4-1	5-2	1-2	2-0	1-2	3-1	4-3
Distillery FC	6-3	5-1	1-0	0-1	2-0	2-1	■	3-2	2-3	2-1	2-3	4-1	7-3	5-0
Glenavon FC	3-2	1-1	2-2	1-3	5-1	2-0	3-4	■	3-4	0-1	2-3	3-2	3-1	5-4
Glentoran FC	3-1	2-2	4-0	2-2	4-1	2-3	2-2	7-3	■	4-5	2-1	5-1	1-2	10-3
Larne FC	2-3	2-2	4-4	2-7	2-2	2-0	1-3	2-2	2-3	■	0-4	4-3	3-4	2-3
Linfield FC	6-1	6-0	4-1	2-2	3-0	0-2	3-2	4-1	4-3	1-2	■	3-1	5-1	8-1
Newry Town FC	1-2	2-2	2-1	1-3	1-2	3-0	6-3	1-1	0-1	2-1	3-4	■	2-0	4-2
Portadown FC	1-4	3-5	3-4	0-7	2-1	2-3	3-3	3-2	2-4	2-1	1-2	1-0	■	2-2
Queen's Island FC	4-4	0-7	2-1	2-10	3-3	3-9	2-3	4-8	2-4	2-4	2-8	1-2	1-6	■

	Irish League	Pd	Wn	Dw	Ls	GF	GA	Pts	
1.	BELFAST CELTIC FC (BELFAST)	26	22	4	-	116	23	48	
2.	Linfield FC (Belfast)	26	19	1	6	88	44	39	
3.	Glentoran FC (Belfast)	26	15	3	8	82	62	33	
4.	Distillery FC (Belfast)	26	15	2	9	71	58	32	
5.	Coleraine FC (Coleraine)	26	13	4	9	63	53	30	
6.	Ballymena FC (Ballymena)	26	10	8	8	64	54	28	
7.	Bangor FC (Bangor)	26	10	6	10	49	54	26	
8.	Glenavon FC (Lurgan)	26	8	8	10	61	63	24	
9.	Ards FC (Newtownards)	26	9	5	12	55	64	23	
10.	Newry Town FC (Newry)	26	9	4	13	47	58	22	
11.	Portadown FC (Portadown)	26	10	2	14	52	76	22	
12.	Larne FC (Larne)	26	8	4	14	51	72	20	
13.	Cliftonville FC (Belfast)	26	3	4	19	32	73	10	
14.	Queen's Island FC (Belfast)	26	2	3	21	53	130	7	#
		364	153	58	153	884	884	364	

\# Queen's Island FC (Belfast) were not re-elected to the league for the next season.

Elected: Derry City FC (Londonderry)

IRISH CUP FINAL (Solitude, Belfast – 30/03/1929)

BALLYMENA FC (BALLYMENA)   2-1   Belfast Celtic FC (Belfast)

Shiels, McCambridge   *J. Mahood*

Ballymena: Gough, McNinch, McDiarmid, J. Reid, D. Reid, Howard, Clarke, Mitchell, Shiels, McCambridge, Cassidy.

Belfast: Diffen, Wallace, Fulton, Moore, Hamill, Pollock, Gallagher, Curran, S. Mahood, J. Mahood.

Semi-finals

Ballymena FC (Ballymena)	3-0	Coleraine FC (Coleraine)
Belfast Celtic FC (Belfast)	3-0	Linfield FC (Belfast)

Quarter-finals

Ballymena FC (Ballymena)	4-1	Broadway United FC
Belfast Celtic FC (Belfast)	3-3, 7-1	Glenavon FC (Lurgan)
Coleraine FC (Coleraine)	3-0	Portadown FC (Portadown)
Linfield FC (Belfast)	6-2	Cliftonville FC (Belfast)

1929-30

Irish League 1929-30 Season	Ards	Ballymena	Bangor	Belfast Celtic	Cliftonville	Coleraine	Derry City	Distillery	Glenavon	Glentoran	Larne	Linfield	Newry Town	Portadown
Ards FC		0-2	4-4	1-2	2-1	2-3	1-2	1-1	3-5	1-5	2-1	1-3	3-2	4-2
Ballymena FC	1-3		4-0	1-1	7-1	0-1	4-0	6-3	5-0	2-1	3-1	1-4	3-0	2-2
Bangor FC	2-0	3-1		3-1	6-3	1-1	0-3	2-1	3-3	2-3	2-3	1-0	2-0	4-3
Belfast Celtic FC	6-1	4-3	1-2		7-2	1-1	4-0	1-5	4-3	1-2	4-1	2-5	1-4	5-1
Cliftonville FC	2-3	0-2	0-0	1-1		4-2	4-2	1-2	2-5	2-3	1-2	0-3	1-5	4-3
Coleraine FC	6-1	2-1	2-0	3-5	3-0		1-2	2-5	5-1	1-2	7-5	0-0	4-1	8-0
Derry City FC	2-2	1-1	3-2	3-1	4-3	0-0		1-1	2-0	1-2	2-1	2-6	2-0	5-2
Distillery FC	6-3	3-1	0-2	2-3	3-1	2-0	4-2		2-0	2-5	3-0	2-5	4-3	3-3
Glenavon FC	4-1	3-1	5-2	4-4	1-0	1-3	2-3	2-3		2-1	3-1	7-1	6-1	2-2
Glentoran FC	6-1	1-2	6-6	4-0	5-2	4-0	2-0	4-3	2-1		4-3	3-3	5-2	3-3
Larne FC	3-3	1-2	2-5	1-3	1-2	2-4	2-2	3-1	1-2	0-1		1-5	3-1	3-1
Linfield FC	2-2	4-7	3-1	3-1	1-0	7-1	2-0	4-2	5-3	3-1	7-1		6-1	3-3
Newry Town FC	3-1	2-0	1-3	0-2	2-3	1-0	2-3	2-0	3-1	3-2	2-2	2-4		5-0
Portadown FC	1-1	5-3	5-3	1-3	2-0	1-3	6-5	4-2	3-4	4-4	5-3	1-5	5-3	

	Irish League	Pd	Wn	Dw	Ls	GF	GA	Pts
1.	LINFIELD FC (BELFAST)	26	19	4	3	94	46	42
2.	Glentoran FC (Belfast)	26	16	4	6	79	53	36
3.	Coleraine FC (Coleraine)	26	14	4	8	66	47	32
4.	Belfast Celtic FC (Belfast)	26	13	4	9	68	57	30
5.	Ballymena FC (Ballymena)	26	13	3	10	65	46	29
6.	Bangor FC (Bangor)	26	12	5	9	61	58	29
7.	Derry City FC (Londonderry)	26	12	5	9	52	55	29
8.	Glenavon FC (Lurgan)	26	12	3	11	70	63	27
9.	Distillery FC (Belfast)	26	12	3	11	65	61	27
10.	Portadown FC (Portadown)	26	7	7	12	68	90	21
11.	Newry Town FC (Newry)	26	9	1	16	51	66	19
12.	Ards FC (Newtownards)	26	6	6	14	47	77	18
13.	Larne FC (Larne)	26	5	3	18	47	77	13
14.	Cliftonville FC (Belfast)	26	5	2	19	40	77	12
		364	155	54	155	873	873	364

No clubs promoted or relegated

IRISH CUP FINAL   (Celtic Park, Belfast – 29/03/1930)

LINFIELD FC (BELFAST)	4-3	Ballymena FC (Ballymena)
Bambrick 4		*Shiels 2, Reid*

Linfield: Lawson, Brown, Watson, McCleery, Jones, Sloan, Houston, McCracken, Bambrick, Grice, McCaw.
Ballymena: Gough, McNinch, McDiarmid, Baskett, Reid, Howard, Kilpatrick, Cassidy, Shiels, Gilmore, Murphy.

Semi-finals

Ballymena FC (Ballymena)	3-2	Newry Town FC (Newry)
Linfield FC (Belfast)	2-1	Glentoran FC (Belfast)

Quarter-finals

Belfast Celtic FC (Belfast)	2-3	Ballymena FC (Ballymena)
Coleraine FC (Coleraine)	0-1	Linfield FC (Belfast)
Glentoran FC (Belfast)	2-2, 4-2	Larne FC (Larne)
Newry Town FC (Newry)	2-1	Glenavon FC (Lurgan)

1930-31

Irish League 1930-31 Season	Ards	Ballymena	Bangor	Belfast Celtic	Cliftonville	Coleraine	Derry City	Distillery	Glenavon	Glentoran	Larne	Linfield	Newry Town	Portadown
Ards FC		3-6	5-4	1-3	2-3	3-3	4-4	3-1	6-1	1-4	0-0	5-1	6-2	5-4
Ballymena FC	5-1		1-4	4-1	2-2	2-3	4-1	4-0	6-1	2-4	3-1	2-2	6-1	1-3
Bangor FC	3-3	2-6		3-4	2-1	3-2	1-2	3-3	4-4	0-3	2-2	1-6	5-0	6-2
Belfast Celtic FC	3-2	4-1	3-1		1-1	4-3	1-3	3-1	4-1	2-4	6-0	4-4	5-2	3-2
Cliftonville FC	5-2	4-3	4-2	0-5		1-4	3-0	4-3	3-1	0-5	2-0	0-1	1-4	3-2
Coleraine FC	1-4	1-1	2-3	0-1	2-0		0-2	3-3	7-0	0-2	2-2	1-2	5-3	1-1
Derry City FC	0-1	1-2	3-3	1-2	5-0	2-0		2-3	5-2	4-4	0-0	6-2	1-0	1-0
Distillery FC	1-0	1-2	3-1	2-1	2-1	4-3	9-0		5-1	2-3	3-1	3-3	9-1	5-0
Glenavon FC	3-4	1-1	2-1	0-2	2-1	2-0	4-2	1-4		1-5	2-1	0-1	6-1	1-1
Glentoran FC	4-2	2-2	3-1	4-3	5-2	2-0	4-1	2-0	3-2		6-2	1-1	5-3	4-3
Larne FC	1-2	4-0	2-0	2-2	4-6	5-2	0-3	2-4	4-2	0-9		2-3	2-1	3-2
Linfield FC	7-2	2-1	2-1	1-2	4-1	3-0	3-0	1-1	3-1	0-2	3-1		4-1	7-1
Newry Town FC	0-1	0-1	5-1	5-5	2-4	1-3	2-0	1-8	0-1	1-5	2-2	1-5		2-1
Portadown FC	0-0	1-7	2-5	4-1	5-2	0-0	7-1	0-2	1-5	4-1	7-1	2-2	8-4	

	Irish League	**Pd**	**Wn**	**Dw**	**Ls**	**GF**	**GA**	**Pts**
1.	GLENTORAN FC (BELFAST)	26	22	3	1	96	39	47
2.	Linfield FC (Belfast)	26	16	6	4	73	42	38
3.	Belfast Celtic FC (Belfast)	26	16	4	6	75	52	36
4.	Distillery FC (Belfast)	26	15	4	7	82	46	34
5.	Ballymena FC (Ballymena)	26	13	5	8	75	50	31
6.	Ards FC (Newtownards)	26	11	5	10	68	69	27
7.	Derry City FC (Londonderry)	26	10	4	12	50	61	24
8.	Cliftonville FC (Belfast)	26	11	2	13	54	70	24
9.	Portadown FC (Portadown)	26	7	5	14	63	73	19
10.	Bangor FC (Bangor)	26	7	5	14	62	75	19
11.	Glenavon FC (Lurgan)	26	8	3	15	47	75	19
12.	Coleraine FC (Coleraine)	26	6	6	14	48	56	18
13.	Larne FC (Larne)	26	6	6	14	44	74	18
14.	Newry Town FC (Newry)	26	4	2	20	45	100	10
		364	152	60	152	882	882	364

No clubs promoted or relegated

IRISH CUP FINAL (The Oval, Belfast – 28/03/1931)
LINFIELD FC (BELFAST)   3-0   Ballymena FC (Ballymena)
Hewitt, Houston, McCracken

Linfield: Higgs, Pyper, Curran, McCleery, Jones, Sloan, Houston, McCracken, Hewitt, Grice, McCaw.
Ballymena: McKeen, McNinch, McCandless, Reid, Stewart, Dalrymple, Cassidy, Gilmore, Shiels, Murphy.

Semi-finals

Ballymena FC (Ballymena)	2-1	Derry City FC (Londonderry)
Linfield FC (Belfast)	5-1	Glentoran FC (Belfast)

Quarter-finals

Ballymena FC (Ballymena)	2-2, 2-0	Bangor FC (Bangor)
Belfast Celtic FC (Belfast)	1-2	Linfield FC (Belfast)
Derry City FC (Londonderry)	5-0	Glenavon FC (Lurgan)
Glentoran FC (Belfast)	6-2	Coleraine FC (Coleraine)

1931-32

Irish League 1931-32 Season	Ards	Ballymena	Bangor	Belfast Celtic	Cliftonville	Coleraine	Derry City	Distillery	Glenavon	Glentoran	Larne	Linfield	Newry Town	Portadown
Ards FC		1-1	2-2	2-1	2-2	3-4	1-2	3-1	4-1	3-2	4-1	2-5	2-0	3-4
Ballymena FC	6-2		6-4	6-0	3-5	7-0	0-0	4-0	4-1	5-0	2-0	2-0	6-2	2-3
Bangor FC	3-0	2-3		1-3	0-1	1-3	1-4	2-4	0-1	3-3	0-0	1-5	1-4	5-3
Belfast Celtic FC	3-0	2-1	0-0		4-6	2-2	0-1	3-0	7-1	4-0	5-1	4-2	3-2	0-0
Cliftonville FC	9-2	1-1	3-1	0-2		4-1	0-1	3-0	4-2	0-5	1-1	0-3	3-0	3-2
Coleraine FC	4-0	4-1	2-5	1-0	3-1		1-1	6-3	2-1	3-3	4-1	2-2	3-1	8-4
Derry City FC	6-3	2-2	4-1	1-0	6-1	1-0		3-2	5-1	1-2	6-0	1-1	1-0	2-1
Distillery FC	1-1	2-0	1-1	0-0	4-3	2-2	4-4		4-2	3-3	5-2	2-3	2-1	3-2
Glenavon FC	3-2	0-4	1-1	0-2	1-4	1-4	1-4	1-0		2-2	4-2	2-3	2-2	2-0
Glentoran FC	6-2	3-0	3-1	2-1	1-1	3-2	1-1	5-2	3-1		8-2	0-1	2-3	3-1
Larne FC	5-4	3-0	5-4	1-1	1-1	1-4	2-1	4-7	2-4	2-2		1-6	4-1	2-2
Linfield FC	4-1	2-0	4-1	0-1	2-0	4-1	3-0	4-2	3-1	4-3	6-0		4-1	2-0
Newry Town FC	4-0	1-1	1-0	2-4	3-1	1-1	0-2	4-1	1-1	2-5	1-2	3-1		1-0
Portadown FC	2-3	1-0	2-0	3-4	4-2	1-0	2-1	2-2	5-5	4-3	2-2	3-3	1-2	

	Irish League	Pd	Wn	Dw	Ls	GF	GA	Pts
1.	LINFIELD FC (BELFAST)	26	19	3	4	77	34	41
2.	Derry City FC (Londonderry)	26	16	6	4	61	30	38
3.	Belfast Celtic FC (Belfast)	26	14	5	7	56	35	33
4.	Coleraine FC (Coleraine)	26	13	6	7	67	54	32
5.	Glentoran FC (Glentoran)	26	12	7	7	73	54	31
6.	Ballymena FC (Ballymena)	26	12	5	9	67	41	29
7.	Cliftonville FC (Belfast)	26	11	5	10	59	55	27
8.	Distillery FC (Belfast)	26	8	7	11	57	68	23
9.	Portadown FC (Portadown)	26	8	6	12	54	63	22
10.	Newry Town FC (Newry)	26	9	4	13	43	53	22
11.	Larne FC (Larne)	26	6	7	13	47	85	19
12.	Ards FC (Newtownards)	26	7	4	15	52	82	18
13.	Glenavon FC (Lurgan)	26	6	5	15	42	74	17
14.	Bangor FC (Bangor)	26	3	6	17	41	68	12
		364	144	76	144	796	796	364

No clubs promoted or relegated

IRISH CUP FINAL   (Celtic Park, Belfast – 26/03/1932)

GLENTORAN FC (BELFAST)   2-1   Linfield FC (Belfast)
McKenzie, Burnison pen.   *Burns*

Glentoran: Bennett, Allen, Gibson, Turnbull, Mathieson, McClements, Morgan, Geary, Roberts, Borland, Lucas.
Linfield: Lawson, Pyper, Curran, Buchanan, Jones, McCleery, Houston, McCracken, Bambrick, Donnelly, McCaw.

Semi-finals

| Glentoran FC (Belfast) | 2-1 | Portadown FC (Portadown) |
| Linfield FC (Belfast) | 2-2, 2-2, 2-1 | Belfast Celtic FC (Belfast) |

Quarter-finals

Bangor FC (Bangor)	2-3	Portadown FC (Portadown)
Belfast Celtic FC (Belfast)	3-3, 3-1	Derry City FC (Londonderry)
Glentoran FC (Belfast)	2-2, 3-1	Ballymena FC (Ballymena)
Linfield FC (Belfast)	5-2	Ards FC (Newtownards)

1932-33

Irish League 1932-33 Season	Ards	Ballymena	Bangor	Belfast Celtic	Cliftonville	Coleraine	Derry City	Distillery	Glenavon	Glentoran	Larne	Linfield	Newry Town	Portadown
Ards FC		0-4	2-1	1-1	2-2	1-2	1-0	5-6	3-2	4-4	2-3	1-1	6-0	1-1
Ballymena FC	8-2		1-3	1-1	1-1	2-1	3-1	1-3	3-1	2-3	2-1	0-1	2-1	5-1
Bangor FC	1-4	5-3		1-3	3-1	3-2	0-1	0-1	1-1	0-3	3-2	1-1	6-1	1-2
Belfast Celtic FC	4-0	7-2	4-1		5-1	3-2	5-1	4-1	2-1	4-1	1-3	1-2	5-1	6-2
Cliftonville FC	3-4	6-1	2-6	1-3		2-2	0-4	1-1	1-2	5-2	4-2	4-2	5-5	5-1
Coleraine FC	5-0	3-0	4-2	1-1	3-1		0-2	2-1	3-2	1-2	4-1	4-5	1-2	11-1
Derry City FC	2-0	1-0	0-1	1-3	3-1	3-0		3-7	2-1	2-2	4-0	2-0	8-0	1-0
Distillery FC	5-0	2-2	5-3	2-0	2-1	1-0	2-1		6-4	3-4	2-0	2-1	5-3	5-1
Glenavon FC	2-1	0-1	3-1	2-3	4-1	4-4	2-3	2-4		1-1	4-1	1-2	5-1	1-2
Glentoran FC	7-5	6-1	2-5	2-4	4-0	0-2	3-5	1-1	2-1		5-0	1-5	7-1	2-1
Larne FC	6-3	2-2	5-6	2-6	3-2	4-3	0-1	1-3	4-3	2-4		1-4	9-2	0-5
Linfield FC	6-0	2-0	1-2	1-2	4-0	2-2	4-1	4-0	4-3	4-2	9-0		6-1	5-0
Newry Town FC	4-1	3-5	2-3	0-3	3-3	4-4	2-1	1-5	2-3	1-2	3-1	2-2		1-0
Portadown FC	3-2	1-4	0-1	1-0	2-1	1-3	2-6	2-0	1-1	1-2	1-2	1-5	4-1	

	Irish League	Pd	Wn	Dw	Ls	GF	GA	Pts
1.	BELFAST CELTIC FC (BELFAST)	26	19	3	4	81	34	41
2.	Distillery FC (Belfast)	26	18	3	5	75	47	39
3.	Linfield FC (Belfast)	26	17	4	5	83	34	38
4.	Derry City FC (Londonderry)	26	16	1	9	59	39	33
5.	Glentoran FC (Belfast)	26	14	4	8	74	61	32
6.	Bangor FC (Bangor)	26	13	2	11	60	56	28
7.	Coleraine FC (Coleraine)	26	11	5	10	69	50	27
8.	Ballymena FC (Ballymena)	26	11	4	11	56	58	26
9.	Glenavon FC (Lurgan)	26	7	4	15	56	59	18
10.	Portadown FC (Portadown)	26	8	2	16	37	72	18
11.	Larne FC (Larne)	26	8	1	17	55	88	17
12.	Ards FC (Newtownards)	26	6	5	15	51	83	17
13.	Cliftonville FC (Belfast)	26	5	6	15	54	74	16
14.	Newry Town FC (Newry)	26	5	4	17	47	102	14
		364	158	48	158	857	857	364

No clubs promoted or relegated

IRISH CUP FINAL   (Windsor Park, Belfast – 08/04/1933)

GLENTORAN FC (BELFAST)   1-1   Distillery FC (Belfast)
Roberts   *Storer*

Glentoran: Harris, Little, Gibson, Turnbull, Craig, Leathem, McNeill, Crooks, Roberts, Doherty, Hutchinson.
Distillery: Newlands, Smith, Gillespie, Gray, Jones, Mitchell, Storer, Sinnamon, McAdam, McLarnon, Kirby.

IRISH CUP FINAL REPLAY (Windsor Park, Belfast – 12/04/1933)

GLENTORAN FC (BELFAST)   1-1   Distillery FC (Belfast)
McNeill   *Kirby*

Glentoran: Harris, Little, Gibson, Turnbull, Craig, Leathem, McNeill, Crooks, Roberts, Doherty, Hutchinson.
Distillery: Newlands, Smith, Gillespie, Gray, Jones, Mitchell, Storer, O'Neill, McAdam, McLarnon, Kirby.

IRISH CUP FINAL 2ND REPLAY (Windsor Park, Belfast – 28/04/1933)

GLENTORAN FC (BELFAST)   3-1   Distillery FC (Belfast)
Doherty, Roberts, Crooks   *McLarnon*

Glentoran: Harris, Lyttle, Gibson, Turnbull, Craig, Arrigan, Doherty, Crooks, Roberts, Leatham, Fitzsimmons.
Distillery: Newlands, Smith, Gillespie, Gray, Lawless, Jones, Storer, McLarnon, McAdam, Mitchell, Kirby.

Semi-finals

Distillery FC (Belfast)	2-0	Cliftonville FC (Belfast)
Glentoran FC (Belfast)	2-1	Coleraine FC (Coleraine)

Quarter-finals

Cliftonville FC (Belfast)	1-0	Belfast Celtic FC (Belfast)
Coleraine FC (Coleraine)	1-1, 3-1	Linfield FC (Belfast)
Derry City FC (Londonderry)	1-2	Distillery FC (Belfast)
Glentoran FC (Belfast)	4-1	Portadown FC (Portadown)

1933-34

Irish League 1933-34 Season	Ards	Ballymena	Bangor	Belfast Celtic	Cliftonville	Coleraine	Derry City	Distillery	Glenavon	Glentoran	Larne	Linfield	Newry Town	Portadown
Ards FC	■	2-1	2-0	2-2	3-2	2-0	2-2	3-2	4-0	0-2	1-0	1-4	5-1	2-0
Ballymena FC	2-2	■	5-0	2-1	1-4	4-2	2-1	4-2	3-3	3-1	4-2	2-4	7-0	1-0
Bangor FC	3-2	2-3	■	2-2	3-4	1-2	1-1	3-5	2-1	3-2	2-2	1-4	3-0	3-2
Belfast Celtic FC	3-3	3-2	0-1	■	5-1	5-2	3-2	3-0	2-0	4-0	6-1	2-5	3-2	3-1
Cliftonville FC	0-2	0-3	2-1	2-4	■	2-1	4-1	0-4	3-2	0-2	2-1	0-6	2-3	4-2
Coleraine FC	2-1	0-0	3-2	2-3	4-2	■	2-1	2-4	1-2	1-3	4-2	2-2	4-1	0-1
Derry City FC	2-0	2-2	2-0	0-1	5-1	1-0	■	0-1	3-3	2-1	1-0	2-0	1-2	2-3
Distillery FC	2-1	1-0	1-0	1-2	5-1	3-3	3-0	■	2-2	0-1	3-1	1-2	6-1	0-1
Glenavon FC	2-1	7-2	1-0	3-2	1-2	5-1	0-1	1-6	■	2-1	0-0	0-2	3-1	2-1
Glentoran FC	6-2	1-1	5-2	4-2	5-2	3-1	1-0	3-0	1-0	■	4-0	0-3	3-0	3-3
Larne FC	1-3	0-3	3-2	1-5	2-4	4-1	0-0	2-4	1-2	1-4	■	3-3	5-3	2-2
Linfield FC	5-0	3-0	2-1	3-1	3-0	2-0	2-1	3-0	8-1	0-1	8-1	■	1-0	5-0
Newry Town FC	1-1	2-2	0-3	0-6	6-2	3-0	1-1	2-2	2-1	1-1	1-2	0-2	■	1-1
Portadown FC	1-0	1-0	2-2	0-1	6-1	2-0	3-3	0-3	2-1	0-4	2-0	1-6	4-3	■

	Irish League	Pd	Wn	Dw	Ls	GF	GA	Pts	
1.	LINFIELD FC (BELFAST)	26	22	2	2	88	21	46	
2.	Belfast Celtic FC (Belfast)	26	17	3	6	74	42	37	
3.	Glentoran FC (Belfast)	26	16	3	7	59	36	35	
4.	Distillery FC (Belfast)	26	14	3	9	61	41	31	
5.	Ballymena FC (Ballymena)	26	12	6	8	59	46	30	#
6.	Ards FC (Newtownards)	26	11	5	10	47	46	27	
7.	Portadown FC (Portadown)	26	10	5	11	41	52	25	
8.	Glenavon FC (Lurgan)	26	10	4	12	45	54	24	
9.	Derry City FC (Londonderry)	26	8	7	11	37	38	23	
10.	Cliftonville FC (Belfast)	26	11	-	15	50	78	22	
11.	Bangor FC (Bangor)	26	7	4	15	43	58	18	
12.	Coleraine FC (Coleraine)	26	7	3	16	40	61	17	
13.	Newry Town FC (Newry)	26	5	6	15	37	71	16	
14.	Larne FC (Larne)	26	4	5	17	37	74	13	
		364	154	56	154	718	718	364	

Ballymena FC (Ballymena) were suspended by the Irish League for refusing to submit their financial records to inspection by the management committee. Ballymena Crusaders FC (Ballymena) applied for the vacant league position but were rejected. They then merged with Ballymena FC as Ballymena United FC (Ballymena), applied once more and were elected to the league, playing home games at the same venue and with the same nucleus of players/officials as the former Ballymena FC (Ballymena).

No clubs were promoted or relegated

IRISH CUP FINAL   (The Oval, Belfast – 14/04/1934)

LINFIELD FC (BELFAST)   5-0   Cliftonville FC (Belfast)
Bambrick, Caiels, Mackie, Donnelly, McCracken

Linfield: Eckersley, Richmond, Richardson, Edwards, Jones, McCleery, Mackie, McCracken, Bambrick, Donnelly, Caiels.
Cliftonville: Hill, Haire, McGuire, McNeill, Leckey, Mitchell, Billingsley, Millar, Hewitt, Wishart, McCaw.

Semi-finals

| Glentoran FC (Belfast) | 2-4 | Cliftonville FC (Belfast) |
| Linfield FC (Belfast) | 7-0 | Belfast Celtic FC (Belfast) |

Quarter-finals

Ballymena FC (Ballymena)	1-4	Belfast Celtic FC (Belfast)
Bangor FC (Bangor)	0-2	Glentoran FC (Belfast)
Cliftonville FC (Belfast)	4-0	Derry City FC (Londonderry)
Linfield FC (Belfast)	2-0	Portadown FC (Portadown)

1934-35

Irish League 1934-35 Season	Ards	Ballymena U.	Bangor	Belfast Celtic	Cliftonville	Coleraine	Derry City	Distillery	Glenavon	Glentoran	Larne	Linfield	Newry Town	Portadown
Ards FC	■	2-2	8-1	1-4	2-5	2-0	0-3	1-3	2-2	3-4	1-2	0-4	5-2	4-4
Ballymena United FC	5-1	■	4-4	0-3	5-1	3-1	0-2	1-4	5-1	0-3	1-1	1-3	5-2	1-3
Bangor FC	1-4	1-4	■	0-7	1-2	4-0	1-5	3-2	1-1	2-7	2-2	0-4	0-3	1-2
Belfast Celtic FC	9-0	3-0	8-1	■	6-2	5-1	4-1	5-2	1-1	3-1	2-3	1-2	8-2	1-1
Cliftonville FC	8-2	4-1	0-0	1-4	■	1-3	2-1	1-1	1-4	3-2	2-2	0-1	3-2	0-5
Coleraine FC	3-0	2-1	0-0	1-2	3-1	■	1-3	0-2	2-1	0-2	3-4	1-1	4-1	2-4
Derry City FC	4-2	7-3	5-3	2-1	3-0	5-2	■	3-1	2-1	2-2	2-1	1-2	3-0	2-0
Distillery FC	2-1	3-2	0-0	1-7	0-1	3-1	1-1	■	1-3	2-0	1-0	1-1	2-1	0-1
Glenavon FC	1-0	1-1	5-0	2-3	2-1	4-2	0-1	2-2	■	2-2	1-3	1-3	4-2	0-2
Glentoran FC	6-0	1-1	5-3	3-2	4-1	2-1	2-1	1-3	3-1	■	4-1	2-2	4-3	2-1
Larne FC	3-0	4-0	3-0	0-0	4-2	3-2	1-1	0-5	3-2	0-4	■	2-5	2-1	1-2
Linfield FC	6-0	6-0	7-1	2-1	5-0	5-2	0-0	2-1	3-0	1-0	2-1	■	3-0	3-1
Newry Town FC	2-3	2-0	7-3	2-5	2-1	5-2	2-3	5-4	8-0	1-3	4-1	2-1	■	0-2
Portadown FC	5-1	0-2	3-3	4-1	4-2	2-4	0-1	1-0	1-1	3-1	3-1	0-2	2-2	■

	Irish League	Pd	Wn	Dw	Ls	GF	GA	Pts
1.	LINFIELD FC (BELFAST)	26	21	4	1	76	19	46
2.	Derry City FC (Londonderry)	26	18	4	4	64	32	40
3.	Belfast Celtic FC (Belfast)	26	17	3	6	96	36	37
4.	Glentoran FC (Belfast)	26	16	4	6	70	42	36
5.	Portadown FC (Portadown)	26	14	5	7	56	38	33
6.	Distillery FC (Belfast)	26	11	5	10	47	44	27
7.	Larne FC (Larne)	26	11	5	10	48	52	27
8.	Glenavon FC (Lurgan)	26	7	7	12	43	55	21
9.	Newry Town FC (Newry)	26	9	1	16	63	73	19
10.	Ballymena United FC (Ballymena)	26	7	5	14	48	65	19
11.	Cliftonville FC (Belfast)	26	8	3	15	45	69	19
12.	Coleraine FC (Coleraine)	26	7	2	17	43	66	16
13.	Ards FC (Newtownards)	26	5	3	18	45	91	13
14.	Bangor FC (Bangor)	26	2	7	17	36	98	11
		364	153	58	153	780	780	364

No clubs promoted or relegated

IRISH CUP FINAL   (Windsor Park, Belfast – 06/04/1935)

GLENTORAN FC (BELFAST)   0-0   Larne FC (Larne)

Glentoran: Lewis, Millar, McCaw, Arrigan, Beck, Leathem, Goodwin, Aicken, McNeill, Tyson, Smith.
Larne: Kenny, Craigie, McIlveen, Swann, Mathieson, Gemmell, McGuffie, Dodds, Byrne, Lyness, Thompson.

IRISH CUP FINAL REPLAY   (Windsor Park, Belfast – 10/04/1935)

GLENTORAN FC (BELFAST)   0-0   Larne FC (Larne)

Glentoran: Lewis, Millar, McDiarmid, Arrigan, Leathem, McCaw, Goodwin, Aicken, Neill, Duncan, Smith.
Larne: Kenny, Craigie, McIlveen, Swann, Mathieson, Gemmell, McGuffie, Dodds, Byrne, Lyness, Thompson.

IRISH CUP FINAL 2ND REPLAY   (Windsor Park, Belfast – 30/04/1935)

GLENTORAN FC (BELFAST)   1-0   Larne FC (Larne)

Goodwin

Glentoran: Lewis, Millar, McDiarmid, Arrigan, Beck, Leathem, Goodwin, Aitken, McNeill, Duncan, Smith.
Larne: Kenny, Craigie, McIlveen, Swann, Mathieson, Gemmell, McGuffie, Dodds, Byrne, Lyness, Thomson.

Semi-finals

Glentoran FC (Belfast)	3-0	Ballymena United FC (Ballymena)
Larne FC (Larne)	1-0	Belfast Celtic FC (Belfast)

Quarter-finals

Distillery FC (Belfast)	2-3	Ballymena United FC (Ballymena)
Glentoran FC (Belfast)	4-2	Linfield FC (Belfast)
Larne FC (Larne)	4-4, 2-2, 2-0	Newry Town FC (Newry)
Portadown FC (Portadown)	0-2	Belfast Celtic FC (Belfast)

1935-36

Irish League 1935-36 Season	Ards	Ballymena U.	Bangor	Belfast Celtic	Cliftonville	Coleraine	Derry City	Distillery	Glenavon	Glentoran	Larne	Linfield	Newry Town	Portadown
Ards FC		1-5	5-1	0-3	2-3	2-1	0-2	2-7	3-1	2-1	3-3	0-4	2-3	2-2
Ballymena United FC	1-1		4-3	1-3	2-1	1-0	2-2	1-0	2-1	2-4	3-2	1-1	2-3	2-2
Bangor FC	0-3	2-1		1-3	1-2	1-2	1-1	1-2	2-1	3-2	0-2	1-1	2-2	8-2
Belfast Celtic FC	2-1	2-0	4-1		4-2	1-0	2-6	2-0	2-0	4-0	9-1	2-1	5-1	2-0
Cliftonville FC	6-0	5-4	2-1	0-4		0-1	2-4	0-0	3-3	2-4	0-0	1-7	5-1	2-0
Coleraine FC	6-0	1-0	2-3	0-2	0-0		2-4	0-0	2-2	0-1	0-0	0-2	1-2	2-4
Derry City FC	8-1	1-0	5-0	0-0	4-0	1-1		6-0	4-2	3-0	2-1	2-0	2-1	1-0
Distillery FC	4-0	1-0	0-3	0-1	4-2	3-2	3-2		5-2	4-2	6-0	2-2	2-1	3-5
Glenavon FC	3-1	2-0	3-4	0-4	4-1	1-0	1-1	1-1		1-2	0-4	0-3	0-2	0-1
Glentoran FC	9-6	2-2	1-2	0-1	1-3	4-0	2-3	1-1	1-0		6-0	1-2	2-5	1-1
Larne FC	3-2	3-1	3-2	3-0	4-1	4-1	2-4	4-1	1-6	1-2		2-1	2-2	1-0
Linfield FC	5-1	3-2	7-0	2-2	2-1	3-0	8-1	4-1	2-0	0-1	2-1		4-3	2-0
Newry Town FC	7-1	5-1	8-1	2-2	2-3	2-1	4-0	6-1	3-3	2-3	5-0	2-1		4-2
Portadown FC	4-3	8-1	4-3	1-0	2-2	1-3	1-2	2-0	2-3	0-4	6-2	1-3	2-2	

	Irish League	Pd	Wn	Dw	Ls	GF	GA	Pts
1.	BELFAST CELTIC FC (BELFAST)	26	20	3	3	66	23	43
2.	Derry City FC (Londonderry)	26	18	5	3	71	36	41
3.	Linfield FC (Belfast)	26	17	4	5	72	28	38
4.	Newry Town FC (Newry)	26	14	5	7	80	50	33
5.	Glentoran FC (Belfast)	26	12	3	11	57	50	27
6.	Distillery FC (Belfast)	26	11	5	10	51	52	27
7.	Larne FC (Larne)	26	11	4	11	49	65	26
8.	Portadown FC (Portadown)	26	9	5	12	53	58	23
9.	Cliftonville FC (Belfast)	26	9	5	12	49	61	23
10.	Ballymena United FC (Ballymena)	26	7	5	14	41	59	19
11.	Bangor FC (Bangor)	26	8	3	15	47	72	19
12.	Glenavon FC (Lurgan)	26	6	5	15	40	56	17
13.	Coleraine FC (Coleraine)	26	5	5	16	28	44	15
14.	Ards FC (Newtownards)	26	5	3	18	44	94	13
		364	152	60	152	748	748	364

No clubs promoted or relegated

IRISH CUP FINAL   (Celtic Park, Belfast – 04/04/1936)

LINFIELD FC (BELFAST)　　　　　　　0-0　　　　　　　Derry City FC (Londonderry)

Linfield: Frame, Hare, Richardson, Edwards, Bowden, McCleery, Foye, Donnelly, Hume, Baird, McCormick.
Derry: Wallace, Hobson, Ross, Doherty, Carlyle, Martin, Smith, Grant, Renfrew, Duffy, Kelly.

IRISH CUP FINAL REPLAY   (Celtic Park, Belfast – 08/04/1936)

LINFIELD FC (BELFAST)　　　　　　　2-1　　　　　　　Derry City FC (Londonderry)
Baird, McCormick　　　　　　　　　　　　　　　　　　　　　　　　　　　　　　　　*Kelly*

Derry: Wallace, Hobson, Ross, Doherty, Carlisle, Martin, Smith, Grant, Renfrew, Duffy, Kelly.
Linfield: Frame, Haire, Richardson, Edwards, Bowden, McCleery, Foye, Donnelly, Hume, Baird, McCormick.

Semi-finals

| Derry City FC (Londonderry) | 3-0 | Glentoran FC (Belfast) 2nd XI |
| Linfield FC (Belfast) | 1-0 | Belfast Celtic FC (Belfast) |

Quarter-finals

Belfast Celtic FC (Belfast)	1-1, 1-1, 0-0, 5-1	Newry Town FC (Newry)
Distillery FC (Belfast)	1-3	Glentoran FC (Belfast) 2nd XI
Glentoran FC (Belfast)	0-4	Derry City FC (Londonderry)
Linfield FC (Belfast)	0-0, 3-1	Portadown FC (Portadown)

1936-37

Irish League 1936-37 Season	Ards	Ballymena U.	Bangor	Belfast Celtic	Cliftonville	Coleraine	Derry City	Distillery	Glenavon	Glentoran	Larne	Linfield	Newry Town	Portadown
Ards FC		6-1	0-1	0-5	3-1	1-1	4-5	3-1	0-4	2-0	5-0	2-6	0-2	1-3
Ballymena United FC	4-1		2-5	0-2	1-3	1-0	1-4	3-1	1-3	4-4	1-3	0-7	1-3	1-3
Bangor FC	1-1	2-0		0-3	1-1	2-1	1-6	4-0	4-3	1-4	1-3	1-7	2-1	1-3
Belfast Celtic FC	10-0	4-0	5-0		4-2	5-0	4-2	2-1	1-0	2-2	2-1	4-0	4-1	1-3
Cliftonville FC	4-2	4-1	0-2	0-1		3-1	2-2	7-4	3-0	3-3	5-3	0-2	2-6	3-3
Coleraine FC	0-2	1-0	0-0	0-6	2-0		1-1	1-0	1-1	0-1	2-2	0-3	2-1	2-1
Derry City FC	3-1	2-0	5-2	2-1	4-0	4-0		5-2	5-2	4-1	4-1	2-1	6-1	4-0
Distillery FC	2-1	2-2	2-1	1-2	1-1	1-2	1-3		4-1	1-0	2-3	0-4	0-3	1-3
Glenavon FC	1-2	5-2	4-0	1-5	4-6	3-2	3-1	4-1		0-1	5-0	2-3	3-1	2-0
Glentoran FC	2-1	8-2	6-1	2-4	1-0	5-3	4-5	0-5	5-2		2-4	2-3	4-2	2-3
Larne FC	9-1	1-2	4-3	1-1	3-4	4-0	0-2	2-1	3-1	4-2		0-3	4-1	3-0
Linfield FC	3-1	4-0	7-2	1-2	2-0	4-1	2-2	5-0	3-0	5-1	2-0		4-0	1-2
Newry Town FC	4-1	5-3	5-1	0-0	7-1	7-0	1-0	3-1	3-2	1-2	0-3	0-0		1-2
Portadown FC	0-1	4-1	2-1	1-1	1-1	3-1	1-2	0-1	2-0	3-1	5-2	1-3	0-0	

	Irish League	Pd	Wn	Dw	Ls	GF	GA	Pts
1.	BELFAST CELTIC FC (BELFAST)	26	20	4	2	86	21	44
2.	Derry City FC (Londonderry)	26	20	3	3	85	37	43
3.	Linfield FC (Belfast)	26	20	2	4	85	25	42
4.	Portadown FC (Portadown)	26	14	4	8	49	38	32
5.	Larne FC (Larne)	26	13	2	11	63	57	28
6.	Newry Town FC (Newry)	26	12	3	11	59	48	27
7.	Glentoran FC (Belfast)	26	11	3	12	65	65	25
8.	Cliftonville FC (Belfast)	26	9	6	11	56	64	24
9.	Glenavon FC (Lurgan)	26	10	1	15	56	59	21
10.	Bangor FC (Bangor)	26	8	3	15	40	80	19
11.	Ards FC (Newtownards)	26	8	2	16	42	73	18
12.	Coleraine FC (Coleraine)	26	6	5	15	24	61	17
13.	Distillery FC (Belfast)	26	6	2	18	36	65	14
14.	Ballymena United FC (Ballymena)	26	4	2	20	34	87	10
		364	161	42	161	780	780	364

No clubs promoted or relegated

IRISH CUP FINAL   (The Oval, Belfast – 10/04/1937)

BELFAST CELTIC FC (BELFAST)   3-0   Linfield FC (Belfast)

Turnbull 3

Belfast: McAlinden, McMillan, Lavery, H. Walker, Leathem, J. Walker, Kernaghan, McArdle, Turnbull, Bruce, McIlroy.

Linfield: Doak, Haire, Richardson, Miles, Bowden, McCleery, Houston, Donnelly, Ramsay, Brownlow, McCormick.

Semi-finals

Belfast Celtic FC (Belfast)	1-1, 3-0	Ballymena United FC (Ballymena)
Linfield FC (Belfast)	2-2, 2-0	Newry Town FC (Newry)

Quarter-finals

Ballymena United FC (Ballymena)	1-0	Derry City FC (Londonderry)
Cliftonville FC (Belfast)	0-1	Belfast Celtic FC (Belfast)
Linfield FC (Belfast)	0-0, 6-1	Glentoran FC (Belfast)
Newry Town FC (Newry)	2-2, 4-3	Portadown FC (Portadown)

1937-38

Irish League 1937-38 Season	Ards	Ballymena U.	Bangor	Belfast Celtic	Cliftonville	Coleraine	Derry City	Distillery	Glenavon	Glentoran	Larne	Linfield	Newry Town	Portadown
Ards FC	■	1-3	2-1	1-4	6-0	2-1	2-5	1-1	1-3	3-4	3-0	0-3	6-2	2-2
Ballymena United FC	1-4	■	2-1	1-0	3-1	6-2	5-0	5-1	7-2	0-1	3-2	2-2	2-2	1-1
Bangor FC	1-3	0-3	■	1-2	3-2	2-1	1-2	3-3	1-2	2-1	4-3	1-2	2-0	1-2
Belfast Celtic FC	6-0	3-1	4-0	■	8-0	4-1	6-1	3-3	6-0	6-1	5-1	2-1	1-1	4-0
Cliftonville FC	1-1	1-3	1-3	1-4	■	3-0	1-2	1-3	1-1	1-3	4-3	0-2	1-1	0-8
Coleraine FC	3-1	3-6	1-1	0-3	8-2	■	1-2	2-0	2-2	2-4	3-2	0-4	2-2	0-2
Derry City FC	3-0	9-1	4-1	1-0	4-0	4-0	■	3-0	2-0	3-0	7-1	7-1	3-1	3-0
Distillery FC	3-1	4-4	3-2	1-0	0-0	4-1	1-3	■	2-1	3-1	5-2	1-5	1-2	2-1
Glenavon FC	4-1	2-0	3-2	1-1	2-2	0-3	1-4	2-1	■	0-4	3-4	1-3	2-4	0-2
Glentoran FC	2-0	1-2	1-5	1-4	3-2	1-1	3-3	5-3	2-0	■	3-2	2-0	4-2	1-2
Larne FC	1-1	2-6	3-0	0-4	3-1	1-1	2-3	4-2	1-1	3-8	■	0-4	2-1	3-2
Linfield FC	6-0	1-1	4-1	0-2	1-1	8-0	6-1	2-3	3-2	5-2	6-3	■	4-1	2-5
Newry Town FC	4-1	5-2	5-0	3-3	6-0	5-0	4-1	1-2	4-1	2-3	4-0	0-2	■	0-0
Portadown FC	2-0	4-2	3-0	3-3	5-0	4-2	2-1	6-0	2-0	1-3	3-0	1-1	4-1	■

Play-off

Derry City FC (Londonderry)	2-2, 1-3	**BELFAST CELTIC FC (BELFAST)**

	Irish League	Pd	Wn	Dw	Ls	GF	GA	Pts
1.	Belfast Celtic FC (Belfast)	26	18	5	3	88	24	41
1.	Derry City FC (Londonderry)	26	20	1	5	81	40	41
3.	Portadown FC (Portadown)	26	16	5	5	67	32	37
4.	Linfield FC (Belfast)	26	16	5	5	78	38	37
5.	Ballymena United FC (Ballymena)	26	14	5	7	72	55	33
6.	Glentoran FC (Belfast)	26	15	2	9	64	57	32
7.	Newry Town FC (Newry)	26	10	6	10	63	49	26
8.	Distillery FC (Belfast)	26	10	6	10	51	61	26
9.	Ards FC (Newtownards)	26	7	4	15	43	66	18
10.	Glenavon FC (Lurgan)	26	6	5	15	36	65	17
11.	Bangor FC (Bangor)	26	7	2	17	39	62	16
12.	Larne FC (Larne)	26	6	3	17	48	87	15
13.	Coleraine FC (Coleraine)	26	5	5	16	40	75	15
14.	Cliftonville FC (Belfast)	26	2	6	18	27	86	10
		364	152	60	152	797	797	364

No clubs promoted or relegated

IRISH CUP FINAL   (Solitude, Belfast – 09/04/1938)

BELFAST CELTIC FC (BELFAST)   0-0   Bangor FC (Bangor)

Belfast: K. McAlinden, Lavery, Fulton, O'Connor, Leathem, Walker, Kernaghan, Walker, Turnbull, Bruce, McIlroy.

Bangor: Hewitt, Graham, Clayton, Jones, Fullerton, Yeats, Morrow, Couser, Russell, Robinson, McCartney.

IRISH CUP FINAL REPLAY   (Solitude, Belfast – 07/05/1938)

BELFAST CELTIC FC (BELFAST)   2-0   Bangor FC (Bangor)

J. McAlinden, Bruce

Bangor: Hewitt, John Graham, Clayton, Jones, Fullerton, Yeates, Morrow, James Graham, Russell, Robinson, McCartney.

Belfast: K. McAlinden, Lavery, Fulton, H. Walker, Leathem, J. Walker, Kernaghan, J. McAlinden, Kelly, Bruce, McIlroy.

Semi-finals

Bangor FC (Bangor)	2-2, 3-1	Derry City FC (Londonderry)
Belfast Celtic FC (Belfast)	1-1, 3-1	Glentoran FC (Belfast)

Quarter-finals

Bangor FC (Bangor)	2-0	Linfield Swifts FC (Linfield)
Belfast Celtic FC (Belfast)	0-0, 0-0, 1-0	Ballymena United FC (Ballymena)
Derry City FC (Londonderry)	2-1	Newry Town FC (Newry)
Glentoran FC (Belfast)	1-1, 0-0, 2-1	Glenavon FC (Lurgan)

1938-39

Irish League 1938-39 Season	Ards	Ballymena U.	Bangor	Belfast Celtic	Cliftonville	Coleraine	Derry City	Distillery	Glenavon	Glentoran	Larne	Linfield	Newry Town	Portadown
Ards FC	■	2-6	2-0	2-3	5-2	4-4	3-1	4-2	4-2	2-1	3-2	4-1	4-2	3-3
Ballymena United FC	1-1	■	2-3	0-8	7-2	4-0	1-0	3-0	1-1	1-0	7-3	2-1	1-0	2-4
Bangor FC	1-1	3-3	■	1-3	3-0	0-0	1-5	1-1	2-2	2-4	0-0	3-2	2-3	4-3
Belfast Celtic FC	8-1	1-2	10-1	■	3-0	8-1	3-4	2-0	3-1	4-3	6-1	1-2	4-1	2-1
Cliftonville FC	4-3	0-3	1-2	1-10	■	5-2	1-5	3-2	2-3	4-3	1-4	0-3	0-0	0-2
Coleraine FC	2-5	1-2	2-0	0-1	0-4	■	1-3	1-2	4-1	3-5	2-3	2-4	1-1	3-1
Derry City FC	5-0	3-5	8-0	2-2	2-1	4-1	■	5-0	3-2	4-0	5-0	1-1	0-0	6-2
Distillery FC	2-0	0-0	7-1	1-0	2-1	5-2	1-4	■	1-2	4-5	6-0	0-2	3-3	2-2
Glenavon FC	2-4	7-0	1-1	2-1	2-1	5-2	3-2	5-1	■	2-3	4-3	6-2	2-2	5-2
Glentoran FC	2-1	1-3	3-2	1-6	4-2	4-0	4-2	2-0	4-3	■	3-1	3-2	0-0	2-9
Larne FC	2-2	2-2	1-0	1-1	4-0	4-3	4-2	0-2	3-0	2-5	■	1-4	0-1	3-2
Linfield FC	1-0	1-2	4-1	1-2	0-0	4-0	2-4	1-0	3-2	2-1	5-0	■	4-1	5-0
Newry Town FC	1-1	3-1	1-2	0-2	4-3	3-1	4-3	1-5	1-2	5-1	3-1	1-0	■	2-2
Portadown FC	6-2	7-2	2-1	2-3	3-0	5-2	5-1	6-4	2-0	3-1	4-0	3-1	3-0	■

	Irish League	Pd	Wn	Dw	Ls	GF	GA	Pts
1.	BELFAST CELTIC FC (BELFAST)	26	19	2	5	97	32	40
2.	Ballymena United FC (Ballymena)	26	15	5	6	63	54	35
3.	Derry City FC (Londonderry)	26	15	3	8	84	47	33
4.	Portadown FC (Portadown)	26	15	3	8	84	56	33
5.	Linfield FC (Belfast)	26	14	2	10	58	40	30
6.	Glentoran FC (Belfast)	26	14	1	11	65	69	29
7.	Glenavon FC (Lurgan)	26	12	4	10	67	57	28
8.	Ards FC (Newtownards)	26	11	6	9	63	66	28
9.	Newry Town FC (Newry)	26	9	8	9	43	48	26
10.	Distillery FC (Belfast)	26	9	4	13	53	56	22
11.	Larne FC (Larne)	26	8	4	14	45	73	20
12.	Bangor FC (Bangor)	26	6	7	13	37	71	19
13.	Cliftonville FC (Belfast)	26	5	2	19	38	81	12
14.	Coleraine FC (Coleraine)	26	3	3	20	40	87	9
		364	155	54	155	837	837	364

No clubs promoted or relegated

IRISH CUP FINAL   (Solitude, Belfast – 29/04/1939)

LINFIELD FC (BELFAST)　　　　2-0　　　　Ballymena United FC (Ballymena)

Finlay, Marshall

Linfield: Doak, Thompson, Richardson, Waddell, Perry, Rosbotham, Brownlow, Donnelly, Marshall, Finlay, McCormick.

Ballymena: Redmond, Vincent, McDaid, Wallace, McCartney, Surgenor, Kirby, Horner, Sclater, Olphert, Moore.

Semi-finals

Ballymena United FC (Ballymena)	3-2	Portadown FC (Portadown)
Linfield FC (Belfast)	4-0	Cliftonville FC (Belfast)

Quarter-finals

Ballymena United FC (Ballymena)	3-1	Belfast Celtic FC (Belfast)
Bangor FC (Bangor)	2-4	Portadown FC (Portadown)
Cliftonville FC (Belfast)	3-0	Glenavon FC (Lurgan)
Linfield FC (Belfast)	3-1	Newry Town FC (Newry)

1939-40

Irish League 1939-40 Season	Ards	Ballymena U.	Bangor	Belfast Celtic	Cliftonville	Coleraine	Derry City	Distillery	Glenavon	Glentoran	Larne	Linfield	Newry Town	Portadown
Ards FC		0-2	3-1	3-3	3-1	5-0	1-3	1-4	0-1	2-1	7-1	2-3	1-1	5-4
Ballymena United FC	5-0		6-0	1-5	4-3	6-1	4-1	4-0	2-2	2-3	5-1	2-1	8-2	2-1
Bangor FC	2-5	2-2		1-3	3-1	4-2	1-3	1-0	5-1	0-4	4-1	2-0	4-1	1-2
Belfast Celtic FC	3-0	3-3	6-0		6-2	6-1	3-0	4-0	4-2	4-2	0-0	5-0	12-0	0-0
Cliftonville FC	1-3	0-1	2-3	0-7		1-2	2-1	7-2	1-2	0-2	3-3	1-6	3-2	2-4
Coleraine FC	3-1	2-4	5-1	1-3	4-1		2-1	5-4	1-4	3-7	3-1	0-4	3-1	2-1
Derry City FC	6-2	5-2	5-2	0-0	6-1	0-0		2-1	9-0	3-2	6-0	1-2	4-1	3-5
Distillery FC	1-2	3-3	3-1	1-3	4-1	1-3	1-3		4-2	2-3	5-2	1-3	7-0	1-1
Glenavon FC	5-1	4-2	6-2	0-3	8-1	3-0	0-1	2-1		4-3	3-2	3-3	2-0	2-3
Glentoran FC	8-1	4-2	5-1	0-3	8-2	4-1	6-1	6-2	6-1		6-2	3-2	6-1	0-3
Larne FC	4-0	2-4	1-1	0-2	1-0	0-1	2-8	4-1	0-5	0-2		1-1	2-1	2-7
Linfield FC	4-0	2-1	1-1	0-2	5-1	3-1	1-0	3-1	5-5	1-2	3-1		3-0	0-5
Newry Town FC	2-0	1-3	3-0	0-1	3-1	1-1	2-0	1-1	3-2	1-9	1-1	3-4		1-1
Portadown FC	3-1	4-2	6-1	1-0	6-2	1-0	3-1	3-2	6-0	2-2	4-2	3-3	7-0	

	Irish League	Pd	Wn	Dw	Ls	GF	GA	Pts
1.	BELFAST CELTIC FC (BELFAST)	26	20	5	1	91	18	45
2.	Portadown FC (Portadown)	26	18	5	3	86	37	41
3.	Glentoran FC (Belfast)	26	19	1	6	104	46	39
4.	Ballymena United FC (Ballymena)	26	15	4	7	82	52	34
5.	Linfield FC (Belfast)	26	14	5	7	63	47	33
6.	Derry City FC (Londonderry)	26	14	2	10	73	46	30
7.	Glenavon FC (Lurgan)	26	13	3	10	69	68	29
8.	Coleraine FC (Coleraine)	26	11	2	13	47	68	24
9.	Ards FC (Newtownards)	26	9	2	15	49	72	20
10.	Bangor FC (Bangor)	26	8	3	13	44	77	19
11.	Distillery FC (Belfast)	26	6	3	17	53	70	15
12.	Newry Town FC (Newry)	26	5	5	16	32	86	15
13.	Larne FC (Larne)	26	4	5	17	36	83	13
14.	Cliftonville FC (Belfast)	26	3	1	22	40	99	7
		364	159	46	159	869	869	364

The Irish League was suspended from 1940-41 to 1946-47 due to World War 2. However, some regional leagues were contested during this period with the Irish League re-starting for season 1947-48.

IRISH CUP FINAL   (Windsor Park, Belfast – 20/04/1940)

BALLYMENA UNITED FC (BALLYMENA)   2-0   Glenavon FC (Lurgan)

Moore, Sclater

Ballymena: Redmond, Vincent, Swann, Barr, McCartney, Rosbotham, Grant, Olphert, Sclater, Weir, Moore.
Glenavon: Kelly, Weir, Hoy, Magill, Clayton, Fraham, Holbeach, Robinson, Craig, Duffy, McCunnie.

Semi-finals

Ballymena United FC (Ballymena)	2-0	Belfast Celtic FC (Belfast)
Glenavon FC (Lurgan)	2-0	Linfield FC (Belfast)

Quarter-finals

Ballymena United FC (Ballymena)	3-2	Dundela FC (Belfast)
Belfast Celtic FC (Belfast)	3-0	Derry City FC (Londonderry)
Belfast Celtic FC (Belfast) 2nd XI	0-3	Glenavon FC (Lurgan)
Larne FC (Larne)	1-2	Linfield FC (Belfast)

1940-41

Belfast & District League 1940-41 Season	Belfast Celtic	Cliftonville	Derry City	Distillery	Glenavon	Glentoran	Linfield	Portadown
Belfast Celtic FC		9-1	1-2	4-0	13-0	1-2	5-2	6-0
		3-1	8-2	3-2	5-2	8-2	2-4	3-1
Cliftonville FC	0-1		2-5	1-3	3-2	1-3	0-5	0-8
	1-3		4-5	1-7	1-1	0-4	3-4	2-5
Derry City FC	0-4	2-1		1-2	5-3	0-4	0-4	2-2
	0-1	2-1		1-4	2-3	2-2	2-2	2-5
Distillery FC	2-7	7-1	6-0		5-0	6-3	5-1	2-2
	0-0	5-1	5-2		2-2	2-3	2-3	1-2
Glenavon FC	1-5	1-2	6-1	2-1		1-0	---	0-4
	0-3	6-3	3-4	0-1		1-1	1-1	1-4
Glentoran FC	1-1	6-2	5-0	5-0	8-0		1-2	4-2
	3-3	6-3	4-0	6-1	1-2		3-1	7-4
Linfield FC	1-0	2-1	7-2	1-1	2-0	1-4		2-0
	0-2	3-1	1-2	1-3	6-1	3-3		3-4
Portadown FC	---	5-1	6-2	3-1	8-0	6-5	1-4	
	2-2	4-2	4-0	1-1	3-1	4-3	3-3	

	Belfast & District League	**Pd**	**Wn**	**Dw**	**Ls**	**GF**	**GA**	**Pts**	
1.	BELFAST CELTIC FC (BELFAST)	27	19	4	4	104	32	42	
2.	Portadown FC (Portadown)	27	17	4	6	92	58	38	#
3.	Glentoran FC (Belfast)	28	16	5	7	99	57	37	
4.	Linfield FC (Belfast)	27	14	4	9	67	51	32	
5.	Distillery FC (Belfast)	28	13	5	10	77	57	31	
6.	Derry City FC (Londonderry)	28	8	3	17	48	100	19	
7.	Glenavon FC (Lurgan)	28	6	4	17	40	95	16	#
8.	Cliftonville FC (Belfast)	28	2	1	25	40	117	5	
		220	95	30	95	567	567	220	

Note: The matches Glenavon FC vs Linfield FC and Portadown FC vs Belfast Celtic FC were not played.

Glenavon FC (Lurgan) and Portadown FC (Portadown) resigned from the league which was reduced to 6 clubs for the next season.

IRISH CUP FINAL (Windsor Park, Belfast – 26/04/1941)

BELFAST CELTIC FC (BELFAST)   1-0   Linfield FC (Belfast)

O'Connor

Belfast: Breen, McMillan, Fulton, Walker, Vernon, Leathem, Kernaghan, Kelly, O'Connor, McAlinden, McIlroy.
Linfield: Redmond, Kirkwood, McNickle, McKeown, Brolly, Wright, Donnelly, Barker, Marshall, Sheen, Baird.

Semi-finals

Belfast Celtic FC (Belfast)	5-2	Glenavon FC (Lurgan)
Linfield FC (Belfast)	3-3, 5-2	Distillery FC (Belfast)

Quarter-finals

Belfast Celtic FC (Belfast)	3-2	Bangor FC (Bangor)
Derry City FC (Londonderry)	0-1	Distillery FC (Belfast)
Glenavon FC (Lurgan)	3-3, 5-0	Cliftonville FC (Belfast)
Portadown FC (Portadown)	0-3	Linfield FC (Belfast)

1941-42

Belfast & District League 1941-42 Season	Belfast Celtic	Cliftonville	Derry City	Distillery	Glentoran	Linfield
Belfast Celtic FC		3-1	1-0	5-2	4-0	0-0
		9-0	10-1	1-1	2-1	0-3
Cliftonville FC	2-4		2-2	2-0	0-5	5-5
	0-2		6-1	1-2	1-3	1-4
Derry City FC	0-0	1-0		2-0	1-1	2-2
	1-4	2-1		1-4	0-2	1-2
Distillery FC	0-2	1-1	3-3		5-1	2-2
	1-1	4-1	8-2		1-1	0-2
Glentoran FC	4-1	3-1	7-0	2-1		0-3
	1-3	4-1	7-1	4-2		3-4
Linfield FC	2-2	3-1	9-1	1-2	3-7	
	3-3	6-2	4-1	3-2	3-3	

	Belfast & District League	**Pd**	**Wn**	**Dw**	**Ls**	**GF**	**GA**	**Pts**
1.	BELFAST CELTIC FC (BELFAST)	20	12	6	2	57	23	30
2.	Linfield FC (Belfast)	20	11	7	2	64	38	29
3.	Glentoran FC (Belfast)	20	11	3	6	59	37	25
4.	Distillery FC (Belfast)	20	6	6	8	41	38	18
5.	Derry City FC (Londonderry)	20	3	5	12	23	73	11
6.	Cliftonville FC (Belfast)	20	2	3	15	29	64	7
		120	45	30	45	273	273	120

No clubs promoted or relegated

IRISH CUP FINAL   (Celtic Park, Belfast – 18/04/1942)

LINFIELD FC (BELFAST) 3-1 Glentoran FC (Belfast)

Thompson 2, Peppitt *Keddie*

Linfield: Redmond, Kirkwood, Feeney, McKeown, Mould, Brolly, Thompson, Wright, Peppitt, Ormiston, Baker.
Glentoran: Hinton, Gager, Aston, McDermott, Bray, Kirkham, Wright, Keddie, Robinson, Matthias, Douglas.

Semi-finals

Ards FC (Newtownards)	0-2	Glentoran FC (Belfast)
Linfield FC (Belfast)	6-0	Distillery FC (Belfast)

Quarter-finals

Bangor FC (Bangor) 2nd XI	1-2, 1-4	Ards FC (Newtownards)
Cliftonville FC (Belfast)	0-3, 0-4	Distillery FC (Belfast)
Glentoran FC (Belfast)	4-0, 0-2	Royal Irish Fusiliers Regiment
Linfield FC (Belfast)	5-1, 4-1	Inniskilling Fusiliers Regiment

1942-43

Belfast & District League 1942-43 Season	Belfast Celtic	Cliftonville	Derry City	Distillery	Glentoran	Linfield
Belfast Celtic FC		6-1	4-0	5-1	3-0	1-4
		4-0	4-0	1-1	2-1	2-1
Cliftonville FC	1-3		3-0	0-4	4-2	0-4
	0-2		1-1	2-1	2-2	0-1
Derry City FC	0-1	4-2		3-2	4-2	1-4
	0-0	1-1		2-0	2-6	0-2
Distillery FC	3-2	4-2	3-2		2-1	2-0
	1-2	4-1	1-2		5-2	0-0
Glentoran FC	3-4	9-3	3-3	2-1		2-1
	2-1	6-2	3-2	1-3		1-3
Linfield FC	2-2	5-1	6-2	2-0	4-3	
	1-0	5-0	3-2	2-4	5-3	

	Belfast & District League	**Pd**	**Wn**	**Dw**	**Ls**	**GF**	**GA**	**Pts**
1.	LINFIELD FC (BELFAST)	20	14	2	4	55	26	30
2.	Belfast Celtic FC (Belfast)	20	13	3	4	50	22	29
3.	Distillery FC (Belfast)	20	10	2	8	42	34	22
4.	Glentoran FC (Belfast)	20	7	2	11	54	56	16
5.	Derry City FC (Londonderry)	20	6	3	11	32	51	15
6.	Cliftonville FC (Belfast)	20	3	2	15	26	70	8
		120	53	14	53	259	259	120

No clubs promoted or relegated

IRISH CUP FINAL   (Windsor Park, Belfast – 17/04/1943)

BELFAST CELTIC FC (BELFAST)   1-0   Glentoran FC (Belfast)
Hollinger

Belfast: Kelly, McMillan, Fulton, Walker, Vernon, Douglas, Kernaghan, O'Connor, Byrne, Townsend, Hollinger.
Glentoran: Beale, Hickman, Henderson, McDermott, Dykes, Stevenson, Wright, Beattie, Kelly, Grant, Douglas.

Semi-finals

Belfast Celtic FC (Belfast)	4-2	Larne FC (Larne)
Glentoran FC (Belfast)	4-2	Ards FC (Newtownards)

Quarter-finals

Alexander Works FC	1-2, 2-3	Belfast Celtic FC (Belfast)
Ards FC (Newtownards)	2-1, 5-0	Infantry Training Centre
Glentoran FC (Belfast)	7-2, 8-0	Royal Irish Fusiliers Regiment
Larne FC (Larne) received a bye		

1943-44

Belfast & District League 1943-44 Season	Belfast Celtic	Cliftonville	Derry City	Distillery	Glentoran	Linfield
Belfast Celtic FC		3-0	9-0	4-3	3-1	3-1
		7-1	4-0	1-1	5-3	0-2
Cliftonville FC	0-5		2-1	3-1	4-2	0-2
	1-1		7-0	0-5	3-5	0-3
Derry City FC	1-1	2-1		3-5	2-1	---
	1-2	1-0		3-4	4-2	2-6
Distillery FC	1-1	1-0	5-3		1-3	2-2
	3-2	0-2	3-1		3-1	6-1
Glentoran FC	0-1	3-1	5-4	4-2		2-2
	0-1	3-1	5-0	3-1		1-3
Linfield FC	---	2-1	5-2	8-1	4-1	
	2-2	4-2	3-5	2-4	5-5	

	Belfast & District League	**Pd**	**Wn**	**Dw**	**Ls**	**GF**	**GA**	**Pts**
1.	BELFAST CELTIC FC (BELFAST)	19	12	5	2	55	21	29
2.	Linfield FC (Belfast)	18	11	3	4	57	38	25
3.	Distillery FC (Belfast)	20	10	3	7	52	47	23
4.	Glentoran FC (Belfast)	20	8	1	11	49	50	17
5.	Cliftonville FC (Belfast)	20	5	1	14	29	51	11
6.	Derry City FC (Londonderry)	19	5	1	13	35	70	11
		116	51	14	51	277	277	116

The matches Linfield FC vs Glentoran FC and Derry City FC vs Linfield FC were not played.

No clubs promoted or relegated

IRISH CUP FINAL   (Windsor Park, Belfast – 22/04/1944)

BELFAST CELTIC FC (BELFAST)　　　　3-1　　　　　　　　　　Linfield FC (Belfast)
Bonnar, McAlinden, A. Kelly　　　　　　　　　　　　　　　　　　　　　　*Cochrane*

Belfast: H. Kelly, McMillan, Cullen, Walker, Vernon, O'Connor, Collins, McAlinden, Byrne, A. Kelly, Bonnar.
Linfield: Twoomey, Bryson, Feeney, H. Walsh, Stark, McWilliams, Cochrane, McCrory, D. Walsh, Pearson, Lockhart.

Semi-finals

Belfast Celtic FC (Belfast)	3-0	Infantry Training Centre
Linfield FC (Belfast)	0-0, 2-0	Cliftonville FC (Belfast)

Quarter-finals

Bangor FC (Bangor) 2nd XI	0-1, 2-2	Infantry Training Centre
Belfast Celtic FC (Belfast)	3-0, 4-1	Distillery FC (Belfast)
Cliftonville FC (Belfast)	2-2, 3-0	Ards FC (Newtownards)
Linfield FC (Belfast)	4-2, 4-1	Larne FC (Larne)

1944-45

Belfast & District League 1944-45 Season	Belfast Celtic	Cliftonville	Derry City	Distillery	Glentoran	Linfield
Belfast Celtic FC		1-0	3-1	4-2	4-1	1-1
		2-0	2-2	6-2	7-3	3-0
Cliftonville FC	1-2		1-4	1-3	2-3	0-6
	0-2		2-3	0-1	2-1	0-4
Derry City FC	1-0	2-3		3-1	2-1	0-2
	3-3	3-1		0-5	4-0	0-5
Distillery FC	2-2	4-2	4-2		3-5	0-4
	1-5	3-1	0-1		5-0	1-3
Glentoran FC	1-2	9-3	6-2	2-1		1-2
	1-2	6-2	6-3	3-4		1-5
Linfield FC	2-2	6-0	5-2	7-1	3-3	
	3-1	4-2	3-3	7-1	9-2	

	Belfast & District League	**Pd**	**Wn**	**Dw**	**Ls**	**GF**	**GA**	**Pts**
1.	LINFIELD FC (BELFAST)	20	15	4	1	81	24	34
2.	Belfast Celtic FC (Belfast)	20	13	5	2	54	27	31
3.	Derry City FC (Londonderry)	20	8	3	9	41	53	19
4.	Distillery FC (Belfast)	20	8	1	11	44	58	17
5.	Glentoran FC (Belfast)	20	7	1	12	55	67	15
6.	Cliftonville FC (Belfast)	20	2	-	18	23	69	4
		120	53	14	53	298	298	120

No clubs promoted or relegated

IRISH CUP FINAL   (Celtic Park, Belfast – 14/04/1945)

LINFIELD FC (BELFAST)   4-2   Glentoran FC (Belfast)
McCrory 2, Lockhart, Cochrane   *Hill, McIlvenny*

Linfield: Breen, Henderson, Feeney, H. Walsh, Bryson, McWilliams, Cochrane, McCrory, D. Walsh, Robinson, Lockhart.
Glentoran: Vernon, McIlroy, Gilmore, McDermott, Dykes, Wright, McIlvenny, Hill, Nimmick, Langton, Deakin.

Semi-finals

Glentoran FC (Belfast)	3-0	Distillery FC (Belfast)
Linfield FC (Belfast)	4-0	Derry City FC (Londonderry)

Quarter-finals

Derry City FC (Londonderry)	5-0, 3-2	Cliftonville FC (Belfast)
Distillery FC (Belfast)	4-1, 3-4	Belfast Celtic FC (Belfast)
Larne FC (Larne)	3-4, 3-5	Glentoran FC (Belfast)
Linfield FC (Belfast)	8-0, 2-0	Ards FC (Newtownards)

1945-46

Belfast & District League 1945-46 Season	Belfast Celtic	Cliftonville	Derry City	Distillery	Glentoran	Linfield
Belfast Celtic FC		4-1	2-1	5-0	3-1	3-0
		5-0	5-0	4-3	2-2	0-2
Cliftonville FC	0-4		4-1	1-1	1-1	2-3
	0-3		3-2	0-6	2-3	1-3
Derry City FC	2-2	8-2		1-0	1-2	1-4
	1-4	5-2		4-1	4-3	3-5
Distillery FC	1-3	1-1	8-4		3-3	3-2
	0-0	4-2	2-1		4-1	1-6
Glentoran FC	2-5	5-0	5-4	1-3		0-3
	2-2	1-1	9-2	2-2		1-7
Linfield FC	0-1	8-1	4-3	8-2	5-0	
	2-1	5-0	5-0	3-2	4-2	

	Belfast & District League	Pd	Wn	Dw	Ls	GF	GA	Pts
1.	LINFIELD FC (BELFAST)	20	17	-	3	79	27	34
2.	Belfast Celtic FC (Belfast)	20	14	4	2	58	20	32
3.	Distillery FC (Belfast)	20	7	5	8	47	52	19
4.	Glentoran FC (Belfast)	20	5	6	9	46	58	16
5.	Derry City FC (Londonderry)	20	5	1	14	48	72	11
6.	Cliftonville FC (Belfast)	20	2	4	14	24	73	8
		120	50	20	50	302	302	120

Elected: Coleraine FC (Coleraine), Ballymena United FC (Ballymena)

The league was extended to 8 clubs for next season

IRISH CUP FINAL (Celtic Park, Belfast – 13/04/1946)

LINFIELD FC (BELFAST) 3-0 Distillery FC (Belfast)

Walsh 2, McCrory

Linfield: Breen, Henderson, Feeney, Jones, Bryson, McWilliams, McKenna, McCrory, Walsh, Russell, Lockhart.
Distillery: Smyth, Crossley, McAuley, Collins, Bowler, Currie, O'Connor, Kernaghan, Lonsdale, Brennan, Walker.

Semi-finals

Distillery FC (Belfast)	0-0, 1-0	Belfast Celtic FC (Belfast) 2nd XI
Linfield FC (Belfast)	2-0	Belfast Celtic FC (Belfast)

Quarter-finals

Belfast Celtic FC (Belfast) 2nd XI	0-0, 3-1	Cliftonville FC (Belfast)
Derry City FC (Londonderry)	0-3, 2-7	Glentoran FC (Belfast)
Distillery FC (Belfast)	2-1, 2-0	Linfield Swifts FC (Belfast)
Linfield FC (Belfast)	2-0, 3-3	Ards FC (Newtownards)

1946-47

Belfast & District League 1946-47 Season	Ballymena U.	Belfast Celtic	Cliftonville	Coleraine	Derry City	Distillery	Glentoran	Linfield
Ballymena United FC		2-4	4-3	3-0	3-3	2-0	3-5	3-5
		1-1	5-1	1-1	3-2	1-0	1-1	0-1
Belfast Celtic FC	1-1		4-1	2-3	2-0	6-1	1-3	2-3
	10-1		6-1	3-2	8-1	4-0	2-1	2-0
Cliftonville FC	2-2	1-2		1-2	1-0	0-6	2-5	3-5
	5-5	0-2		3-3	1-2	3-4	0-5	1-0
Coleraine FC	3-0	0-2	2-1		4-0	1-3	0-0	2-2
	1-0	3-6	4-3		4-2	2-0	0-2	2-4
Derry City FC	2-1	0-2	4-1	3-0		4-2	2-3	0-2
	3-4	2-9	6-2	4-1		1-0	0-3	3-1
Distillery FC	6-1	2-4	10-1	3-4	2-2		2-1	0-3
	0-2	1-2	2-3	2-2	4-1		2-1	2-1
Glentoran FC	3-1	3-0	5-2	7-2	2-1	3-1		1-2
	5-1	4-2	9-3	6-1	4-3	4-1		2-4
Linfield FC	6-0	1-2	5-0	2-0	7-1	5-1	2-3	
	2-1	2-3	5-1	10-5	4-1	5-2	4-2	

	Belfast & District League	Pd	Wn	Dw	Ls	GF	GA	Pts
1.	BELFAST CELTIC FC (BELFAST)	28	21	2	5	95	40	44
2.	Glentoran FC (Belfast)	28	20	2	6	93	46	42
3.	Linfield FC (Belfast)	28	20	1	7	93	45	41
4.	Coleraine FC (Coleraine)	28	10	5	13	54	75	25
5.	Ballymena United FC (Ballymena)	28	8	7	13	52	76	23
6.	Distillery FC (Belfast)	28	9	2	17	59	69	20
7.	Derry City FC (Londonderry)	28	9	2	17	53	80	20
8.	Cliftonville FC (Belfast)	28	3	3	22	46	114	9
		224	100	24	100	545	545	224

The Irish League restarted the next season with the above 8 clubs plus the following elected clubs:
Ards FC (Newtownards), Bangor FC (Bangor), Glenavon FC (Lurgan), Portadown FC (Portadown)

IRISH CUP FINAL (Windsor Park, Belfast – 26/04/1947)

BELFAST CELTIC FC (BELFAST)　　　　1-0　　　　　　　　　　Glentoran FC (Belfast)
Tully

Belfast: K. McAlinden, McMillan, Aherne, Walker, Currie, R. Lawler, Campbell, Tully, McMorran, Denver, Douglas.
Glentoran: McKee, Kane, Neill, Blanchflower, Waters, Hughes, Wright, Kelly, McCormack, J. Lawler, Lavery.

Semi-finals

Belfast Celtic FC (Belfast)	1-0	Linfield FC (Belfast)
Glentoran FC (Belfast)	1-1, 1-1, 2-1	Ballymena United FC (Ballymena)

Quarter-finals

Cliftonville FC (Belfast)	0-2, 0-3	Ballymena United FC (Ballymena)
Coleraine FC (Coleraine)	4-1, 0-3, 0-3	Linfield FC (Belfast)
Derry City FC (Londonderry)	0-1, 2-5	Belfast Celtic FC (Belfast)
Distillery FC (Belfast)	1-0, 0-1, 1-2	Glentoran FC (Belfast)

1947-48

Irish League 1947-48 Season	Ards	Ballymena U.	Bangor	Belfast Celtic	Cliftonville	Coleraine	Derry City	Distillery	Glenavon	Glentoran	Linfield	Portadown
Ards FC	■	2-2	1-2	2-5	1-3	3-2	4-1	1-2	2-4	1-1	2-1	3-0
Ballymena United FC	0-1	■	2-0	4-3	5-2	3-2	6-0	2-1	4-2	1-1	1-2	5-2
Bangor FC	1-2	3-7	■	2-5	1-1	2-2	4-0	3-2	2-5	2-3	1-4	1-3
Belfast Celtic FC	6-0	2-0	3-2	■	3-0	5-2	5-1	5-0	3-1	0-0	3-0	6-2
Cliftonville FC	3-4	1-1	2-3	2-4	■	0-1	3-0	2-0	3-3	2-1	0-0	2-1
Coleraine FC	1-1	4-0	3-0	1-8	4-0	■	3-0	0-2	2-2	2-2	1-2	5-2
Derry City FC	6-2	1-1	0-2	1-5	1-3	2-5	■	0-2	1-2	2-3	0-7	1-0
Distillery FC	2-0	2-2	3-1	0-2	3-0	0-2	2-0	■	2-0	2-2	0-4	1-0
Glenavon FC	1-1	1-2	1-1	1-3	3-2	2-2	4-0	0-2	■	0-5	1-1	5-1
Glentoran FC	4-1	2-2	4-0	1-3	3-1	3-0	4-0	0-2	1-3	■	0-2	1-1
Linfield FC	3-1	3-1	1-1	3-1	3-1	2-2	2-0	4-1	4-1	1-1	■	3-0
Portadown FC	4-2	1-1	1-2	1-4	2-3	5-2	1-1	2-4	1-3	1-2	0-3	■

Irish League

#	Club	Pd	Wn	Dw	Ls	GF	GA	Pts
1.	BELFAST CELTIC FC (BELFAST)	22	19	1	2	84	26	39
2.	Linfield FC (Belfast)	22	15	5	2	55	19	35
3.	Ballymena United FC (Ballymena)	22	10	7	5	52	38	27
4.	Distillery FC (Belfast)	22	12	2	8	35	32	26
5.	Glentoran FC (Belfast)	22	9	8	5	44	29	26
6.	Coleraine FC (Coleraine)	22	8	6	8	48	46	22
7.	Glenavon FC (Lurgan)	22	8	6	8	45	45	22
8.	Ards FC (Newtownards)	22	7	4	11	37	54	18
9.	Cliftonville FC (Belfast)	22	7	4	11	36	47	18
10.	Bangor FC (Bangor)	22	6	4	12	36	55	16
11.	Portadown FC (Portadown)	22	3	3	16	31	60	9
12.	Derry City FC (Londonderry)	22	2	2	18	18	70	6
		264	106	52	106	521	521	264

Top goalscorer 1947-48

1) James JONES   (Belfast Celtic FC)   28

Note: The match Bangor FC 2-5 Celtic FC was abandoned after 76 minutes, but the result was allowed to stand.

No clubs promoted or relegated

IRISH CUP FINAL   (Celtic Park, Belfast)

LINFIELD FC (BELFAST)   3-0   Coleraine FC (Coleraine)

Thompson, O'Connor o.g., Simpson

Linfield: A. Russell, McCune, McMichael, Liggett, Bryson, Walsh, Thompson, Bardsley, Simpson, J. Russell, McKenna.

Coleraine: K. McAlinden, O'Connor, Gilmore, Masters, McCavana, Doherty, O'Reilly, Nolan, Clarke, McDowell, Mahood.

Semi-finals

| Coleraine FC (Coleraine) | 3-3, 3-2 | Belfast Celtic FC (Belfast) |
| Linfield FC (Belfast) | 5-1 | Glenavon FC (Lurgan) |

Quarter-finals

Belfast Celtic FC (Belfast)	4-1	Brantwood FC (Belfast)
Coleraine FC (Coleraine)	1-0	Derry City FC (Londonderry)
Glenavon FC (Lurgan)	3-0	Distillery FC (Belfast)
Linfield FC (Belfast)	3-2	Bangor FC (Bangor)

1948-49

Irish League 1948-49 Season	Ards	Ballymena U.	Bangor	Belfast Celtic	Cliftonville	Coleraine	Derry City	Distillery	Glenavon	Glentoran	Linfield	Portadown
Ards FC		8-0	2-4	4-4	1-2	7-0	3-1	0-1	0-2	2-1	0-4	2-2
Ballymena United FC	1-0		1-1	0-5	3-4	5-2	3-2	7-5	0-0	1-1	0-3	1-1
Bangor FC	2-3	2-2		0-1	2-1	1-0	4-1	5-2	1-1	3-0	3-3	2-3
Belfast Celtic FC	4-3	3-2	3-0		4-3	4-0	8-0	10-2	3-1	0-3	0-1	5-1
Cliftonville FC	3-2	1-1	2-2	2-5		6-0	1-1	2-1	5-2	1-0	1-3	5-0
Coleraine FC	4-1	1-2	3-1	1-0	3-0		1-2	0-6	1-1	1-3	0-2	2-4
Derry City FC	2-3	1-2	3-1	4-3	2-1	7-1		2-2	1-2	0-1	1-3	3-2
Distillery FC	2-1	6-2	5-0	1-2	0-1	2-0	2-3		2-0	2-1	3-2	2-2
Glenavon FC	1-2	2-2	4-2	1-0	2-2	4-1	4-1	2-2		1-2	0-3	2-2
Glentoran FC	2-0	4-2	2-1	0-0	2-0	3-2	2-2	4-1	7-1		1-4	2-1
Linfield FC	5-1	4-2	1-2	1-1	0-0	3-1	3-0	5-2	1-1	2-0		3-1
Portadown FC	2-1	2-0	2-4	2-4	2-1	2-1	0-1	5-0	3-1	1-4	1-2	

	Irish League	Pd	Wn	Dw	Ls	GF	GA	Pts	
1.	LINFIELD FC (BELFAST)	22	16	4	2	58	21	36	
2.	Belfast Celtic FC (Belfast)	22	14	3	5	69	32	31	#
3.	Glentoran FC (Belfast)	22	13	3	6	45	28	29	
4.	Cliftonville FC (Belfast)	22	9	5	8	44	38	23	
5.	Bangor FC (Bangor)	22	8	5	9	43	45	21	
6.	Distillery FC (Belfast)	22	9	3	10	51	56	21	
7.	Portadown FC (Portadown)	22	8	4	10	41	48	20	
8.	Glenavon FC (Lurgan)	22	6	8	8	35	43	20	
9.	Derry City FC (Londonderry)	22	8	3	11	40	52	19	
10.	Ballymena United FC (Ballymena)	22	6	7	9	39	58	19	
11.	Ards FC (Newtownards)	22	7	2	13	46	49	16	
12.	Coleraine FC (Coleraine)	22	4	1	17	25	66	9	
		264	108	48	108	536	536	624	

Belfast Celtic FC (Belfast) resigned from the league as a result of "trouble" at some of their matches, including the Boxing Day match in which Celtic player Jimmy Jones had his leg broken after being attacked by spectators.

Top goalscorer 1948-49

1) William SIMPSON   (Linfield FC)   19

Elected: Crusaders FC (Belfast)

IRISH CUP FINAL   (Windsor Park, Belfast – 16/04/1949)

DERRY CITY FC (LONDONDERRY)   3-1   Glentoran FC (Belfast)
Colvan, Cannon, Hermon   *Peacock*

Derry: Muir, Cully, Brennan, Doherty, Ferris, McCreary, Hermon, Aitken, Cannon, Colvan, Kelly.
Glentoran: Moore, Neill, McCarthy, Ferran, Hughes, Blanchflower, Nimmick, Peacock, McFarlane, Kerr, Feeney.

Semi-finals

Derry City FC (Londonderry)	2-0	Distillery FC (Belfast)
Glentoran FC (Belfast)	2-2, 1-1, 3-0	Portadown FC (Portadown)

Quarter-finals

Cliftonville FC (Belfast)	1-3	Glentoran FC (Belfast)
Derry City FC (Londonderry)	1-1, 3-3, 1-1, 1-0	Bangor FC (Bangor)
Distillery FC (Belfast)	2-1	Coleraine FC (Coleraine)
Portadown FC (Portadown)	3-1	Glenavon FC (Lurgan)

1949-50

Irish League 1949-50 Season	Ards	Ballymena U.	Bangor	Cliftonville	Coleraine	Crusaders	Derry City	Distillery	Glenavon	Glentoran	Linfield	Portadown
Ards FC	■	1-1	2-2	0-0	3-1	5-2	0-1	2-2	0-2	3-4	0-2	1-1
Ballymena United FC	0-0	■	1-2	6-0	4-1	1-3	1-1	0-3	1-1	1-5	1-3	1-2
Bangor FC	1-2	3-0	■	1-3	2-1	1-2	2-3	2-3	0-1	0-4	0-2	7-0
Cliftonville FC	6-0	2-2	1-2	■	1-3	2-7	0-3	1-4	2-4	0-6	1-4	3-3
Coleraine FC	1-0	0-1	2-4	3-0	■	2-2	3-6	1-3	6-4	0-5	2-3	3-2
Crusaders FC	2-6	0-1	0-4	0-5	2-2	■	0-4	1-1	4-1	0-4	2-2	2-3
Derry City FC	1-3	5-1	2-0	3-0	0-0	2-0	■	2-4	0-1	1-1	2-2	1-0
Distillery FC	1-2	2-1	1-1	4-1	3-1	2-1	1-2	■	5-1	1-4	0-2	1-0
Glenavon FC	3-0	3-1	0-1	2-2	4-0	9-0	6-2	3-2	■	2-3	1-2	1-1
Glentoran FC	2-1	5-0	1-0	4-2	2-1	4-2	2-0	2-3	3-1	■	2-3	2-1
Linfield FC	3-1	6-1	4-2	2-1	7-2	4-1	1-2	1-0	2-0	1-1	■	2-2
Portadown FC	0-2	1-3	1-1	2-1	3-3	4-4	1-1	0-2	1-1	2-4	3-6	■

Play-off

LINFIELD FC (BELFAST)	2-0	Glentoran FC (Belfast)

	Irish League	Pd	Wn	Dw	Ls	GF	GA	Pts
1.	Linfield FC (Belfast)	22	17	4	1	64	27	38
1.	Glentoran FC (Belfast)	22	18	2	2	70	25	38
3.	Distillery FC (Belfast)	22	13	3	6	48	31	29
4.	Derry City FC (Londonderry)	22	12	5	5	44	29	29
5.	Glenavon FC (Lurgan)	22	10	4	8	51	38	24
6.	Ards FC (Newtownards)	22	7	6	9	34	38	20
7.	Bangor FC (Bangor)	22	8	3	11	38	36	19
8.	Ballymena United FC (Ballymena)	22	5	5	12	29	49	15
9.	Portadown FC (Portadown)	22	3	9	10	33	52	15
10.	Coleraine FC (Coleraine)	22	5	4	13	38	61	14
11.	Crusaders FC (Belfast)	22	4	5	13	37	69	13
12.	Cliftonville FC (Belfast)	22	3	4	15	34	65	10
		264	105	54	105	520	520	264

No club promoted or relegated

Top goalscorer 1949-50

1) Samuel HUGHES   (Glentoran FC)   23

IRISH CUP FINAL (Windsor Park, Belfast – 22/04/1950)

LINFIELD FC (BELFAST)   2-1   Distillery FC (Belfast)
Thompson, McDowell   *Mycock*

Linfield: Russell, McCune, Houston, Smyth, Hamill, Walsh, Thompson, Currie, Simpson, McDowell, Dickson.
Distillery: Smyth, Wilson, Mills, Casement, Lonsdale, Gray, Dodds, Mulholland, McClinton, Mycock, Kelly.

Semi-finals

Distillery FC (Belfast)   5-1   Linfield Swifts FC (Belfast)
Linfield FC (Belfast)   1-0   Derry City FC (Londonderry)

Quarter-finals

Crusaders FC (Belfast)   1-7   Distillery FC (Belfast)
Derry City FC (Londonderry)   2-0   Ards FC (Newtownards)
Linfield FC (Belfast)   3-0   Glentoran FC (Belfast)
Linfield Swifts FC (Belfast)   3-0   Bangor FC (Bangor)

1950-51

Irish League 1950-51 Season	Ards	Ballymena U.	Bangor	Cliftonville	Coleraine	Crusaders	Derry City	Distillery	Glenavon	Glentoran	Linfield	Portadown
Ards FC		1-1	3-0	3-0	1-3	1-2	1-2	3-5	1-2	1-5	0-3	3-2
Ballymena United FC	4-2		0-2	4-0	2-3	1-2	2-1	2-2	1-5	0-2	3-2	0-2
Bangor FC	1-1	4-1		4-3	1-5	0-3	2-2	1-2	0-1	1-6	3-5	1-4
Cliftonville FC	3-1	2-0	4-0		2-3	3-2	2-0	2-3	1-0	0-4	0-2	4-4
Coleraine FC	5-0	3-0	3-1	6-1		6-1	4-1	0-3	1-1	1-0	1-0	2-0
Crusaders FC	8-1	3-3	1-2	4-4	4-2		3-2	1-1	1-4	1-1	1-1	1-0
Derry City FC	3-2	3-1	1-1	3-2	1-0	0-1		1-1	0-3	1-2	0-6	1-0
Distillery FC	2-1	1-2	6-0	2-3	2-2	2-0	3-1		1-4	1-5	0-1	3-1
Glenavon FC	4-0	4-0	2-0	4-2	6-2	4-0	1-1	6-2		1-3	1-1	2-7
Glentoran FC	7-2	2-0	2-1	5-3	3-2	4-1	4-1	2-1	3-0		1-1	3-0
Linfield FC	3-0	1-1	3-2	3-0	2-1	6-0	3-2	4-2	3-1	2-1		4-2
Portadown FC	1-0	7-2	4-1	3-1	3-0	3-2	6-0	3-0	1-2	0-2	2-1	

	Irish League	Pd	Wn	Dw	Ls	GF	GA	Pts
1.	GLENTORAN FC (BELFAST)	22	18	2	2	66	21	38
2.	Linfield FC (Belfast)	22	15	4	3	57	24	34
3.	Glenavon FC (Lurgan)	22	14	3	5	58	31	31
4.	Coleraine FC (Coleraine)	22	13	2	7	55	35	28
5.	Portadown FC (Portadown)	22	12	1	9	55	35	25
6.	Distillery FC (Belfast)	22	9	4	9	45	44	22
7.	Crusaders FC (Belfast)	22	8	5	9	42	51	21
8.	Cliftonville FC (Belfast)	22	7	2	13	42	60	16
9.	Derry City FC (Londonderry)	22	6	4	12	27	50	16
10.	Ballymena United FC (Ballymena)	22	5	4	13	30	54	14
11.	Bangor FC (Bangor)	22	4	3	15	28	62	11
12.	Ards FC (Newtownards)	22	3	2	17	28	66	8
		264	114	36	114	533	533	264

Top goalscorers 1950-51

1) Walter ALLEN (Portadown FC) 23
   Samuel HUGHES (Glentoran FC) 23

No clubs promoted or relegated

IRISH CUP FINAL (Windsor Park, Belfast – 28/04/1951)

GLENTORAN FC (BELFAST)　　　3-1　　　Ballymena United FC (Ballymena)

S. Hughes 2, Williamson　　　　　　　　　　　　　　　　　　　　　　*Currie*

Glentoran: Moore, Dunlop, McCarthy, Mulholland, T. Hughes, Ferran, Cunningham, Ewing, S. Hughes, Williamson, Feeney.

Ballymena: Rodgers, Trevorrow, Barr, Gray, Murphy, Douglas, Morrison, Anderson, Ewart, O'Hara, Currie.

Semi-finals

Ballymena United FC (Ballymena)	2-1	Portadown FC (Portadown)
Glentoran FC (Belfast)	3-1	Linfield FC (Belfast)

Quarter-finals

Ards FC (Newtownards)	0-1	Portadown FC (Portadown)
Cliftonville FC (Belfast)	2-2, 0-1	Ballymena United FC (Ballymena)
Glentoran FC (Belfast)	3-0	Brantwood FC (Belfast)
Linfield FC (Belfast)	0-0, 3-2	Crusaders FC (Belfast)

1951-52

Irish League 1951-52 Season	Ards	Ballymena U.	Bangor	Cliftonville	Coleraine	Crusaders	Derry City	Distillery	Glenavon	Glentoran	Linfield	Portadown
Ards FC		4-1	1-2	0-0	3-5	3-0	4-1	2-2	3-4	1-3	3-1	1-2
Ballymena United FC	3-1		4-0	2-1	1-1	3-1	2-1	3-3	0-1	2-2	2-0	0-2
Bangor FC	2-3	5-4		2-1	1-1	0-2	1-1	0-0	0-3	1-1	1-6	3-2
Cliftonville FC	4-3	2-2	1-0		1-3	2-1	2-2	1-2	1-4	2-3	0-1	2-1
Coleraine FC	0-1	5-1	4-2	3-1		7-2	2-1	2-1	1-1	2-1	1-0	1-3
Crusaders FC	1-3	1-1	5-2	1-0	1-1		3-0	0-1	0-3	0-1	0-5	2-1
Derry City FC	4-0	2-2	0-1	3-0	3-2	2-3		0-2	0-3	3-1	2-1	2-1
Distillery FC	4-3	2-2	2-0	1-1	0-0	1-2	2-2		1-0	3-0	2-2	2-1
Glenavon FC	1-1	2-1	1-0	6-2	5-0	5-0	5-0	1-2		8-3	5-0	2-2
Glentoran FC	8-1	1-3	6-0	3-1	3-2	4-1	4-0	3-0	1-2		4-3	2-2
Linfield FC	0-0	2-2	1-2	1-0	0-1	1-1	1-1	1-1	0-3	1-0		1-1
Portadown FC	1-2	5-0	2-2	3-2	1-0	5-5	2-3	2-1	1-2	1-3	2-1	

	Irish League	Pd	Wn	Dw	Ls	GF	GA	Pts	
1.	GLENAVON FC (LURGAN)	22	17	3	2	67	19	37	
2.	Coleraine FC (Coleraine)	22	11	5	6	44	33	27	PO
3.	Distillery FC (Belfast)	22	9	9	4	35	28	27	PO
4.	Glentoran FC (Belfast)	22	12	3	7	57	39	27	PO
5.	Ballymena United FC (Ballymena)	22	7	8	7	41	44	22	
6.	Portadown FC (Portadown)	22	8	5	9	43	39	21	
7.	Ards FC (Newtownards)	22	8	4	10	43	40	20	
8.	Derry City FC (Londonderry)	22	7	5	10	33	44	19	
9.	Crusaders FC (Belfast)	22	7	4	11	32	51	18	
10.	Linfield FC (Belfast)	22	5	7	10	29	34	17	
11.	Bangor FC (Bangor)	22	6	5	11	27	51	17	
12.	Cliftonville FC (Belfast)	22	4	4	14	27	47	12	
		264	101	62	101	478	478	264	

2nd Place Play-off

Distillery FC (Belfast) 1-1 Coleraine FC (Coleraine)
(Coleraine took 2nd place on better goal-average in the league)
Glentoran FC (Belfast) 1-2 Distillery FC (Belfast)
Coleraine FC (Coleraine) received a bye

Top goalscorer 1951-52

1) James JONES   (Glenavon FC)   27

No clubs promoted or relegated

IRISH CUP FINAL   (Windsor Park, Belfast – 26/04/1952)

ARDS FC (NEWTOWNARDS)   1-0   Glentoran FC (Belfast)

Thompson

Ards: O'Connell, Moore, Hamill, Tucker, Robinson, Corbett, Lawther, Thompson, Drake, McDowell, Walker.
Glentoran: Clarke, Lucas, King, Neill, T. Hughes, McFarlane, Lowry, Ewing, S. Hughes, Williamson, Feeney.

Semi-finals

Ards FC (Newtownards)	1-0	Ballymena United FC (Ballymena)
Glentoran FC (Belfast)	0-0, 2-2, 0-0, 1-0	Linfield FC (Belfast)

Quarter-finals

Brantwood FC (Belfast)	0-1	Ards FC (Newtownards)
Cliftonville FC (Belfast)	2-2, 0-3	Ballymena United FC (Ballymena)
Glentoran FC (Belfast)	3-3, 1-1, 3-0	Glenavon FC (Lurgan)
Linfield FC (Belfast)	4-0	Portadown FC (Portadown)

1952-53

Irish League 1952-53 Season	Ards	Ballymena U.	Bangor	Cliftonville	Coleraine	Crusaders	Derry City	Distillery	Glenavon	Glentoran	Linfield	Portadown
Ards FC	■	1-3	2-1	3-1	6-4	1-1	3-0	0-1	1-0	1-1	1-1	0-0
Ballymena United FC	4-0	■	3-1	6-1	1-1	5-3	3-0	4-0	4-1	0-1	2-2	4-0
Bangor FC	2-2	1-2	■	1-2	0-3	0-3	0-0	1-0	2-5	0-2	2-1	3-2
Cliftonville FC	2-1	1-4	4-1	■	3-2	3-1	1-0	3-2	2-1	2-4	1-4	1-4
Coleraine FC	2-2	2-1	3-1	4-0	■	1-1	0-3	1-2	2-1	2-5	0-2	2-1
Crusaders FC	2-1	1-2	5-2	4-2	2-2	■	4-0	3-0	1-2	4-2	1-1	2-2
Derry City FC	1-3	3-1	4-1	2-2	0-2	3-0	■	2-2	2-4	2-3	1-3	3-0
Distillery FC	0-0	2-4	3-0	0-0	3-1	2-0	2-0	■	0-2	1-1	0-1	1-0
Glenavon FC	4-3	5-2	3-0	4-4	0-2	2-0	5-1	0-1	■	0-3	2-2	3-2
Glentoran FC	3-0	4-1	6-0	7-1	2-2	2-0	2-0	1-3	1-1	■	3-1	4-1
Linfield FC	2-0	3-0	5-1	3-0	6-1	0-0	4-0	2-0	2-0	1-1	■	1-1
Portadown FC	0-1	1-1	1-0	3-1	1-1	1-1	2-0	1-1	2-4	2-1	1-0	■

	Irish League	**Pd**	**Wn**	**Dw**	**Ls**	**GF**	**GA**	**Pts**
1.	GLENTORAN FC (BELFAST)	22	14	5	3	59	25	33
2.	Linfield FC (Belfast)	22	12	7	3	47	18	31
3.	Ballymena United FC (Ballymena)	22	13	3	6	57	34	29
4.	Glenavon FC (Lurgan)	22	11	3	8	49	39	25
5.	Distillery FC (Belfast)	22	9	5	8	26	27	23
6.	Coleraine FC (Coleraine)	22	8	6	8	40	43	22
7.	Crusaders FC (Belfast)	22	7	7	8	39	36	21
8.	Ards FC (Newtownards)	22	7	7	8	32	35	21
9.	Cliftonville FC (Belfast)	22	8	3	11	37	61	19
10.	Portadown FC (Portadown)	22	6	7	9	28	35	19
11.	Derry City FC (Londonderry)	22	5	3	14	27	47	13
12.	Bangor FC (Bangor)	22	3	2	17	20	61	8
		264	103	58	103	461	461	264

Top goalscorer 1952-53
1) Samuel HUGHES   (Glentoran FC)   28

No clubs promoted or relegated

IRISH CUP FINAL   (Solitude, Belfast)
LINFIELD FC (BELFAST)   5-0   Coleraine FC (Coleraine)
Thompson 2, Walker, McDowell, Dickson
Linfield: Russell, Keith, Lewis, G. Nixon, Hamill, McMillan, Thompson, McDowell, Walker, Dickson, Lunn.
Coleraine: Watt, Montgomery, Canning, Brolly, McCavana, McDermott, Cuneen, Colvan, O'Kane, Doherty, McCormick.

Semi-finals
Coleraine FC (Coleraine)	5-0	Glentoran FC (Belfast) 2nd XI
Linfield FC (Belfast)	2-1	Glentoran FC (Belfast)

Quarter-finals
Ards FC (Newtownards)	4-5	Glentoran FC (Belfast)
Crusaders FC (Belfast)	0-1	Coleraine FC (Coleraine)
Glentoran FC (Belfast) 2nd XI	2-0	Bangor FC (Bangor)
Portadown FC (Portadown)	1-2	Linfield FC (Belfast)

1953-54

Irish League 1953-54 Season	Ards	Ballymena U.	Bangor	Cliftonville	Coleraine	Crusaders	Derry City	Distillery	Glenavon	Glentoran	Linfield	Portadown
Ards FC	■	1-2	1-3	4-2	1-4	3-2	3-2	1-0	3-4	0-4	1-2	4-1
Ballymena United FC	2-0	■	2-0	2-0	5-1	1-2	5-2	1-1	4-4	1-4	2-2	1-4
Bangor FC	0-2	2-1	■	1-0	5-1	4-2	2-1	1-0	1-3	2-0	1-1	3-0
Cliftonville FC	3-2	0-3	4-2	■	1-6	2-3	2-3	1-3	1-5	1-6	1-4	0-2
Coleraine FC	1-1	1-2	1-1	5-2	■	3-3	2-1	3-2	3-0	1-1	1-1	3-2
Crusaders FC	2-0	1-1	4-0	4-0	0-6	■	5-3	3-0	1-3	1-3	4-5	4-2
Derry City FC	6-1	1-3	2-0	1-1	4-2	1-3	■	1-1	0-0	2-3	0-2	3-1
Distillery FC	2-2	4-0	6-0	1-2	5-2	3-3	3-2	■	5-2	2-3	0-1	2-2
Glenavon FC	4-2	1-2	3-1	2-0	6-1	2-4	5-1	0-1	■	5-3	4-2	4-0
Glentoran FC	2-0	4-1	3-2	5-1	4-1	5-3	1-0	2-1	5-3	■	0-2	4-1
Linfield FC	4-0	3-3	3-0	1-1	4-0	1-1	3-0	2-1	2-1	3-2	■	2-1
Portadown FC	1-0	2-3	2-3	2-1	1-1	1-4	2-0	1-2	3-7	1-3	2-6	■

	Irish League	Pd	Wn	Dw	Ls	GF	GA	Pts
1.	LINFIELD FC (BELFAST)	22	15	6	1	56	26	36
2.	Glentoran FC (Belfast)	22	17	1	4	67	34	35
3.	Glenavon FC (Lurgan)	22	13	2	7	68	45	28
4.	Ballymena United FC (Ballymena)	22	11	5	6	47	40	27
5.	Crusaders FC (Belfast)	22	11	4	7	60	49	26
6.	Bangor FC (Bangor)	22	10	2	10	34	42	22
7.	Coleraine FC (Coleraine)	22	8	6	8	49	52	22
8.	Distillery FC (Belfast)	22	8	5	9	45	36	21
9.	Ards FC (Newtownards)	22	6	2	14	32	53	14
10.	Derry City FC (Londonderry)	22	5	3	14	36	50	13
11.	Portadown FC (Portadown)	22	5	2	15	34	60	12
12.	Cliftonville FC (Belfast)	22	3	2	17	26	67	8
		264	112	40	112	554	554	264

Top goalscorer 1953-54

1) James JONES   (Glenavon FC)   32

No clubs promoted or relegated

IRISH CUP FINAL   (Windsor Park, Belfast – 24/04/1954)

DERRY CITY FC (LONDONDERRY)   2-2   Glentoran FC (Belfast)
Delaney, Brady   *Cunningham, Feeney*

IRISH CUP FINAL REPLAY   (Windsor Park, Belfast – 29/04/1954)

DERRY CITY FC (LONDONDERRY)   0-0   Glentoran FC (Belfast)

IRISH CUP FINAL 2ND REPLAY   (Windsor Park, Belfast – 10/05/1954)

DERRY CITY FC (LONDONDERRY)   1-0   Glentoran FC (Belfast)
O'Neill

Derry: Heffron, Wilson, Houston, Brolly, Curran, Smyth, Brady, Delaney, Forsythe, Toner, O'Neill.
Glentoran: Bond, McCarthy, King, Neill, Murdough, Lewis, Lowry, Scott, Hughes, Cunningham, Feeney.

Semi-finals

Derry City FC (Londonderry)   2-2, 2-1   Linfield FC (Belfast)
Glentoran FC (Belfast)   2-1   Distillery FC (Belfast)

Quarter-finals

Coleraine FC (Coleraine)   2-2, 0-1   Distillery FC (Belfast)
Derry City FC (Londonderry)   1-1, 2-0   Bangor FC (Bangor)
Glentoran FC (Belfast)   4-1   Ards FC (Newtownards)
Linfield FC (Belfast)   2-0   Ballymena United FC (Ballymena)

1954-55

Irish League 1954-55 Season	Ards	Ballymena U.	Bangor	Cliftonville	Coleraine	Crusaders	Derry City	Distillery	Glenavon	Glentoran	Linfield	Portadown
Ards FC	■	4-3	5-1	4-5	6-1	4-0	4-2	4-0	0-1	3-1	1-3	3-3
Ballymena United FC	2-2	■	1-3	2-3	4-2	2-0	2-1	2-2	2-3	0-4	2-3	3-3
Bangor FC	1-1	2-2	■	0-5	2-2	3-1	2-1	2-1	1-4	2-3	2-2	2-0
Cliftonville FC	1-1	1-0	5-1	■	1-2	0-1	5-1	2-0	0-4	1-2	1-1	3-3
Coleraine FC	4-1	3-0	2-5	3-2	■	3-0	4-2	4-0	1-3	1-1	2-1	2-0
Crusaders FC	2-2	1-3	2-3	1-4	1-2	■	0-0	5-1	0-4	1-5	2-3	2-0
Derry City FC	0-1	1-1	2-1	2-1	5-2	0-2	■	1-0	1-2	2-1	1-2	1-1
Distillery FC	2-3	3-1	0-2	2-1	1-3	5-3	4-0	■	2-2	1-3	1-1	3-1
Glenavon FC	4-0	3-1	4-2	1-1	1-0	0-1	7-4	3-1	■	3-1	1-1	5-3
Glentoran FC	3-2	4-1	5-3	1-3	3-1	1-2	6-1	1-4	2-5	■	1-2	4-2
Linfield FC	2-2	2-0	3-2	2-0	2-1	3-0	1-0	0-0	2-0	3-0	■	5-2
Portadown FC	4-0	2-1	2-1	4-5	5-1	0-2	0-3	0-2	1-1	3-2	0-2	■

Play-off

LINFIELD FC (BELFAST)   2-0   Glenavon FC (Lurgan)

	Irish League	Pd	Wn	Dw	Ls	GF	GA	Pts
1.	Linfield FC (Belfast)	22	15	6	1	46	21	36
1.	Glenavon FC (Lurgan)	22	16	4	2	61	27	36
3.	Cliftonville FC (Belfast)	22	10	4	8	50	38	24
4.	Ards FC (Newtownards)	22	9	6	7	53	45	24
5.	Coleraine FC (Coleraine)	22	11	2	9	46	46	24
6.	Glentoran FC (Belfast)	22	11	1	10	54	46	23
7.	Bangor FC (Bangor)	22	8	4	10	43	53	20
8.	Distillery FC (Belfast)	22	7	4	11	35	44	18
9.	Crusaders FC (Belfast)	22	7	2	13	29	48	16
10.	Portadown FC (Portadown)	22	5	5	12	39	53	15
11.	Derry City FC (Londonderry)	22	6	3	13	31	49	15
12.	Ballymena United FC (Ballymena)	22	4	5	13	35	52	13
		264	109	46	109	522	522	264

Top goalscorer 1954-55

1) Fay COYLE   (Coleraine FC)   20

No clubs promoted or relegated

IRISH CUP FINAL (Windsor Park, Belfast – 23/04/1955)

DUNDELA FC (BELFAST)   3-0   Glenavon FC (Lurgan)

Ervine 2, Greenwood

Dundela: J. Smyth, R. Smyth, Stewart, McAuley, Lynch, Millar, Greenwood, Reid, Ervine, Kavanagh, Gourley.
Glenavon: Durkan, Greer, Armstrong, Corr, Liggett, Cush, Masters, Denver, Jones, Campbell, McVeigh.

Semi-finals

Dundela FC (Belfast)	2-1	Crusaders FC (Belfast)
Glenavon FC (Lurgan)	5-0	Glentoran FC (Belfast)

Quarter-finals

Crusaders FC (Belfast)	2-1	Linfield FC (Belfast)
Dundela FC (Belfast)	1-0	Cliftonville FC (Belfast)
Glenavon FC (Lurgan)	1-1, 1-1, 1-0	Ards FC (Newtownards)
Glentoran FC (Belfast)	2-0	Portadown FC (Portadown)

1955-56

Irish League 1955-56 Season	Ards	Ballymena U.	Bangor	Cliftonville	Coleraine	Crusaders	Derry City	Distillery	Glenavon	Glentoran	Linfield	Portadown
Ards FC	■	4-3	2-4	3-2	1-1	5-2	1-2	3-2	1-0	2-3	0-1	4-0
Ballymena United FC	3-2	■	2-3	1-2	0-4	2-1	1-3	3-1	1-4	4-1	1-3	1-4
Bangor FC	1-1	6-2	■	4-2	4-4	8-3	4-1	2-2	4-6	4-2	0-4	2-3
Cliftonville FC	1-6	3-1	0-1	■	1-2	1-1	3-2	1-4	1-7	0-1	0-4	0-0
Coleraine FC	1-0	5-1	3-4	4-1	■	1-2	3-1	2-1	1-2	2-3	1-1	4-2
Crusaders FC	3-0	6-0	1-1	1-1	2-2	■	3-2	0-1	2-1	2-3	2-5	1-0
Derry City FC	3-1	1-2	2-1	5-2	2-2	4-1	■	2-2	1-4	1-2	1-2	1-1
Distillery FC	1-2	5-1	2-2	0-3	5-2	3-0	2-1	■	2-1	0-0	1-3	2-2
Glenavon FC	6-0	3-1	3-1	1-2	9-6	5-1	5-2	3-1	■	4-4	0-1	4-0
Glentoran FC	2-1	2-3	2-3	3-4	0-1	2-1	4-2	0-0	4-2	■	1-1	0-1
Linfield FC	2-1	1-2	4-3	4-1	2-1	3-0	3-1	5-0	1-0	1-0	■	2-0
Portadown FC	2-4	5-1	3-7	6-2	2-4	3-1	5-1	2-2	1-7	1-4	0-3	■

	Irish League	Pd	Wn	Dw	Ls	GF	GA	Pts
1.	LINFIELD FC (BELFAST)	22	19	2	1	56	16	40
2.	Glenavon FC (Lurgan)	22	14	1	7	77	38	29
3.	Bangor FC (Bangor)	22	11	5	6	69	54	27
4.	Coleraine FC (Coleraine)	22	10	5	7	56	46	25
5.	Glentoran FC (Belfast)	22	10	4	8	43	40	24
6.	Distillery FC (Belfast)	22	7	7	8	39	40	21
7.	Ards FC (Newtownards)	22	9	2	11	44	45	20
8.	Portadown FC (Portadown)	22	7	4	11	43	57	18
9.	Derry City FC (Londonderry)	22	6	4	12	42	54	16
10.	Crusaders FC (Belfast)	22	6	4	12	36	53	16
11.	Cliftonville FC (Belfast)	22	5	4	13	33	62	14
12.	Ballymena United FC (Ballymena)	22	7	-	15	36	69	14
		264	111	42	111	574	574	264

Top goalscorer 1955-56

1)	James JONES	(Glenavon FC)	26

No clubs promoted or relegated

IRISH CUP FINAL   (Windsor Park, Belfast – 21/04/1956)

DISTILLERY FC (BELFAST) 2-2 Glentoran FC (Belfast)
McEvoy, Curry *Fogarty, Nolan*

IRISH CUP FINAL REPLAY   (Windsor Park, Belfast – 26/04/1956)

DISTILLERY FC (BELFAST) 1-1 Glentoran FC (Belfast)
Tait *Nolan*

IRISH CUP FINAL 2ND REPLAY   (Windsor Park, Belfast – 30/04/1956)

DISTILLERY FC (BELFAST) 1-0 Glentoran FC (Belfast)
Curry

Distillery: Beare, Magee, Brennan, Twinem, Watters, Tait, Curry, Hepburn, Dugan, Dougan, Hamilton.
Glentoran: McMahon, McCarthy, Lucas, Neill, Murdough, Dubois, Lowry, Fogarty, Mulvey, Bruce, Nolan.

Semi-finals

Distillery FC (Belfast)	1-0	Cliftonville FC (Belfast)
Glentoran FC (Belfast)	4-0	Portadown FC (Portadown)

Quarter-finals

Ards FC (Newtownards)	1-2	Cliftonville FC (Belfast)
Crusaders FC (Belfast)	0-4	Distillery FC (Belfast)
Linfield FC (Belfast)	1-2	Portadown FC (Portadown)
Linfield Swifts FC (Belfast)	0-3	Glentoran FC (Belfast)

1956-57

Irish League 1956-57 Season	Ards	Ballymena U.	Bangor	Cliftonville	Coleraine	Crusaders	Derry City	Distillery	Glenavon	Glentoran	Linfield	Portadown
Ards FC		2-1	5-4	4-3	5-1	3-1	4-2	8-1	1-2	3-3	1-1	4-1
Ballymena United FC	0-5		2-3	4-3	1-1	5-2	1-2	2-4	0-4	1-3	1-6	6-1
Bangor FC	0-3	1-1		3-0	2-3	1-1	5-0	6-1	0-4	1-1	4-2	1-1
Cliftonville FC	0-7	2-1	2-6		3-4	0-2	4-1	1-6	1-1	2-4	1-4	1-3
Coleraine FC	2-1	4-1	4-2	2-2		2-5	2-1	2-3	5-2	3-1	3-3	4-2
Crusaders FC	1-0	3-1	0-1	4-1	2-3		3-1	0-2	2-1	3-1	0-5	4-2
Derry City FC	0-2	3-0	1-1	4-1	2-0	4-1		4-1	2-2	2-1	3-4	2-2
Distillery FC	3-1	5-1	3-2	2-0	1-5	2-2	2-0		1-3	2-2	1-4	2-2
Glenavon FC	1-0	5-0	3-0	6-1	4-0	2-0	7-1	8-1		3-1	3-2	5-0
Glentoran FC	1-0	7-2	3-1	2-1	3-2	3-1	4-0	3-0	2-1		1-3	5-4
Linfield FC	2-2	3-1	2-1	5-1	3-1	4-0	3-2	1-1	1-1	2-2		3-2
Portadown FC	4-4	3-3	2-2	4-1	2-1	2-1	2-4	5-3	1-3	2-3	0-2	

Irish League	Pd	Wn	Dw	Ls	GF	GA	Pts
1. GLENAVON FC (LURGAN)	22	16	3	3	71	22	35
2. Linfield FC (Belfast)	22	14	6	2	67	32	34
3. Glentoran FC (Belfast)	22	13	4	5	56	39	30
4. Ards FC (Newtownards)	22	12	4	6	65	34	28
5. Coleraine FC (Coleraine)	22	11	3	8	54	51	25
6. Distillery FC (Belfast)	22	9	4	9	47	62	22
7. Bangor FC (Bangor)	22	7	6	9	47	44	20
8. Crusaders FC (Belfast)	22	9	2	11	38	46	20
9. Derry City FC (Londonderry)	22	8	3	11	41	52	19
10. Portadown FC (Portadown)	22	5	6	11	47	66	16
11. Ballymena United FC (Ballymena)	22	3	3	16	35	72	9
12. Cliftonville FC (Belfast)	22	2	2	18	31	79	6
	264	109	46	109	599	599	264

Top goalscorer 1956-57

1) James JONES   (Glenavon FC)   33

No clubs promoted or relegated

IRISH CUP FINAL   (Windsor Park, Belfast – 13/04/1957)

GLENAVON FC (LURGAN)   2-0   Derry City FC (Londonderry)

Houston o.g., Jones

Glenavon: Rea, Armstrong, Lyske, Corr, Davis, Cush, Wilson, McVeigh, Jones, Campbell, Elwood.
Derry: Heffron, Kinnen, Houston, Brolly, Travers, Smyth, Wright, Crossan, Campbell, P. Coyle, Nash.

Semi-finals

Derry City FC (Londonderry)	0-0, 1-0	Linfield FC (Belfast)
Glenavon FC (Lurgan)	1-0	Distillery FC (Belfast)

Quarter-finals

Derry City FC (Londonderry)	3-0	Ards FC (Newtownards)
Distillery FC (Belfast)	1-1, 4-4, +:−	Portadown FC (Portadown)
Glentoran FC (Belfast)	2-2, 1-2	Linfield FC (Belfast)
Newry Town FC (Newry)	1-4	Glentoran FC (Belfast)

1957-58

Irish League 1957-58 Season	Ards	Ballymena U.	Bangor	Cliftonville	Coleraine	Crusaders	Derry City	Distillery	Glenavon	Glentoran	Linfield	Portadown
Ards FC	■	3-0	5-2	7-2	3-4	6-1	2-1	2-2	3-4	5-1	3-0	3-2
Ballymena United FC	1-1	■	1-3	4-0	2-2	4-2	2-1	3-2	3-2	5-1	3-1	1-0
Bangor FC	1-2	0-2	■	5-1	2-1	1-1	4-0	2-1	1-2	2-9	1-2	2-0
Cliftonville FC	3-4	2-4	1-1	■	4-4	4-3	0-2	3-2	0-1	2-6	1-7	1-2
Coleraine FC	1-3	4-2	6-1	2-1	■	1-3	1-0	1-2	2-8	2-1	4-3	2-3
Crusaders FC	1-4	5-2	1-2	4-2	2-4	■	2-4	2-3	1-0	0-1	2-6	0-3
Derry City FC	0-1	1-2	4-1	6-1	2-2	2-1	■	2-2	2-3	0-1	3-2	2-2
Distillery FC	1-1	0-5	2-3	3-2	2-2	0-1	2-2	■	2-4	1-3	1-0	0-6
Glenavon FC	0-3	2-1	5-0	6-3	2-1	1-0	7-1	3-0	■	5-1	2-3	5-2
Glentoran FC	0-1	3-1	3-0	7-0	5-1	5-2	5-1	3-2	0-1	■	0-2	2-1
Linfield FC	4-4	5-1	5-3	4-1	3-3	2-3	0-2	3-3	4-1	3-1	■	3-4
Portadown FC	1-2	1-2	3-3	2-1	5-3	0-1	1-2	0-3	2-3	1-1	1-1	■

	Irish League	Pd	Wn	Dw	Ls	GF	GA	Pts
1.	ARDS FC (NEWTOWNARDS)	22	16	4	2	68	32	36
2.	Glenavon FC (Lurgan)	22	17	-	5	67	35	34
3.	Ballymena United FC (Ballymena)	22	13	2	7	51	41	28
4.	Glentoran FC (Belfast)	22	12	1	9	50	38	25
5.	Linfield FC (Belfast)	22	11	3	8	68	48	25
6.	Bangor FC (Bangor)	22	9	3	10	40	48	21
7.	Coleraine FC (Coleraine)	22	8	5	9	53	59	21
8.	Derry City FC (Londonderry)	22	8	4	10	40	44	20
9.	Portadown FC (Portadown)	22	7	3	12	43	48	17
10.	Distillery FC (Belfast)	22	5	6	11	36	53	16
11.	Crusaders FC (Belfast)	22	7	1	14	38	57	15
12.	Cliftonville FC (Belfast)	22	2	2	18	35	86	6
		264	115	34	115	589	589	264

Top goalscorer 1957-58

1) Jackie MILBURN   (Linfield FC)   29

No clubs promoted or relegated

IRISH CUP FINAL   (The Oval, Belfast)

BALLYMENA UNITED FC (BALLYMENA)   2-0   Linfield FC (Belfast)

McGhee, Russell

Ballymena: Bond, Trevorrow, Johnston, Brown, Lowry, Cubitt, Egan, Forsyth, McGhee, McCrae, Russell.
Linfield: Russell, Gilliland, Graham, Rodgers, Hamill, Fletcher, Robinson, Parke, Milburn, Dickson, Braithwaite.

Semi-finals

Ballymena United FC (Ballymena)	3-0	Derry City FC (Londonderry)
Linfield FC (Belfast)	4-2	Glenavon FC (Lurgan)

Quarter-finals

Ballymena United FC (Ballymena)	3-1	Ards FC (Newtownards)
Bangor FC (Bangor)	2-3	Derry City FC (Londonderry)
Glenavon FC (Lurgan)	3-1	Linfield Swifts FC (Belfast)
Linfield FC (Belfast)	6-4	Portadown FC (Portadown)

1958-59

Irish League 1958-59 Season	Ards	Ballymena U.	Bangor	Cliftonville	Coleraine	Crusaders	Derry City	Distillery	Glenavon	Glentoran	Linfield	Portadown
Ards FC	■	1-4	1-0	7-0	5-3	1-2	3-1	3-5	2-3	2-3	0-3	1-0
Ballymena United FC	3-3	■	2-0	5-0	4-2	4-1	2-3	4-2	0-0	2-3	2-1	1-3
Bangor FC	2-3	0-2	■	1-0	5-0	0-3	3-0	1-1	0-2	3-2	2-3	4-3
Cliftonville FC	1-5	4-1	2-4	■	0-3	1-3	0-3	3-1	2-5	0-2	0-4	1-8
Coleraine FC	1-2	4-0	3-3	6-1	■	4-0	2-0	2-2	2-1	1-1	4-0	1-2
Crusaders FC	5-1	0-2	3-0	3-0	0-1	■	2-5	4-4	2-3	2-1	3-2	3-1
Derry City FC	0-6	1-4	1-0	1-1	0-1	2-1	■	1-3	1-6	0-4	1-4	2-1
Distillery FC	1-1	3-4	2-0	5-1	4-4	2-2	3-1	■	1-2	2-6	2-3	0-3
Glenavon FC	2-3	3-1	2-1	6-0	3-0	1-1	2-2	7-0	■	7-1	3-6	2-3
Glentoran FC	1-1	4-0	3-1	8-3	3-2	3-3	2-0	3-3	1-2	■	2-1	0-1
Linfield FC	5-1	5-0	4-0	9-0	3-1	1-2	2-0	3-0	2-0	4-2	■	1-0
Portadown FC	6-1	3-4	5-0	2-0	6-0	1-1	3-2	5-3	1-4	1-1	2-3	■

	Irish League	Pd	Wn	Dw	Ls	GF	GA	Pts
1.	LINFIELD FC (BELFAST)	22	17	-	5	69	27	34
2.	Glenavon FC (Lurgan)	22	14	3	5	66	32	31
3.	Glentoran FC (Belfast)	22	11	5	6	56	41	27
4.	Portadown FC (Portadown)	22	12	2	8	60	35	26
5.	Ballymena United FC (Ballymena)	22	12	2	8	51	46	26
6.	Crusaders FC (Belfast)	22	10	5	7	46	40	25
7.	Ards FC (Newtownards)	22	10	3	9	53	51	23
8.	Coleraine FC (Coleraine)	22	9	4	9	47	45	22
9.	Distillery FC (Belfast)	22	5	7	10	49	63	17
10.	Bangor FC (Bangor)	22	6	2	14	30	47	14
11.	Derry City FC (Londonderry)	22	6	2	14	27	55	14
12.	Cliftonville FC (Belfast)	22	2	1	19	20	92	5
		264	114	36	114	574	574	264

Top goalscorer 1958-59

1) Jackie MILBURN   (Linfield FC)   26

No clubs promoted or relegated

IRISH CUP FINAL   (Windsor Park, Belfast – 18/04/1959)

GLENAVON FC (LURGAN)	1-1	Ballymena United FC (Ballymena)
Jones		Lowry pen.

Glenavon: Rea, Armstrong, Cummings, Lawther, Forde, Hughes, Wilson, Magee, Jones, Campbell, McVeigh.
Ballymena: Bond, Trevorrow, Johnston, Brown, Lowry, Cubitt, Walsh, McCrae, McGhee, Russell, Clarke

IRISH CUP FINAL REPLAY   (Windsor Park, Belfast – 29/04/1959)

GLENAVON FC (LURGAN)	2-0	Ballymena United FC (Ballymena)
Wilson, Magee		

Ballymena: Bond, Trevorrow, Johnston, Brown, Lowry, Cubitt, Walsh, McCrae, McGhee, Russell, Clarke.
Glenavon: Rea, Armstrong, Cummings, Masters, Forde, Hughes, Wilson, Magee, Jones, Campbell, McVeigh.

Semi-finals

Ballymena United FC (Ballymena)	2-1	Linfield FC (Belfast)
Glenavon FC (Lurgan)	5-1	Distillery FC (Belfast)

Quarter-finals

Distillery FC (Belfast)	1-0	Derry City FC Londonderry)
Glenavon FC (Lurgan)	2-0	Glentoran FC (Belfast)
Linfield FC (Belfast)	4-2	Ards FC (Newtownards)
Portadown FC (Portadown)	1-1, 0-1	Ballymena United FC (Ballymena)

1959-60

Irish League 1959-60 Season	Ards	Ballymena U.	Bangor	Cliftonville	Coleraine	Crusaders	Derry City	Distillery	Glenavon	Glentoran	Linfield	Portadown
Ards FC	■	1-1	1-4	4-1	2-0	4-1	2-1	4-5	2-0	1-2	2-5	2-0
Ballymena United FC	2-1	■	2-0	3-1	4-4	1-2	2-0	1-3	0-4	5-3	2-4	2-2
Bangor FC	5-1	1-0	■	3-2	1-2	2-2	3-3	0-2	1-3	2-2	3-2	1-2
Cliftonville FC	2-0	0-4	1-3	■	1-0	0-1	0-4	0-1	0-1	0-5	3-7	0-2
Coleraine FC	1-3	2-5	4-3	4-3	■	3-2	1-0	1-3	0-6	1-2	1-1	2-4
Crusaders FC	2-2	3-2	1-0	4-1	5-0	■	3-0	1-1	1-3	1-3	5-1	1-1
Derry City FC	1-4	6-1	2-4	5-0	1-2	5-2	■	1-0	0-2	0-2	1-3	2-2
Distillery FC	3-0	1-2	0-0	5-2	5-2	2-3	3-2	■	3-5	1-2	4-4	4-1
Glenavon FC	4-0	1-4	5-2	5-1	4-2	5-0	2-4	1-2	■	0-0	2-1	1-0
Glentoran FC	5-1	2-0	3-1	3-1	4-1	3-0	2-2	1-2	3-4	■	7-3	1-1
Linfield FC	2-0	4-1	2-0	7-1	2-1	1-1	2-0	3-3	2-5	3-2	■	1-1
Portadown FC	0-0	1-5	3-0	4-2	1-1	4-2	2-1	2-2	0-4	1-3	1-3	■

	Irish League	Pd	Wn	Dw	Ls	GF	GA	Pts
1.	GLENAVON FC (LURGAN)	22	17	1	4	67	28	35
2.	Glentoran FC (Belfast)	22	14	4	4	60	31	32
3.	Distillery FC (Belfast)	22	12	5	5	55	38	29
4.	Linfield FC (Belfast)	22	12	5	5	63	46	29
5.	Ballymena United FC (Ballymena)	22	10	3	9	49	46	23
6.	Crusaders FC (Belfast)	22	9	5	8	43	44	23
7.	Portadown FC (Portadown)	22	7	8	7	35	40	22
8.	Ards FC (Newtownards)	22	8	3	11	37	47	19
9.	Bangor FC (Bangor)	22	7	4	11	39	45	18
10.	Derry City FC (Londonderry)	22	6	3	13	41	44	15
11.	Coleraine FC (Coleraine)	22	6	3	13	35	62	15
12.	Cliftonville FC (Belfast)	22	2	-	20	22	75	4
		264	110	44	110	546	546	264

Top goalscorer 1959-60

1) James JONES   (Glenavon FC)   29

No clubs promoted or relegated

IRISH CUP FINAL   (The Oval, Belfast)

LINFIELD FC (BELFAST)   5-1   Ards FC (Newtownards)

Ferguson 2, Milburn 2, Gough   *Welsh*

Linfield: Irvine, Gilliland, Graham, Wilson, Hamill, Gough, Stewart, Dickson, Milburn, Ferguson, Braithwaite.
Ards: Moffatt, Patterson, Hunter, McCullough, Reynolds, Hamill, Humphries, Welsh, McCrory, Ewing, Boyd.

Semi-finals

| Ards FC (Newtownards) | 1-0 | Derry City FC (Londonderry) |
| Linfield FC (Belfast) | 5-2 | Distillery FC (Belfast) |

Quarter-finals

Distillery FC (Belfast)	5-2	Ballymena United FC (Ballymena)
Glentoran FC (Belfast)	1-1, 2-3	Derry City FC (Londonderry)
Linfield FC (Belfast)	5-3	Glenavon FC (Lurgan)
Portadown FC (Portadown) 2nd XI	2-4	Ards FC (Newtownards)

1960-61

Irish League 1960-61 Season	Ards	Ballymena U.	Bangor	Cliftonville	Coleraine	Crusaders	Derry City	Distillery	Glenavon	Glentoran	Linfield	Portadown
Ards FC	■	1-1	4-2	6-3	7-2	2-0	5-1	3-0	3-2	2-1	1-4	0-2
Ballymena United FC	1-1	■	5-2	8-2	1-3	1-1	3-0	1-5	6-0	2-1	2-1	3-3
Bangor FC	1-6	2-0	■	6-4	5-5	1-4	2-3	1-4	1-2	1-4	0-3	3-3
Cliftonville FC	1-5	1-3	4-2	■	2-4	3-1	0-1	1-6	2-3	0-3	1-4	1-3
Coleraine FC	1-3	0-1	4-7	5-0	■	1-1	2-1	1-5	2-3	1-1	3-5	1-2
Crusaders FC	1-2	1-0	1-1	2-1	2-1	■	4-1	1-0	0-0	1-2	0-0	1-3
Derry City FC	3-6	1-3	0-5	0-2	2-3	1-3	■	1-0	1-1	2-1	2-4	1-5
Distillery FC	3-2	3-4	2-2	9-2	5-3	1-1	7-2	■	0-2	1-7	5-4	0-4
Glenavon FC	3-4	1-1	3-2	10-2	2-0	1-2	1-3	5-2	■	3-2	5-1	1-1
Glentoran FC	2-0	4-0	3-0	7-0	4-1	3-0	5-3	1-3	2-0	■	0-1	1-0
Linfield FC	2-2	1-2	3-0	3-0	5-3	1-1	5-1	8-1	3-1	3-2	■	3-1
Portadown FC	3-1	4-3	2-2	2-1	4-0	3-2	1-1	5-1	2-2	2-2	1-1	■

Play-off
LINFIELD FC (BELFAST)   3-2   Portadown FC (Portadown)

	Irish League	Pd	Wn	Dw	Ls	GF	GA	Pts
1.	Linfield FC (Belfast)	22	14	4	4	65	34	32
1.	Portadown FC (Portadown)	22	12	8	2	56	31	32
3.	Ards FC (Newtownards)	22	14	3	5	66	39	31
4.	Glentoran FC (Belfast)	22	13	2	7	58	26	28
5.	Ballymena United FC (Ballymena)	22	11	5	6	51	38	27
6.	Glenavon FC (Lurgan)	22	10	5	7	51	42	25
7.	Crusaders FC (Belfast)	22	8	7	7	30	29	23
8.	Distillery FC (Belfast)	22	10	2	10	63	61	22
9.	Bangor FC (Bangor)	22	4	5	13	48	69	13
10.	Coleraine FC (Coleraine)	22	5	3	14	46	68	13
11.	Derry City FC (Londonderry)	22	5	2	15	31	68	12
12.	Cliftonville FC (Belfast)	22	3	-	19	33	93	6
		264	109	46	109	598	598	264

Top goalscorer 1960-61
1) Trevor THOMPSON   (Glentoran FC)   22

IRISH CUP FINAL   (Solitude, Belfast – 22/04/1961)
GLENAVON FC (LURGAN)   5-1   Linfield FC (Belfast)
Campbell 3, Jones 2   *Ferguson*

Glenavon: Kinkead, Hughes, Armstrong, Dugan, McKinstry, Magee, Wilson, Johnston, Jones, Campbell, Weatherup.

Linfield: Irvine, Gilliland, Graham, Wilson, Parke, Gough, Stewart, Ferguson, Walker, Dickson, Braithwaite.

Semi-finals

Glenavon FC (Lurgan)	3-2	Crusaders FC (Belfast)
Linfield FC (Belfast)	4-2	Ballyclare Comrades FC (Ballyclare)

Quarter-finals

Ards FC (Newtownards)	0-4	Glenavon FC (Lurgan)
Ballymena United FC (Ballymena)	1-3	Ballyclare Comrades FC (Ballyclare)
Distillery FC (Belfast)	1-1, 2-2, 1-3	Crusaders FC (Belfast)
Linfield FC (Belfast)	5-1	Bangor FC (Bangor)

1961-62

Irish League 1961-62 Season	Ards	Ballymena U.	Bangor	Cliftonville	Coleraine	Crusaders	Derry City	Distillery	Glenavon	Glentoran	Linfield	Portadown
Ards FC		1-1	1-1	5-1	3-2	4-1	2-0	3-1	4-3	4-2	2-4	2-1
Ballymena United FC	1-2		2-1	7-0	1-1	1-1	2-0	3-2	3-3	1-1	4-2	1-3
Bangor FC	2-0	0-4		2-0	1-3	3-2	3-3	4-5	1-3	4-1	0-1	2-6
Cliftonville FC	1-3	1-3	0-0		0-0	1-2	2-2	4-5	1-1	1-2	0-5	0-4
Coleraine FC	0-1	0-1	4-0	2-1		4-1	4-2	2-3	1-2	1-1	2-0	1-1
Crusaders FC	3-0	1-2	3-0	6-0	3-1		1-0	2-1	1-3	1-0	3-2	3-4
Derry City FC	0-0	0-0	1-0	5-0	0-1	1-1		2-2	2-2	0-1	0-2	0-1
Distillery FC	2-2	1-4	2-4	6-0	4-2	2-3	2-3		2-2	4-3	4-6	2-1
Glenavon FC	5-1	2-2	5-2	2-2	7-2	1-1	4-0	5-1		2-3	2-1	3-4
Glentoran FC	1-0	1-2	2-0	6-0	2-1	0-1	5-1	3-0	4-4		1-1	2-2
Linfield FC	3-2	6-1	4-1	3-1	4-3	9-0	0-0	2-2	2-0	3-1		2-1
Portadown FC	3-3	3-1	4-0	2-1	1-0	4-2	3-0	2-3	2-1	2-3	2-0	

Play-off

LINFIELD FC (BELFAST)	3-1	Portadown FC (Portadown)

	Irish League	Pd	Wn	Dw	Ls	GF	GA	Pts
1.	Linfield FC (Belfast)	22	14	3	5	62	32	31
1.	Portadown FC (Portadown)	22	14	3	5	56	32	31
3.	Ballymena United FC (Ballymena)	22	11	7	4	47	32	29
4.	Ards FC (Newtownards)	22	11	5	6	46	38	27
5.	Glenavon FC (Lurgan)	22	9	8	5	62	43	26
6.	Crusaders FC (Belfast)	22	11	3	8	42	43	25
7.	Glentoran FC (Belfast)	22	10	5	7	45	35	25
8.	Distillery FC (Belfast)	22	8	4	10	56	62	20
9.	Coleraine FC (Coleraine)	22	7	4	11	37	39	18
10.	Derry City FC (Londonderry)	22	3	8	11	22	38	14
11.	Bangor FC (Bangor)	22	5	3	14	31	56	13
12.	Cliftonville FC (Belfast)	22	-	5	17	17	73	5
		264	103	58	103	523	523	264

Top goalscorer 1961-62

1) Michael LYNCH (Ards FC) 20

IRISH CUP FINAL   (The Oval, Belfast)

LINFIELD FC (BELFAST)   4-0   Portadown FC (Portadown)

Dickson 2, Barr, Braithwaite

Linfield: Irvine, Gilliland, Graham, Wilson, Hatton, Parke, Stewart, Ferguson, Barr, Dickson, Braithwaite.
Portadown: Kydd, Burke, Loughlin, Cush, Beattie, Campbell, Gillespie, McMillen, Gorman, Wilson, Callan.

Semi-finals

Linfield FC (Belfast)	3-1	Bangor FC (Bangor)
Portadown FC (Portadown)	3-1	Glenavon FC (Lurgan)

Quarter-finals

Bangor FC (Bangor)	1-0	Glentoran FC (Belfast)
Cliftonville FC (Belfast)	2-4	Linfield FC (Belfast)
Crusaders FC (Belfast)	3-3, 0-2	Portadown FC (Portadown)
Glenavon FC (Lurgan)	2-1	Coleraine FC (Coleraine)

1962-63

Irish League 1962-63 Season	Ards	Ballymena U.	Bangor	Cliftonville	Coleraine	Crusaders	Derry City	Distillery	Glenavon	Glentoran	Linfield	Portadown
Ards FC		2-2	3-0	1-4	1-2	1-2	1-5	2-3	1-0	1-6	0-1	0-0
Ballymena United FC	0-0		4-2	5-1	2-2	2-1	5-2	3-1	1-1	4-3	1-1	2-2
Bangor FC	1-3	2-2		2-1	3-1	0-3	1-2	1-3	0-3	0-5	2-5	2-2
Cliftonville FC	3-4	0-1	3-1		0-3	1-5	1-2	0-3	0-0	0-3	0-2	0-4
Coleraine FC	1-2	3-0	0-0	2-2		3-2	2-2	2-1	0-0	2-1	0-3	0-1
Crusaders FC	4-1	4-1	4-0	3-2	3-2		4-0	0-3	4-3	1-4	0-3	0-1
Derry City FC	3-2	1-1	2-0	1-1	1-2	1-1		0-1	1-0	0-1	1-1	3-1
Distillery FC	5-3	6-1	9-1	4-1	0-0	1-0	3-1		1-2	1-1	4-2	2-2
Glenavon FC	2-0	1-1	6-1	6-2	3-3	2-3	4-1	0-2		0-1	3-2	3-0
Glentoran FC	2-1	5-1	2-2	1-1	2-3	1-1	0-2	5-1	2-1		1-1	1-3
Linfield FC	3-1	1-1	1-0	2-0	0-0	2-0	3-2	2-2	2-3	1-1		2-2
Portadown FC	5-0	1-1	1-1	1-1	4-1	8-2	3-1	1-1	3-1	0-1	0-0	

	Irish League	Pd	Wn	Dw	Ls	GF	GA	Pts
1.	DISTILLERY FC (BELFAST)	22	13	5	4	57	30	31
2.	Linfield FC (Belfast)	22	10	9	3	40	24	29
3.	Portadown FC (Portadown)	22	9	10	3	45	25	28
4.	Glentoran FC (Belfast)	22	11	6	5	49	27	28
5.	Ballymena United FC (Ballymena)	22	7	11	4	41	42	25
6.	Crusaders FC (Belfast)	22	11	2	9	47	42	24
7.	Coleraine FC (Coleraine)	22	8	8	6	34	33	24
8.	Glenavon FC (Lurgan)	22	9	5	8	44	31	23
9.	Derry City FC (Londonderry)	22	8	5	9	34	38	21
10.	Ards FC (Newtownards)	22	5	3	14	30	54	13
11.	Cliftonville FC (Belfast)	22	2	5	15	24	56	9
12.	Bangor FC (Bangor)	22	2	5	15	22	65	9
		264	95	74	95	467	467	264

Top goalscorer 1962-63
1) Joe MELDRUM   (Distillery FC)   27

No clubs promoted or relegated

IRISH CUP FINAL   (The Oval, Belfast – 20/04/1963)
LINFIELD FC (BELFAST)   2-1   Distillery FC (Belfast)
Cairns, Braithwaite   *Kennedy*

Linfield: Irvine, Parke, Graham, Andrews, Hatton, Gough, Stewart, Ferguson, Cairns, Dickson, Braithwaite.
Distillery: Kennedy, D. Meldrum, Ellison, Kennedy, White, Gregg, Welsh, Curley, J. Meldrum, Scott, Hamilton.

Semi-finals
Distillery FC (Belfast)   3-1   Ballymena United FC (Ballymena)
Linfield FC (Belfast)   3-1   Crusaders FC (Belfast)

Quarter-finals
Ballymena United FC (Ballymena)   3-1   Glentoran FC (Belfast)
Bangor FC (Bangor)   2-6   Crusaders FC (Belfast)
Coleraine FC (Coleraine)   1-3   Linfield FC (Belfast)
Distillery FC (Belfast)   4-2   Ards FC (Newtownards)

1963-64

Irish League 1963-64 Season	Ards	Ballymena U.	Bangor	Cliftonville	Coleraine	Crusaders	Derry City	Distillery	Glenavon	Glentoran	Linfield	Portadown
Ards FC		2-3	4-0	5-0	1-3	4-2	4-3	2-2	2-4	2-2	3-1	0-1
Ballymena United FC	3-3		1-2	6-0	2-1	3-2	1-3	2-1	3-2	0-3	1-4	4-2
Bangor FC	0-2	2-3		3-3	0-3	2-6	1-3	2-7	4-1	1-5	0-2	1-2
Cliftonville FC	0-6	1-3	3-1		1-2	2-1	0-4	3-4	2-5	0-2	0-2	0-4
Coleraine FC	3-0	1-0	2-1	4-3		2-1	0-1	4-1	2-1	2-2	1-4	2-1
Crusaders FC	3-1	0-2	3-0	4-0	0-2		3-1	1-5	1-2	3-1	2-2	2-1
Derry City FC	6-1	5-5	1-1	3-0	0-0	3-1		2-1	5-2	5-0	1-0	3-1
Distillery FC	6-1	5-2	6-1	3-3	2-2	2-0	0-3		4-0	3-3	0-1	2-2
Glenavon FC	6-0	5-3	4-1	5-1	1-3	0-1	2-1	4-3		0-1	2-1	1-3
Glentoran FC	2-0	3-2	4-0	5-0	0-0	3-2	4-3	3-1	1-1		3-2	4-0
Linfield FC	5-2	1-3	4-2	2-0	3-0	1-1	4-2	3-1	6-2	1-8		2-2
Portadown FC	3-0	4-3	7-0	5-2	0-1	2-1	2-1	2-4	2-1	1-0	2-2	

	Irish League	Pd	Wn	Dw	Ls	GF	GA	Pts
1.	GLENTORAN FC (BELFAST)	22	14	5	3	59	29	33
2.	Coleraine FC (Coleraine)	22	14	4	4	40	25	32
3.	Derry City FC (Londonderry)	22	13	3	6	59	33	29
4.	Linfield FC (Belfast)	22	12	4	6	53	38	28
5.	Portadown FC (Portadown)	22	12	3	7	49	36	27
6.	Ballymena United FC (Ballymena)	22	11	2	9	55	52	24
7.	Distillery FC (Belfast)	22	9	5	8	63	46	23
8.	Glenavon FC (Lurgan)	22	10	1	11	51	50	21
9.	Crusaders FC (Belfast)	22	8	2	12	40	41	18
10.	Ards FC (Newtownards)	22	7	3	12	45	58	17
11.	Bangor FC (Bangor)	22	2	2	18	26	76	6
12.	Cliftonville FC (Belfast)	22	2	2	18	24	80	6
		264	114	36	114	564	564	264

Top goalscorer 1963-64

1) Trevor THOMPSON (Glentoran FC) 21

Note: The Distillery FC 4-0 Glenavon FC match was abandoned after 78 minutes but the result was allowed to stand.

No club promoted or relegated

IRISH CUP FINAL   (Windsor Park, Belfast – 25/04/1964)

DERRY CITY FC (LONDONDERRY)   2-0   Glentoran FC (Belfast)

Wilson, Doherty

Derry: Mahon, Campbell, Cathcart, McGeogh, Crossan, Wood, McKenzie, Doherty, Coyle, Wilson, Seddon.
Glentoran: Finlay, Creighton, Borne, Byrne, McCullough, Bruce, Pavis, Curley, Thompson, Brannigan, Green.

Semi-finals

Derry City FC (Londonderry)	3-0	Banbridge Town FC (Banbridge)
Glentoran FC (Belfast)	2-0	Coleraine FC (Coleraine)

Quarter-finals

Banbridge Town FC (Banbridge)	3-0	Cliftonville FC (Belfast)
Coleraine FC (Coleraine)	3-1	Portadown FC (Portadown)
Crusaders FC (Belfast)	2-2, 0-2	Glentoran FC (Belfast)
Derry City FC (Londonderry)	5-0	Distillery FC (Belfast)

1964-65

Irish League 1964-65 Season	Ards	Ballymena U.	Bangor	Cliftonville	Coleraine	Crusaders	Derry City	Distillery	Glenavon	Glentoran	Linfield	Portadown
Ards FC		2-3	1-1	4-2	1-5	1-4	3-3	0-4	2-0	1-4	0-1	3-0
Ballymena United FC	4-1		3-0	3-1	0-4	1-0	3-5	1-1	3-1	0-2	3-2	0-1
Bangor FC	1-1	4-2		7-0	1-3	2-0	0-2	2-4	2-3	2-2	3-4	4-3
Cliftonville FC	1-2	2-8	1-3		0-5	0-3	1-3	0-4	0-10	0-4	1-5	0-4
Coleraine FC	2-1	2-2	4-1	4-1		4-2	1-2	2-1	3-0	0-0	3-1	1-1
Crusaders FC	1-1	0-0	1-0	5-0	2-0		4-1	3-1	2-1	1-0	1-8	1-1
Derry City FC	5-1	3-3	2-1	10-1	1-0	3-1		2-2	6-1	2-0	2-0	4-3
Distillery FC	2-1	1-2	1-3	6-1	0-2	0-6	2-3		1-4	1-2	4-2	2-0
Glenavon FC	7-2	1-2	3-0	3-2	3-1	2-4	3-0	3-1		6-0	1-1	4-0
Glentoran FC	2-2	3-2	1-1	0-3	3-2	2-1	0-1	2-0	3-2		1-1	1-1
Linfield FC	3-3	5-2	2-1	6-0	1-4	2-2	4-2	0-3	0-3	4-1		2-0
Portadown FC	0-1	3-3	1-3	1-0	2-2	2-2	1-1	3-0	0-0	5-0	1-3	

	Irish League	Pd	Wn	Dw	Ls	GF	GA	Pts
1.	DERRY CITY FC (LONDONDERRY)	22	15	5	2	62	32	35
2.	Coleraine FC (Coleraine)	22	13	4	5	54	26	30
3.	Crusaders FC (Belfast)	22	11	5	6	46	32	27
4.	Glenavon FC (Lurgan)	22	12	2	8	61	35	26
5.	Linfield FC (Belfast)	22	10	5	7	54	40	25
6.	Ballymena United FC (Ballymena)	22	10	5	7	50	44	25
7.	Glentoran FC (Belfast)	22	9	6	7	33	38	24
8.	Bangor FC (Bangor)	22	7	4	11	42	44	18
9.	Distillery FC (Belfast)	22	8	2	12	41	44	18
10.	Portadown FC (Portadown)	22	5	8	9	33	37	18
11.	Ards FC (Newtownards)	22	5	6	11	34	55	16
12.	Cliftonville FC (Belfast)	22	1	-	21	17	100	2
		264	106	52	106	527	527	264

Note: The Linfield FC 0-3 Distillery FC match was abandoned after 83 minutes but the result was allowed to stand.

Top goalscorers 1964-65

1) Dennis GUY   (Glenavon FC)   19
   Kenneth HALLIDAY   (Coleraine FC)   19

No clubs promoted or relegated

IRISH CUP FINAL   (Windsor Park, Belfast – 24/04/1965)

COLERAINE FC (COLERAINE)   2-1   Glenavon FC (Lurgan)
Dunlop, Irwin   *Johnston*

Coleraine: V. Hunter, McCurdy, Campbell, Murray, A. Hunter, Peacock, Kinsella, Curley, Halliday, Dunlop, Irwin.
Glenavon: McNally, Murphy, E. Johnston, Magee, Lowry, Hughes, Watson, E. Magee, Guy, W. Johnston, Weatherup.

Semi-finals

Coleraine FC (Coleraine)	1-0	Glentoran FC (Belfast)
Glenavon FC (Lurgan)	3-3, 3-2	Linfield FC (Belfast)

Quarter-finals

Crusaders FC (Belfast)	0-1	Coleraine FC (Coleraine)
Derry City FC (Londonderry)	2-2, 0-0, 1-2	Linfield FC (Belfast)
Glenavon FC (Lurgan)	6-1	Banbridge Town FC (Banbridge)
Glentoran FC (Belfast)	4-0	Portadown FC (Portadown)

1965-66

Irish League 1965-66 Season	Ards	Ballymena U.	Bangor	Cliftonville	Coleraine	Crusaders	Derry City	Distillery	Glenavon	Glentoran	Linfield	Portadown
Ards FC	■	1-2	1-1	1-1	0-0	2-2	0-3	1-0	1-3	2-3	1-3	1-4
Ballymena United FC	2-2	■	2-0	8-0	1-2	5-2	3-4	3-0	5-5	2-1	0-0	1-0
Bangor FC	2-2	0-0	■	3-1	0-3	1-1	1-0	1-3	2-5	0-4	1-4	4-1
Cliftonville FC	2-1	1-5	1-3	■	3-3	0-4	1-1	0-3	1-6	3-5	0-10	0-6
Coleraine FC	5-1	1-3	6-0	6-2	■	2-2	3-1	3-0	2-0	0-1	0-0	1-1
Crusaders FC	6-1	1-3	4-1	7-1	4-2	■	1-2	1-0	2-1	0-1	2-3	5-0
Derry City FC	4-1	5-1	4-1	4-1	3-2	5-0	■	3-1	1-3	3-2	0-0	5-0
Distillery FC	2-2	1-1	3-1	2-2	3-1	1-2	2-5	■	2-4	0-4	3-3	3-3
Glenavon FC	1-2	0-1	3-1	6-1	2-4	4-1	1-2	2-1	■	8-2	0-1	4-1
Glentoran FC	2-3	0-0	3-1	2-0	2-0	2-1	0-1	7-3	0-0	■	2-0	2-0
Linfield FC	5-1	5-2	3-0	3-0	4-1	6-1	3-2	3-3	1-1	1-2	■	3-0
Portadown FC	0-2	2-1	0-0	7-2	3-5	4-0	5-3	0-3	4-3	1-3	1-2	■

	Irish League	Pd	Wn	Dw	Ls	GF	GA	Pts
1.	LINFIELD FC (BELFAST)	22	14	6	2	68	23	34
2.	Derry City FC (Londonderry)	22	15	2	5	61	33	32
3.	Glentoran FC (Belfast)	22	15	2	5	50	29	32
4.	Ballymena United FC (Ballymena)	22	11	6	5	51	33	28
5.	Glenavon FC (Lurgan)	22	11	3	8	61	28	25
6.	Coleraine FC (Coleraine)	22	10	5	7	52	36	25
7.	Crusaders FC (Belfast)	22	9	3	10	49	47	21
8.	Portadown FC (Portadown)	22	7	3	12	43	53	17
9.	Distillery FC (Belfast)	22	5	6	11	39	52	16
10.	Ards FC (Newtownards)	22	4	6	12	29	54	14
11.	Bangor FC (Bangor)	22	5	4	13	26	59	14
12.	Cliftonville FC (Belfast)	22	1	4	17	23	96	6
		264	107	50	107	553	553	264

Top goalscorer 1965-66

1) Samuel PAVIS (Linfield FC) 28

No clubs promoted or relegated

IRISH CUP FINAL (The Oval, Belfast – 23/04/1966)

GLENTORAN FC (BELFAST)　　　　　2-0　　　　　　　　　　Linfield FC (Belfast)

Conroy 2

Glentoran: Finlay, Creighton, Borne, McCullough, Byrne, Bruce, Conroy, Stewart, Thompson, McDonnell, McAlinden.

Linfield: McFaul, Gilliland, White, Gregg, Hatton. Leishman, Ferguson, Thomas, Pavis, Scott, McCambley.

Semi-finals

Glentoran FC (Belfast)	1-1, 5-0	Coleraine FC (Coleraine)
Linfield FC (Belfast)	2-0	Crusaders FC (Belfast)

Quarter-finals

Ards FC (Newtownards)	1-3	Crusaders FC (Belfast)
Ballymena United FC (Ballymena)	1-2	Coleraine FC (Coleraine)
Distillery FC (Belfast)	1-2	Glentoran FC (Belfast)
Linfield FC (Belfast)	5-1	Brantwood FC (Belfast)

1966-67

Irish League 1966-67 Season	Ards	Ballymena U.	Bangor	Cliftonville	Coleraine	Crusaders	Derry City	Distillery	Glenavon	Glentoran	Linfield	Portadown
Ards FC	■	1-2	2-2	3-1	1-0	3-1	2-3	3-0	1-1	1-3	1-1	3-3
Ballymena United FC	1-1	■	5-1	2-1	4-4	7-3	1-2	4-0	2-0	2-3	2-4	4-1
Bangor FC	1-4	0-2	■	3-1	4-3	0-5	1-2	0-11	1-4	2-4	1-3	5-2
Cliftonville FC	0-1	1-1	3-2	■	1-1	0-0	0-2	2-2	0-2	2-5	2-4	1-9
Coleraine FC	4-2	1-2	4-1	2-0	■	3-2	1-0	2-2	4-1	1-2	0-3	2-2
Crusaders FC	3-2	4-3	5-1	3-2	1-6	■	6-3	3-1	2-1	1-3	4-4	2-1
Derry City FC	0-2	2-1	4-4	4-0	4-1	9-4	■	0-2	2-2	1-0	5-2	1-1
Distillery FC	1-1	1-1	8-3	3-2	2-5	3-1	1-1	■	0-5	2-4	1-4	0-2
Glenavon FC	2-0	4-4	10-0	3-1	2-2	2-5	0-1	0-1	■	1-2	2-1	3-2
Glentoran FC	2-2	5-2	6-0	5-0	2-3	3-2	4-4	2-0	2-2	■	2-2	2-2
Linfield FC	6-2	2-1	2-2	7-2	4-2	2-0	4-1	5-1	2-3	1-1	■	4-1
Portadown FC	1-0	4-1	5-1	4-1	0-2	2-6	3-0	3-2	4-0	2-5	1-3	■

	Irish League	**Pd**	**Wn**	**Dw**	**Ls**	**GF**	**GA**	**Pts**
1.	GLENTORAN FC (BELFAST)	22	14	6	2	67	35	34
2.	Linfield FC (Belfast)	22	14	5	3	70	37	33
3.	Derry City FC (Londonderry)	22	11	5	6	51	42	27
4.	Coleraine FC (Coleraine)	22	10	5	7	53	42	25
5.	Crusaders FC (Belfast)	22	11	2	9	63	60	24
6.	Glenavon FC (Lurgan)	22	9	5	8	50	39	23
7.	Ballymena United FC (Ballymena)	22	9	5	8	54	45	23
8.	Ards FC (Newtownards)	22	7	7	8	37	38	21
9.	Portadown FC (Portadown)	22	8	4	10	46	48	20
10.	Distillery FC (Belfast)	22	6	5	11	44	53	17
11.	Bangor FC (Bangor)	22	3	3	16	35	95	9
12.	Cliftonville FC (Belfast)	22	2	4	16	23	59	8
		264	104	56	104	593	593	264

Top goalscorer 1966-67

1) Samuel PAVIS   (Linfield FC)   25

No clubs promoted or relegated

IRISH CUP FINAL   (Windsor Park, Belfast – 02/04/1967)

CRUSADERS FC (BELFAST)   3-1   Glentoran FC (Belfast)
Trainor, McNeill, McCullough   *Thompson*

Crusaders: Nicholson, Paterson, Lewis, McPolin, Campbell, S. McCullough, Law, Trainer, Meldrum, McNeill, Wilson.

Glentoran: Finlay, Creighton, McKeag, Jackson, W.McCullough, Stewart, Morrow, Bruce, Thompson, Ross, Weatherup.

Semi-finals

Crusaders FC (Belfast)	3-2	Bangor FC (Bangor)
Glentoran FC (Belfast)	1-0	Linfield FC (Belfast)

Quarter-finals

Bangor FC (Bangor)	4-1	Portadown FC (Portadown)
Cliftonville FC (Belfast)	1-4	Linfield FC (Belfast)
Crusaders FC (Belfast)	1-0	Coleraine FC (Coleraine)
Glentoran FC (Belfast)	3-1	Distillery FC (Belfast)

1967-68

Irish League 1967-68 Season	Ards	Ballymena U.	Bangor	Cliftonville	Coleraine	Crusaders	Derry City	Distillery	Glenavon	Glentoran	Linfield	Portadown
Ards FC	■	3-1	2-0	5-0	1-1	2-1	6-1	5-1	2-1	1-6	0-2	1-2
Ballymena United FC	3-1	■	3-1	5-2	3-7	2-2	0-1	3-1	4-3	2-5	4-5	5-2
Bangor FC	1-5	4-4	■	3-2	0-5	4-4	2-4	0-1	2-3	0-5	0-4	3-2
Cliftonville FC	0-1	1-5	6-4	■	0-4	1-3	4-2	0-3	2-8	0-5	1-4	2-2
Coleraine FC	3-1	7-2	2-3	5-1	■	2-2	1-2	3-1	4-1	1-0	5-5	7-1
Crusaders FC	3-5	3-1	5-5	6-2	1-5	■	3-1	3-3	2-2	0-2	1-3	10-3
Derry City FC	2-3	5-1	4-3	6-0	1-2	1-1	■	4-1	2-1	1-4	4-1	4-2
Distillery FC	2-4	0-2	3-1	2-1	3-4	2-1	0-1	■	2-5	1-3	1-5	0-3
Glenavon FC	0-1	3-1	3-1	3-1	0-0	4-4	5-1	0-1	■	0-2	1-6	2-1
Glentoran FC	3-0	2-2	10-1	5-0	2-2	2-1	4-2	4-1	4-2	■	2-2	4-1
Linfield FC	1-1	3-1	11-1	3-0	1-3	5-0	8-1	8-3	1-1	3-1	■	1-0
Portadown FC	0-1	2-1	1-0	1-0	2-3	2-1	2-1	2-1	1-3	1-4	1-3	■

	Irish League	Pd	Wn	Dw	Ls	GF	GA	Pts
1.	GLENTORAN FC (BELFAST)	22	17	3	2	79	24	37
2.	Linfield FC (Belfast)	22	16	4	2	85	32	36
3.	Coleraine FC (Coleraine)	22	15	5	2	76	33	35
4.	Ards FC (Newtownards)	22	14	2	6	51	34	30
5.	Derry City FC (Londonderry)	22	11	1	10	51	54	23
6.	Glenavon FC (Lurgan)	22	9	4	9	51	45	22
7.	Ballymena United FC (Ballymena)	22	8	3	11	55	63	19
8.	Crusaders FC (Belfast)	22	5	8	9	57	59	18
9.	Portadown FC (Portadown)	22	8	1	13	34	57	17
10.	Distillery FC (Belfast)	22	6	1	15	33	62	13
11.	Bangor FC (Bangor)	22	3	3	16	39	89	9
12.	Cliftonville FC (Belfast)	22	2	1	19	26	85	5
		264	114	36	114	637	637	264

Top goalscorer 1967-68

1) Samuel PAVIS   (Linfield FC)   30

No clubs promoted or relegated

IRISH CUP FINAL   (The Oval, Belfast – 27/04/1968)

CRUSADERS FC (BELFAST)   2-0   Linfield FC (Belfast)

Meldrum 2

Crusaders: Nicholson, Anderson, Cathcart, Campbell, McFarlane, McPolin, Brush, Trainor, Meldrum, Jamison, Wilson,

Linfield: McGonigal, Gilliland, Patterson, Andrews, Hatton, Wood, Ferguson, Hamilton, Pavis, Scott, Cathcart (Millen).

Semi-finals

| Crusaders FC (Belfast) | 1-1, 3-2 | Derry City FC (Londonderry) |
| Linfield FC (Belfast) | 2-1 | Ards FC (Newtownards) |

Quarter-finals

Ballyclare Comrades FC (Ballyclare)	0-1	Ards FC (Newtownards)
Bangor FC (Bangor)	0-5	Linfield FC (Belfast)
Crusaders FC (Belfast)	0-0, 2-2, 4-3	Portadown FC (Portadown)
Glentoran FC (Belfast)	2-2, 2-2, 0-1	Derry City FC (Londonderry)

1968-69

Irish League 1968-69 Season	Ards	Ballymena U.	Bangor	Cliftonville	Coleraine	Crusaders	Derry City	Distillery	Glenavon	Glentoran	Linfield	Portadown
Ards FC	■	4-3	2-0	1-0	3-1	1-1	2-1	3-1	4-1	1-2	1-2	5-2
Ballymena United FC	1-4	■	3-0	2-1	5-0	1-3	5-3	2-1	1-1	2-2	1-2	3-2
Bangor FC	0-3	1-1	■	0-1	2-4	1-3	0-2	4-3	2-3	0-2	0-2	2-1
Cliftonville FC	3-3	0-3	2-2	■	0-5	1-3	2-2	1-2	0-4	1-3	0-2	0-2
Coleraine FC	3-3	1-6	2-0	2-0	■	1-1	1-2	5-2	2-0	2-1	0-1	4-0
Crusaders FC	3-3	2-1	2-0	2-2	0-1	■	4-1	1-2	1-0	1-1	0-4	3-1
Derry City FC	3-0	5-1	3-0	6-0	0-1	4-1	■	3-2	4-1	2-1	2-1	4-0
Distillery FC	1-2	2-2	5-1	1-1	2-2	3-6	0-4	■	3-0	1-2	3-7	3-0
Glenavon FC	1-2	2-2	1-2	3-5	2-1	2-4	0-2	4-0	■	1-2	1-5	3-0
Glentoran FC	1-1	2-1	1-2	4-0	0-1	0-2	1-1	1-0	7-1	■	2-1	2-0
Linfield FC	3-0	3-1	4-1	4-1	0-1	3-0	3-1	0-0	3-0	1-3	■	8-1
Portadown FC	1-0	0-1	1-2	2-3	0-3	1-4	1-2	0-2	0-1	0-2	0-2	■

	Irish League	Pd	Wn	Dw	Ls	GF	GA	Pts
1.	LINFIELD FC (BELFAST)	22	17	1	4	61	19	35
2.	Derry City FC (Londonderry)	22	15	2	5	57	27	32
3.	Glentoran FC (Belfast)	22	13	4	5	42	22	30
4.	Coleraine FC (Coleraine)	22	13	3	6	43	30	29
5.	Ards FC (Newtownards)	22	12	5	5	48	34	29
6.	Crusaders FC (Belfast)	22	12	5	5	47	34	29
7.	Ballymena United FC (Ballymena)	22	9	5	8	48	41	23
8.	Distillery FC (Belfast)	22	6	4	12	39	51	16
9.	Glenavon FC (Lurgan)	22	6	2	14	32	52	14
10.	Bangor FC (Bangor)	22	5	2	15	22	51	12
11.	Cliftonville FC (Belfast)	22	3	5	14	24	58	11
12.	Portadown FC (Portadown)	22	2	-	20	15	59	4
		264	113	38	113	478	478	264

Top goalscorer 1968-69

1) Daniel HALE   (Derry City FC)   21

No clubs promoted or relegated

IRISH CUP FINAL   (Windsor Park, Belfast – 19/04/1969)

ARDS FC (NEWTOWNARDS)   0-0   Distillery FC (Belfast)

Ards: Kydd, Johnston, Crothers, Bell, Stewart, Nixon, Cochrane, McAvoy, Brown, Humphries, Shields.

Distillery: Young, Meldrum, Pike, Kennedy, Conlon, McCarroll, Rafferty, McCaffrey, O'Halloran, Brannigan, Lennox.

IRISH CUP FINAL REPLAY (Windsor Park, Belfast – 23/04/1969)

ARDS FC (NEWTOWNARDS)　　　　　4-2　　　　　　　　　　Distillery FC (Belfast)
McAvoy 4　　　　　　　　　　　　　　　　　　　　　　　　　*McCaffrey, Conlon*

Distillery: Young, Patterson, Pike, Kennedy, Conlon, McCarroll, Rafferty, McCafferty, O'Halloran, Brannigan, Lennox.
Ards: Kydd, Johnston, Crothers, Bell, Stewart, Nixon, Shields (Sands), McAvoy, Brown, Humphries, Mowat.

Semi-finals

Ards FC (Newtownards)	1-0	Coleraine FC (Coleraine)
Distillery FC (Belfast)	1-1, 0-0, 2-1	Glentoran FC (Belfast)

Quarter-finals

Ards FC (Newtownards)	4-1	Crusaders FC (Belfast)
Ballymena United FC (Ballymena)	1-2	Distillery FC (Belfast)
Bangor FC (Bangor)	0-1	Coleraine FC (Coleraine)
Glentoran FC (Belfast)	3-2	Derry City FC (Londonderry)

1969-70

Irish League 1969-70 Season	Ards	Ballymena U.	Bangor	Cliftonville	Coleraine	Crusaders	Derry City	Distillery	Glenavon	Glentoran	Linfield	Portadown
Ards FC	■	4-1	2-1	3-1	1-1	2-1	4-0	1-0	0-1	2-3	2-3	4-1
Ballymena United FC	1-2	■	2-2	1-1	1-5	2-0	3-4	0-0	3-1	0-3	0-4	1-3
Bangor FC	2-2	3-4	■	3-1	0-1	3-4	1-1	3-1	1-0	1-1	3-2	2-0
Cliftonville FC	0-2	0-1	0-1	■	3-1	0-2	2-3	1-3	3-3	0-3	1-5	1-2
Coleraine FC	2-1	3-0	2-2	1-0	■	2-1	1-1	6-1	1-3	2-0	3-1	2-3
Crusaders FC	1-1	1-1	1-0	8-3	0-7	■	0-3	2-1	4-1	2-0	1-3	6-2
Derry City FC	3-2	0-2	2-1	2-0	0-1	1-0	■	4-1	0-1	0-0	1-1	0-4
Distillery FC	0-0	1-0	1-1	1-1	0-3	4-3	2-4	■	5-0	0-5	0-1	2-0
Glenavon FC	0-2	3-0	1-1	2-1	4-2	1-1	1-1	0-0	■	2-2	5-2	0-2
Glentoran FC	1-1	0-0	2-0	2-0	2-1	7-2	1-0	3-0	2-0	■	2-2	2-1
Linfield FC	2-2	1-0	4-1	1-1	4-2	4-1	2-4	3-0	1-1	0-2	■	0-3
Portadown FC	1-1	1-1	2-0	1-0	3-1	4-1	1-4	4-2	2-2	1-3	1-2	■

	Irish League	**Pd**	**Wn**	**Dw**	**Ls**	**GF**	**GA**	**Pts**
1.	GLENTORAN FC (BELFAST)	22	14	6	2	46	17	34
2.	Coleraine FC (Coleraine)	22	12	3	7	50	31	27
3.	Ards FC (Newtownards)	22	10	7	3	41	26	27
4.	Linfield FC (Belfast)	22	11	5	6	48	36	27
5.	Derry City FC (Londonderry)	22	11	5	6	38	31	27
6.	Portadown FC (Portadown)	22	11	3	8	42	37	25
7.	Glenavon FC (Lurgan)	22	7	8	7	32	36	22
8.	Bangor FC (Bangor)	22	6	7	9	32	36	19
9.	Crusaders FC (Belfast)	22	8	3	11	42	52	19
10.	Ballymena United FC (Ballymena)	22	5	6	11	24	42	16
11.	Distillery FC (Belfast)	22	5	5	12	25	45	15
12.	Cliftonville FC (Belfast)	22	1	4	17	20	51	6
		264	101	62	101	440	440	264

Top goalscorer 1969-70

1) Des DICKSON (Coleraine FC) 21

No clubs promoted or relegated

IRISH CUP FINAL (Windsor Park, Belfast – 04/04/1970)

LINFIELD FC (BELFAST) 2-1 Ballymena United FC (Ballymena)
Scott 2 *Fleming*

Linfield: Stewart, Gilliland, Patterson, Andrews, Hatton, Bowyer, Viollet, Hamilton, Millen, Scott, Pavis.
Ballymena: Platt, Erwin, Richardson, Torrens, Averell, Russell, Porter, McGowan, Fleming, Martin, McFall.

Semi-finals

Ballymena United FC (Ballymena) 2-0 Coleraine FC (Coleraine)
Linfield FC (Belfast) 2-1 Derry City FC (Londonderry)

Quarter-finals

Ballymena United FC (Ballymena) 2-1 Crusaders FC (Belfast)
Derry City FC (Londonderry) 1-1, 0-0, 3-2 Cliftonville FC (Belfast)
Glenavon FC (Lurgan) 2-4 Coleraine FC (Coleraine)
Linfield FC (Belfast) 2-0 Newry Town FC (Newry)

1970-71

Irish League 1970-71 Season	Ards	Ballymena U.	Bangor	Cliftonville	Coleraine	Crusaders	Derry City	Distillery	Glenavon	Glentoran	Linfield	Portadown
Ards FC		0-1	1-2	2-0	0-2	1-1	3-2	1-4	4-2	2-2	2-1	3-2
Ballymena United FC	0-1		4-0	2-1	1-2	1-1	3-1	2-2	4-2	0-2	1-2	1-1
Bangor FC	0-0	1-1		1-0	2-1	0-3	2-1	3-3	3-6	0-3	0-1	2-0
Cliftonville FC	3-3	2-2	1-3		0-0	0-2	1-1	1-4	3-1	1-5	3-1	4-2
Coleraine FC	2-1	0-2	2-0	3-1		6-0	4-2	1-0	4-2	3-1	1-3	3-2
Crusaders FC	0-0	1-0	0-0	4-1	2-1		1-0	0-4	3-4	0-4	0-4	3-1
Derry City FC	3-1	2-2	1-0	5-2	4-2	4-0		1-3	3-3	0-3	3-3	4-1
Distillery FC	2-1	1-1	0-0	3-0	2-0	3-0	2-1		3-0	1-2	2-5	6-3
Glenavon FC	1-3	2-1	3-0	1-1	4-2	2-2	3-4	0-1		1-2	0-2	1-3
Glentoran FC	4-0	0-2	1-0	5-0	1-1	1-0	2-0	4-1	4-1		0-3	3-0
Linfield FC	3-0	3-0	1-0	2-0	2-1	7-0	3-1	2-0	2-0	1-1		5-0
Portadown FC	0-1	1-3	1-2	1-1	0-2	1-1	2-2	1-4	1-0	0-2	1-2	

	Irish League	Pd	Wn	Dw	Ls	GF	GA	Pts	
1.	LINFIELD FC (BELFAST)	22	18	2	2	58	16	38	
2.	Glentoran FC (Belfast)	22	16	3	3	52	17	35	
3.	Distillery FC (Belfast)	22	13	4	5	51	29	30	**
4.	Coleraine FC (Coleraine)	22	12	2	8	43	32	26	
5.	Ballymena United FC (Ballymena)	22	8	7	7	34	28	23	
6.	Ards FC (Newtownards)	22	8	5	9	30	37	21	
7.	Crusaders FC (Belfast)	22	7	6	9	24	45	20	
8.	Bangor FC (Bangor)	22	7	5	10	21	34	19	
9.	Derry City FC (Londonderry)	22	7	5	10	45	46	19	**
10.	Glenavon FC (Lurgan)	22	5	3	14	39	55	13	
11.	Cliftonville FC (Belfast)	22	3	6	13	26	53	12	
12.	Portadown FC (Portadown)	22	2	4	16	24	55	8	
		264	106	52	106	447	447	264	

** Due to the "civil unrest" in the country, Distillery FC (Belfast) and Derry City FC (Londonderry) were ordered to play several "home" games on neutral ground for security reasons. At the end of the season Distillery FC moved from their traditional home ground, "Grosvenor Park", to share with Crusaders FC (Belfast) at "Seaview Ground" and Derry City FC moved from their home ground "Brandywell Park" in Londonderry to share with Coleraine FC at "The Showgrounds" in Coleraine.

Top goalscorer 1970-71

1) Bryan HAMILTON   (Linfield FC)   18

No clubs promoted or relegated

IRISH CUP FINAL   (Windsor Park, Belfast – 03/04/1971 – 6,000)

DISTILLERY FC (BELFAST)   3-0   Derry City FC (Londonderry)

O'Neill 2, Savage

Distillery: McDonald, McCarroll, Meldrum, Brannigan, Rafferty, Donnelly, Law, Watson, Savage, O'Neill, Lennox.
Derry: McKibbin, Duffy, McLaughlin, McDowell, White, Wood, Rowland, O'Halloran, Ward, Hale, Smith (Hill 49').

Semi-finals

| Derry City FC (Londonderry) | 1-0 | Linfield FC (Belfast) |
| Distillery FC (Belfast) | 1-1, 2-1 | Coleraine FC (Coleraine) |

Quarter-finals

Coleraine FC (Coleraine)	2-0	Ballymena United FC (Ballymena)
Derry City FC (Londonderry)	2-1	Chimney Corner FC (Antrim)
Glenavon FC (Lurgan)	0-2	Distillery FC (Belfast)
Linfield FC (Belfast)	4-1	Crusaders FC (Belfast)

1971-72

Irish League 1971-72 Season	Ards	Ballymena U.	Bangor	Cliftonville	Coleraine	Crusaders	Derry City	Distillery	Glenavon	Glentoran	Linfield	Portadown
Ards FC		1-0	3-1	8-1	4-2	1-0	1-2	2-4	1-0	2-0	1-1	4-3
Ballymena United FC	1-1		2-1	2-0	3-2	4-2	1-1	0-0	2-3	1-2	2-1	1-6
Bangor FC	2-4	0-1		2-2	2-2	0-0	4-4	2-4	0-4	1-2	0-7	0-1
Cliftonville FC	0-2	0-0	2-1		0-4	0-1	2-2	2-1	2-3	0-6	0-5	0-2
Coleraine FC	1-1	4-2	4-0	3-0		5-5	2-0	1-4	4-1	2-1	1-1	3-2
Crusaders FC	4-0	2-1	3-2	3-0	1-0		4-7	2-0	1-1	0-0	2-1	1-5
Derry City FC	0-4	0-5	4-4	4-2	2-2	1-3		0-0	3-3	2-2	1-3	1-3
Distillery FC	1-4	2-0	2-4	4-4	3-3	0-0	2-0		1-1	0-6	2-1	0-3
Glenavon FC	2-2	1-4	3-0	2-1	1-2	0-1	4-3	4-1		0-1	0-2	1-1
Glentoran FC	2-1	1-0	4-0	4-0	1-0	2-0	1-0	2-2	5-0		4-0	0-0
Linfield FC	1-1	2-2	3-0	2-1	3-3	4-1	0-2	3-0	2-1	2-2		2-2
Portadown FC	2-1	2-0	1-2	3-0	3-1	1-0	3-2	0-1	1-1	4-2	1-2	

	Irish League	**Pd**	**Wn**	**Dw**	**Ls**	**GF**	**GA**	**Pts**	
1.	GLENTORAN FC (BELFAST)	22	14	5	3	50	17	33	
2.	Portadown FC (Portadown)	22	13	4	5	49	25	30	
3.	Ards FC (Newtownards)	22	12	5	5	49	30	29	
4.	Linfield FC (Belfast)	22	10	7	5	48	29	27	
5.	Crusaders FC (Belfast)	22	10	5	7	36	35	25	
6.	Coleraine FC (Coleraine)	22	9	7	6	51	40	25	
7.	Ballymena United FC (Ballymena)	22	8	5	9	34	34	21	
8.	Distillery FC (Belfast)	22	7	7	8	34	44	21	**
9.	Glenavon FC (Lurgan)	22	7	6	9	36	40	20	
10.	Derry City FC (Londonderry/Coleraine)	22	4	8	10	41	55	16	**
11.	Bangor FC (Bangor)	22	2	5	15	28	62	9	
12.	Cliftonville FC (Belfast)	22	2	4	16	19	64	8	
		264	98	68	98	475	475	264	

** Due to the "civil unrest" in the country Distillery FC played their "home" games at the ground of Crusaders FC and Derry City FC played "sensitive" home games at Coleraine. During the match between Derry City FC and Ballymena United at Brandywell Park in Londonderry the Ballymena team bus was hijacked, driven away and set on fire by "terrorists".

Top goalscorers 1971-72

1)	Des DICKSON	(Coleraine FC)	15
	Peter WATSON	(Distillery FC)	15

IRISH CUP FINAL   (Windsor Park, Belfast – 22/04/1972 – 8,000)

COLERAINE FC (COLERAINE)　　　　　　　　2-1　　　　　　　　Portadown FC (Portadown)

Dickson, Murray　　　　　　　　　　　　　　　　　　　　　　　　　　　　　　　　*Anderson*

Coleraine: Crossan, McCurdy, Gordon, Curley, Jackson, Murray, Dunlop, Mullan, Healey, Dickson, Jennings.
Portadown: Carlisle, Strain, McFall, Malcolmson, Lunn, Hutton, R.Morrison, McGowan, Anderson, B.Morrison, Fleming.

Semi-finals

Ards FC (Newtownards)	1-1, 0-1	Coleraine FC (Coleraine)
Portadown FC (Portadown)	2-0	Derry City FC (Londonderry)

Quarter-finals

Crusaders FC (Belfast)	1-1, 0-3	Ards FC (Newtownards)
Glentoran FC (Belfast)	2-3	Coleraine FC (Coleraine)
Portadown FC (Portadown)	2-0	Linfield FC (Belfast)
Queen's University FC (Belfast)	2-4	Derry City FC (Londonderry)

1972-73

Irish League 1972-73 Season	Ards	Ballymena U.	Bangor	Cliftonville	Coleraine	Crusaders	Distillery	Glenavon	Glentoran	Larne	Linfield	Portadown
Ards FC		3-1	3-1	7-0	1-1	5-2	1-1	1-3	2-3	2-0	1-1	4-0
Ballymena United FC	0-2		1-0	2-1	2-4	1-1	2-1	1-1	4-1	2-2	0-0	3-1
Bangor FC	1-1	1-0		1-0	1-2	1-1	2-5	1-1	2-3	6-0	0-1	1-3
Cliftonville FC	0-4	1-0	1-1		0-5	0-1	2-3	3-1	0-5	1-3	1-2	1-5
Coleraine FC	0-1	2-1	0-0	1-0		0-3	4-0	4-0	4-1	6-1	4-2	1-3
Crusaders FC	2-1	3-0	2-0	3-0	2-1		1-0	2-0	2-0	6-1	2-0	1-1
Distillery FC	0-2	1-2	2-4	4-2	4-1	0-8		1-0	4-2	1-0	2-2	1-1
Glenavon FC	1-2	4-1	0-0	3-0	0-3	1-0	2-0		4-0	4-1	2-0	2-0
Glentoran FC	0-1	0-1	3-0	9-0	1-3	2-2	3-3	4-0		3-2	0-2	1-1
Larne FC	0-2	2-2	1-1	2-3	2-4	2-5	3-2	2-4	1-5		0-2	2-3
Linfield FC	4-2	2-0	1-3	2-1	3-1	5-1	2-3	1-0	0-1	2-1		3-1
Portadown FC	1-1	2-0	1-1	2-1	3-0	1-0	1-2	1-0	2-1	1-0	3-1	

	Irish League	**Pd**	**Wn**	**Dw**	**Ls**	**GF**	**GA**	**Pts**	
1.	CRUSADERS FC (BELFAST)	22	14	4	4	50	22	32	
2.	Ards FC (Newtownards)	22	13	5	4	49	22	31	
3.	Portadown FC (Portadown)	22	12	5	5	37	27	29	
4.	Coleraine FC (Coleraine0	22	13	2	7	51	31	28	
5.	Linfield FC (Belfast)	22	12	3	7	38	29	27	
6.	Glenavon FC (Lurgan)	22	10	3	9	33	28	23	
7.	Distillery FC (Belfast)	22	9	4	9	40	47	22	**
8.	Glentoran FC (Belfast)	22	9	3	10	48	40	21	
9.	Ballymena United FC (Ballymena)	22	7	5	10	26	35	19	
10.	Bangor FC (Bangor)	22	5	8	9	28	32	18	
11.	Cliftonville FC (Belfast)	22	2	1	18	18	66	7	
12.	Larne FC (Larne)	22	2	3	17	28	67	7	**
		264	109	46	109	446	446	264	

** Derry City FC (Londonderry) resigned from the league in November 1972 due to the refusal of other clubs to play at Brandywell Park because of the security risks caused by the "civil unrest" in the country.

Distillery FC (Belfast) continued to play "home" games at the ground of Crusaders FC (Belfast) and would continue to do so until moving to the town of Lisburn in 1979.

Top goalscorer 1972-73

1) Des DICKSON			(Coleraine FC)		23

Elected: Larne FC (Larne) to replace Derry City FC (Londonderry).

IRISH CUP FINAL   (Windsor Park, Belfast – 28/04/1973 – 10,000)

GLENTORAN FC (BELFAST)		3-2			Linfield FC (Belfast)

Feeney 2 (1 pen.), Jamison						*Malone, Magee*

Glentoran: A. Patterson, Hill, McKeag, Stewart (Walker 45'), Murray, McCreary, Weatherup, Anderson, Hall, Jamison, Feeney.

Linfield: Barclay, Fraser, J. Patterson, Sinclair, McAllister, Bowyer, Nixon, Magee, Millen, Malone, Cathcart (Larmour 45').

Semi-finals

Coleraine FC (Coleraine)	1-2	Linfield FC (Belfast)
Glentoran FC (Belfast)	1-0	Glenavon FC (Lurgan)

Quarter-finals

Coleraine FC (Coleraine)	2-1	Portadown FC (Portadown)
Crusaders FC (Belfast)	1-2	Glentoran FC (Belfast)
Glenavon FC (Lurgan)	3-1	Bangor FC (Bangor)
Larne FC (Larne)	2-2, 0-2	Linfield FC (Belfast)

1973-74

Irish League 1973-74 Season	Ards	Ballymena U.	Bangor	Cliftonville	Coleraine	Crusaders	Distillery	Glenavon	Glentoran	Larne	Linfield	Portadown
Ards FC	■	1-0	2-1	4-1	2-2	3-4	3-1	3-2	3-0	4-3	2-2	0-1
Ballymena United FC	1-0	■	1-2	2-2	1-3	1-0	6-0	0-1	1-2	2-0	1-0	1-1
Bangor FC	3-2	1-2	■	8-2	2-0	1-4	4-0	3-1	1-1	2-0	1-2	0-1
Cliftonville FC	1-4	1-1	0-2	■	1-2	2-1	1-1	0-1	2-1	0-1	0-4	1-2
Coleraine FC	1-0	3-2	1-0	2-1	■	1-0	4-1	2-0	3-2	5-1	1-1	2-0
Crusaders FC	4-3	2-1	2-1	2-0	2-0	■	5-2	2-0	1-1	5-2	1-4	1-1
Distillery FC	1-1	1-5	0-4	2-3	0-1	0-2	■	2-3	3-0	1-4	1-1	1-6
Glenavon FC	1-0	0-1	1-0	2-1	1-2	1-3	4-2	■	2-1	3-1	1-1	0-0
Glentoran FC	1-0	0-2	0-1	1-0	0-2	0-3	4-2	4-0	■	2-3	3-2	1-0
Larne FC	2-2	1-0	1-1	2-0	1-3	1-3	0-1	4-3	1-3	■	0-0	1-7
Linfield FC	4-1	2-3	1-1	8-1	1-0	2-0	3-0	2-3	5-1	0-1	■	1-0
Portadown FC	1-2	3-0	4-1	3-0	1-1	5-1	6-2	1-3	2-0	3-1	3-0	■

	Irish League	Pd	Wn	Dw	Ls	GF	GA	Pts
1.	COLERAINE FC (COLERAINE)	22	16	3	3	41	20	35
2.	Portadown FC (Portadown)	22	13	4	5	51	20	30
3.	Crusaders FC (Belfast)	22	14	2	6	48	32	30
4.	Linfield FC (Belfast)	22	10	6	6	46	25	26
5.	Glenavon FC (Lurgan)	22	11	2	9	33	35	24
6.	Ballymena United FC (Ballymena)	22	10	3	9	34	26	23
7.	Bangor FC (Bangor)	22	10	3	9	40	28	23
8.	Ards FC (Newtownards)	22	9	4	9	42	37	37
9.	Glentoran FC (Belfast)	22	8	2	12	28	39	18
10.	Larne FC (Larne)	22	7	3	12	31	50	17
11.	Cliftonville FC (Belfast)	22	3	3	16	20	56	9
12.	Distillery FC (Belfast)	22	2	3	17	24	70	7
		264	113	38	113	438	438	264

Note: Distillery FC (Belfast) continued to play "home" games at the ground of Crusaders FC (Belfast).

Top goalscorer 1973-74

1) Des DICKSON   (Coleraine FC)   24

No clubs promoted or relegated

IRISH CUP FINAL   (Windsor Park, Belfast – 27/04/1974 – 7,000)

ARDS FC (NEWTOWNARDS)   2-1   Ballymena United FC (Ballymena)

Guy, McAvoy   *Sloan*

Ards: Matthews, Patton, Patterson, Mowat, McCoy, Nixon, McAteer, McAvoy, Guy, Humphries, Cathcart (Graham 60').

Ballymena: McKenzie, Gowdy, McAuley, Stewart, Averell, Brown, Donald, Sloan, Erwin (Todd 82'), McFall, Frickleton.

Semi-finals

Ards FC (Newtownards)	4-2	Glenavon FC (Lurgan)
Ballymena United FC (Ballymena)	1-1, 2-2 (aet)	Larne FC (Larne)
	(Ballymena United won 4-3 on penalties)	

Quarter-finals

Ards FC (Newtownards)	4-2	Bangor FC (Bangor)
Ballymena United FC (Ballymena)	7-1	Crusaders FC (Belfast)
Chimney Corner FC (Antrim)	0-3	Larne FC (Larne)
Coleraine FC (Coleraine)	0-2	Glenavon FC (Lurgan)

1974-75

Irish League 1974-75 Season	Ards	Ballymena U.	Bangor	Cliftonville	Coleraine	Crusaders	Distillery	Glenavon	Glentoran	Larne	Linfield	Portadown
Ards FC	■	0-0	1-0	3-2	1-3	0-1	3-0	4-1	1-2	1-4	2-6	1-1
Ballymena United FC	1-2	■	1-2	4-0	2-1	0-0	2-0	8-0	1-2	4-2	1-1	2-0
Bangor FC	1-1	2-2	■	2-2	2-5	3-1	2-0	4-1	3-1	0-1	3-4	1-1
Cliftonville FC	0-2	3-3	2-4	■	0-3	0-4	3-1	1-0	0-4	1-0	0-1	0-0
Coleraine FC	2-0	3-1	2-3	3-0	■	3-0	3-0	6-1	3-1	2-0	2-0	2-3
Crusaders FC	1-3	1-2	4-2	6-1	2-2	■	2-1	5-0	2-3	2-1	0-2	2-0
Distillery FC	2-0	1-1	0-1	1-1	2-2	2-4	■	0-2	0-3	1-2	0-2	1-2
Glenavon FC	3-1	2-3	2-1	3-2	0-2	0-0	3-3	■	2-4	1-4	2-3	3-1
Glentoran FC	4-0	1-1	0-0	4-0	3-1	1-4	5-1	0-0	■	5-1	1-0	2-0
Larne FC	4-0	0-1	1-1	2-0	2-3	1-2	0-2	4-2	2-3	■	0-2	2-0
Linfield FC	3-1	2-1	2-0	3-1	2-1	1-1	5-1	2-1	4-1	4-2	■	2-2
Portadown FC	2-1	0-2	1-0	1-0	0-4	2-2	5-1	4-2	4-2	0-3	0-2	■

	Irish League	Pd	Wn	Dw	Ls	GF	GA	Pts
1.	LINFIELD FC (BELFAST)	22	17	3	2	53	23	37
2.	Coleraine FC (Coleraine)	22	15	2	5	58	25	32
3.	Glentoran FC (Belfast)	22	14	3	5	52	30	31
4.	Ballymena United FC (Ballymena)	22	10	7	5	43	25	27
5.	Crusaders FC (Belfast)	22	11	5	6	46	30	27
6.	Bangor FC (Bangor)	22	8	6	8	37	35	22
7.	Portadown FC (Portadown)	22	8	5	9	29	37	21
8.	Larne FC (Larne)	22	9	1	12	38	37	19
9.	Ards FC (Newtownards)	22	7	3	12	28	43	17
10.	Glenavon FC (Lurgan)	22	5	3	14	31	62	13
11.	Cliftonville FC (Belfast)	22	3	4	15	19	54	10
12.	Distillery FC (Belfast)	22	2	4	16	20	53	8
		264	109	46	109	454	454	264

Note: Distillery FC (Belfast) continued to play "home" games at the ground of Crusaders FC (Belfast).

Top goalscorer 1974-75

1) Martin MALONE   (Portadown FC)   19

No clubs promoted or relegated

IRISH CUP FINAL   (Showgrounds, Ballymena – 19/04/1975 – 5,600)

COLERAINE FC (COLERAINE)   1-1   Linfield FC (Belfast)
Smith 32'   *Graham 65'*

Coleraine: V. Magee, McCurdy, Gordon, Beckett, Jackson, Murray, Tweed, Jennings, Guy, Smith, Simpson.
Linfield: Barclay, Fraser, McVeigh, E. Magee, Rafferty, Bowyer, Patterson (Campbell 60'), M. Malone, P. Malone, Graham, McKee.

IRISH CUP FINAL REPLAY   (Showgrounds, Ballymena – 23/04/1975 – 5,400)

COLERAINE FC (COLERAINE)   0-0   Linfield FC (Belfast)

Linfield: Barclay, Fraser, McVeigh, E. Magee, Rafferty, Bowyer, Campbell, M. Malone (Bell 66'), P. Malone, Graham, Hunter.
Coleraine: V. Magee, McCurdy, Gordon, Beckett, Jackson, Murray, McNutt, Jennings, Guy, Smith, Cochrane.

IRISH CUP FINAL 2ND REPLAY   (Showgrounds, Ballymena – 29/04/1975 – 5,200)

COLERAINE FC (COLERAINE)   1-0   Linfield FC (Belfast)

Smith 17'

Coleraine: V. Magee, McCurdy, McNutt, Beckett, Jackson, Murray, Cochrane, Jennings, Smith, Dickson, Gordon.
Linfield: Barclay, Fraser, McVeigh, E. Magee, Rafferty, Bowyer, Campbell (Bell 70'), Patterson, P. Malone, Graham, Hunter.

Semi-finals

Brantwood FC (Belfast)	0-6	Coleraine FC (Coleraine)
Carrick Rangers FC (Carrickfergus)	0-6	Linfield FC (Belfast)

Quarter-finals

Brantwood FC (Belfast)	2-1	Glentoran FC (Belfast)
Carrick Rangers FC (Carrickfergus)	2-1	Distillery FC (Belfast)
Cliftonville FC (Belfast)	1-1, 0-5	Coleraine FC (Coleraine)
Linfield FC (Belfast)	3-0	Larne FC (Larne)

1975-76

Irish League 1975-76 Season	Ards	Ballymena U.	Bangor	Cliftonville	Coleraine	Crusaders	Distillery	Glenavon	Glentoran	Larne	Linfield	Portadown
Ards FC	■	1-1	1-2	4-3	3-1	0-3	1-2	2-2	0-3	3-1	1-3	2-4
Ballymena United FC	0-1	■	4-1	1-0	5-1	2-3	1-0	4-1	1-2	3-2	1-1	1-1
Bangor FC	0-0	1-1	■	2-1	1-0	2-2	3-1	2-2	2-0	3-0	0-2	3-1
Cliftonville FC	2-2	2-0	0-0	■	0-1	0-2	2-1	1-1	2-4	1-0	1-5	2-4
Coleraine FC	3-0	4-2	1-1	1-1	■	3-1	1-0	2-1	0-1	2-1	3-0	7-2
Crusaders FC	1-1	2-0	1-0	4-1	0-0	■	2-2	4-0	2-2	1-1	3-2	2-1
Distillery FC	0-2	1-3	1-1	5-2	2-3	0-7	■	1-1	0-5	1-2	0-1	2-0
Glenavon FC	1-3	1-1	0-1	0-3	0-1	1-5	3-1	■	1-1	4-1	0-5	2-1
Glentoran FC	2-3	5-2	3-0	4-1	2-2	0-1	3-0	2-0	■	1-1	3-1	1-0
Larne FC	3-0	0-1	2-3	1-4	1-2	0-2	5-3	3-2	2-1	■	2-4	0-1
Linfield FC	3-0	2-1	3-0	2-0	2-2	0-1	1-1	0-0	1-2	2-3	■	1-1
Portadown FC	3-2	3-1	1-0	2-3	1-2	1-2	5-0	0-1	0-2	1-1	1-2	■

	Irish League	Pd	Wn	Dw	Ls	GF	GA	Pts
1.	CRUSADERS FC (BELFAST)	22	15	6	1	51	19	36
2.	Glentoran FC (Belfast)	22	14	4	4	48	22	32
3.	Coleraine FC (Coleraine)	22	13	5	4	42	27	31
4.	Linfield FC (Belfast)	22	11	5	6	43	25	27
5.	Bangor FC (Bangor)	22	9	7	6	28	27	25
6.	Ballymena United FC (Ballymena)	22	8	5	9	36	35	21
7.	Ards FC (Newtownards)	22	7	5	10	32	43	19
8.	Portadown FC (Portadown)	22	7	3	12	34	39	17
9.	Cliftonville FC (Belfast)	22	6	4	12	32	46	16
10.	Larne FC (Larne)	22	6	3	13	32	45	15
11.	Glenavon FC (Lurgan)	22	4	7	11	24	44	15
12.	Distillery FC (Belfast)	22	3	4	15	24	54	10
		264	103	58	103	426	426	264

Note: Distillery FC (Belfast) continued to play "home" games at the ground of Crusaders FC (Belfast).

Top goalscorer 1975-76

1) Des DICKSON   (Coleraine FC)   23

No clubs promoted or relegated

IRISH CUP FINAL   (The Oval, Belfast – 10/04/1976 – 9,500)

CARRICK RANGERS FC   2-1   Linfield FC (Belfast)
Prenter 25', 64'   *Malone 50 seconds*

Carrick: Cowan, Hamilton, Macklin, Matchett, Whiteside, Brown, Cullen, Connor, McKenzie, Prenter, Allen.
Linfield: Barclay, Fraser, McVeigh, Coyle, Rafferty, Bowyer, Nixon, Lemon (McKee 45'), Bell, M. Malone, Magee.

Semi-finals

| Glentoran FC (Belfast) | 0-2 | Linfield FC (Belfast) |
| Larne FC (Larne) | 3-3, 2-3 | Carrick Rangers FC (Carrickfergus) |

Quarter-finals

Ards FC (Newtownards)	1-1, 1-7	Linfield FC (Belfast)
Coleraine FC (Coleraine)	1-1, 3-3, 1-2	Carrick Rangers FC (Carrickfergus)
Glentoran FC (Belfast)	2-1	Cliftonville FC (Belfast)
Larne FC (Larne)	+:-	Crusaders FC (Belfast)

1976-77

Irish League 1976-77 Season	Ards	Ballymena U.	Bangor	Cliftonville	Coleraine	Crusaders	Distillery	Glenavon	Glentoran	Larne	Linfield	Portadown
Ards FC		2-0	3-2	2-1	4-2	2-1	1-0	2-3	0-1	3-5	3-1	2-1
Ballymena United FC	1-0		0-2	0-1	2-3	0-2	2-0	1-0	0-4	4-1	1-1	2-4
Bangor FC	0-2	1-1		4-2	3-2	2-2	1-2	0-2	1-4	3-3	0-3	1-0
Cliftonville FC	0-1	0-1	1-1		0-0	0-3	0-2	1-3	1-3	2-1	2-1	1-2
Coleraine FC	2-0	3-2	2-0	3-1		3-0	0-0	3-2	0-0	3-0	1-3	3-1
Crusaders FC	4-3	4-1	1-1	6-2	0-2		1-1	1-2	2-0	2-1	0-2	2-1
Distillery FC	0-0	0-0	1-0	4-1	2-4	2-5		0-2	3-4	2-3	1-6	1-2
Glenavon FC	4-1	1-0	3-1	1-2	2-0	1-1	3-2		1-0	1-1	2-1	3-2
Glentoran FC	3-0	3-1	1-0	5-0	4-2	2-1	3-0	1-0		3-1	2-0	3-1
Larne FC	2-0	1-0	3-0	2-1	1-0	3-0	0-1	5-1	2-2		1-2	3-2
Linfield FC	3-1	0-0	2-0	4-0	1-0	0-0	1-1	0-3	3-0	0-1		4-2
Portadown FC	3-2	1-1	3-0	2-1	1-2	2-1	5-0	0-0	0-2	1-2	0-1	

	Irish League	Pd	Wn	Dw	Ls	GF	GA	Pts
1.	GLENTORAN FC (BELFAST)	22	17	2	3	50	19	36
2.	Glenavon FC (Lurgan)	22	14	3	5	40	25	31
3.	Linfield FC (Belfast)	22	12	4	6	39	21	28
4.	Coleraine FC (Coleraine)	22	12	3	7	40	29	27
5.	Larne FC (Larne)	22	12	3	7	42	33	27
6.	Crusaders FC (Belfast)	22	9	5	8	39	33	23
7.	Ards FC (Newtownards)	22	10	1	11	34	39	21
8.	Portadown FC (Portadown)	22	8	2	12	36	37	18
9.	Ballymena United FC (Ballymena)	22	5	5	12	20	34	15
10.	Distillery FC (Belfast)	22	5	5	12	25	44	15
11.	Bangor FC (Bangor)	22	4	5	13	23	43	13
12.	Cliftonville FC (Belfast)	22	4	2	16	20	51	10
		264	112	40	112	408	408	624

Note: Distillery FC (Belfast) continued to play "home" games at the ground of Crusaders FC (Belfast).

Top goalscorer 1976-77

1) Ronald McATEER   (Crusaders FC)   20

No clubs promoted or relegated

IRISH CUP FINAL   (The Oval, Belfast – 10,000)

COLERAINE FC (COLERAINE)   4-1   Linfield FC (Belfast)

Beckett, Dickson, Moffatt, Guy   *Lemon*

Coleraine: V. Magee, Hutton, McNutt, Beckett, Jackson, Connell, Porter, Jennings, Guy, Dickson, Moffatt.
Linfield: Barclay, Parkes, Garrett, Coyle, Rafferty, Lemon, Nixon, Dornan, Bell, Martin, E. Magee.

Semi-finals

Coleraine FC (Coleraine)	0-0, 3-0	Distillery FC (Belfast)
Linfield FC (Belfast)	1-1, 3-2	Larne FC Larne)

Quarter-finals

Ards FC (Newtownards)	0-6	Linfield FC (Belfast)
Crusaders FC (Belfast)	0-1	Coleraine FC (Coleraine)
Glenavon FC (Lurgan)	0-3	Distillery FC (Belfast)
Portadown FC (Portadown)	1-3	Larne FC (Larne)

1977-78

Irish League 1977-78 Season	Ards	Ballymena U.	Bangor	Cliftonville	Coleraine	Crusaders	Distillery	Glenavon	Glentoran	Larne	Linfield	Portadown
Ards FC	■	2-1	1-2	1-2	3-0	3-1	1-2	2-0	1-1	1-0	0-1	3-2
Ballymena United FC	1-3	■	1-0	1-2	2-0	2-1	3-1	0-1	0-2	2-3	0-3	1-3
Bangor FC	1-2	2-2	■	1-1	1-0	4-1	0-1	0-1	0-4	2-3	1-1	2-1
Cliftonville FC	1-1	3-0	2-0	■	1-4	1-0	3-2	0-4	3-1	0-1	1-3	2-1
Coleraine FC	2-0	3-0	2-1	1-2	■	1-2	3-1	3-2	1-1	1-0	0-4	3-3
Crusaders FC	1-2	2-1	2-0	2-2	1-1	■	1-2	0-5	3-3	1-0	0-3	2-0
Distillery FC	2-2	2-2	0-3	1-3	3-1	5-2	■	1-2	0-5	3-1	1-4	1-1
Glenavon FC	5-2	2-1	1-1	1-1	2-0	1-0	4-1	■	2-1	2-1	0-4	3-1
Glentoran FC	4-2	2-0	6-1	5-0	4-1	4-0	2-2	2-0	■	1-0	2-3	2-1
Larne FC	3-1	2-1	1-0	3-2	4-3	0-1	4-0	2-0	0-1	■	1-2	0-4
Linfield FC	6-4	2-1	2-0	3-0	4-2	3-1	7-1	4-2	1-2	1-0	■	2-2
Portadown FC	3-1	3-0	1-0	2-2	0-1	3-0	4-0	3-1	1-4	2-2	1-2	■

	Irish League	Pd	Wn	Dw	Ls	GF	GA	Pts
1.	LINFIELD FC (BELFAST)	22	19	2	1	65	22	40
2.	Glentoran FC (Belfast)	22	15	4	3	59	22	34
3.	Glenavon FC (Lurgan)	22	13	2	7	41	30	28
4.	Cliftonville FC (Belfast)	22	10	5	7	34	38	25
5.	Portadown FC (Portadown)	22	8	5	9	42	34	21
6.	Larne FC (Larne)	22	10	1	11	31	31	21
7.	Ards FC (Newtownards)	22	9	3	10	38	41	21
8.	Coleraine FC (Coleraine)	22	8	3	11	34	41	19
9.	Distillery FC (Belfast)	22	6	4	12	32	59	16
10.	Crusaders FC (Belfast)	22	6	3	13	24	46	15
11.	Bangor FC (Bangor)	22	5	4	13	22	36	14
12.	Ballymena United FC (Ballymena)	22	4	2	16	22	44	10
		264	113	38	113	444	444	264

Note: Distillery FC (Belfast) continued to play "home" games at the ground of Crusaders FC (Belfast).

Top goalscorer 1977-78

1) Warren FEENEY (Glentoran FC) 17

IRISH CUP FINAL   (The Oval, Belfast – 29/04/1978 – 12,000)

LINFIELD FC (BELFAST)   3-1   Ballymena United FC (Ballymena)
Dornan 14', Garrett 39', Rafferty 83'   *Nelson 67'*

Linfield: Barclay, Fraser, Parks, Coyle, Rafferty, Dornan, Nixon, Garrett, Martin, Hamilton, Murray.
Ballymena: Rafferty, Donald, Spence, McCullough, Jackson, Simpson, Nelson, T. Sloan, Johnston, J.Sloan, McLean.

Semi-finals

Ballymena United FC (Ballymena)	1-1, 1-1, 1-1	Crusaders FC (Belfast)(aet 4-1 pen)
Linfield FC (Belfast)	2-1	Portadown FC (Portadown)

Quarter-finals

Ballymena United FC (Ballymena)	1-0	Ards FC (Newtownards)
Bangor FC (Bangor)	0-6	Portadown FC (Portadown)
Crusaders FC (Belfast)	1-0	Larne FC (Larne)
Linfield FC (Belfast)	4-3	Glentoran FC (Belfast)

1978-79

Irish League 1978-79 Season	Ards	Ballymena U.	Bangor	Cliftonville	Coleraine	Crusaders	Distillery	Glenavon	Glentoran	Larne	Linfield	Portadown
Ards FC	■	3-3	1-2	3-2	2-2	3-2	2-0	3-0	4-4	3-2	0-2	3-0
Ballymena United FC	1-3	■	1-1	1-1	1-1	0-0	2-0	0-2	5-1	1-3	1-2	1-0
Bangor FC	2-5	0-0	■	0-0	3-1	2-0	2-0	2-6	0-0	1-3	0-2	1-3
Cliftonville FC	2-1	5-0	3-0	■	2-0	1-0	3-0	1-3	2-4	0-1	0-3	1-1
Coleraine FC	1-2	1-2	1-1	1-1	■	5-0	0-1	4-3	0-0	0-3	0-0	3-0
Crusaders FC	1-0	4-0	2-2	2-2	1-0	■	5-2	1-0	0-2	2-2	1-4	1-2
Distillery FC	0-3	4-2	2-2	2-3	1-2	0-3	■	1-4	1-3	1-3	0-1	1-4
Glenavon FC	3-1	3-2	0-1	2-0	3-0	1-1	1-1	■	3-2	2-1	0-0	1-1
Glentoran FC	1-0	2-0	3-2	1-1	2-1	3-2	2-2	2-2	■	0-2	1-1	1-0
Larne FC	3-3	2-1	2-1	2-0	0-1	1-1	2-0	1-2	1-1	■	3-4	3-5
Linfield FC	1-2	6-1	2-2	2-1	2-3	1-1	2-0	0-0	2-1	3-1	■	3-1
Portadown FC	0-0	2-0	3-1	0-0	0-2	0-0	1-0	5-1	2-0	3-1	2-3	■

	Irish League	**Pd**	**Wn**	**Dw**	**Ls**	**GF**	**GA**	**Pts**	
1.	LINFIELD FC (BELFAST)	22	14	6	2	46	21	34	
2.	Glenavon FC (Lurgan)	22	11	6	5	42	30	28	
3.	Ards FC (Newtownards)	22	11	5	6	47	34	27	
4.	Glentoran FC (Belfast)	22	9	8	5	36	33	26	
5.	Portadown FC (Portadown)	22	10	5	7	35	27	25	
6.	Larne FC (Larne)	22	10	4	8	42	35	24	
7.	Cliftonville FC (Belfast)	22	7	7	8	31	29	21	
8.	Coleraine FC (Coleraine)	22	7	6	9	29	30	20	
9.	Crusaders FC (Belfast)	22	6	8	8	30	33	20	
10.	Bangor FC (Bangor)	22	5	8	9	28	40	18	
11.	Ballymena United FC (Ballymena)	22	4	6	12	25	46	14	
12.	Distillery FC (Belfast)	22	2	3	17	19	52	7	**
		264	96	72	96	410	410	264	

** Distillery FC (Belfast), who had playing "home" games at the ground of Crusaders FC (Belfast) since 1971 because of the "civil unrest" in the country moved out of Belfast to a new stadium "New Grosvenor Park", Ballyskeagh Road, Lambeg, Lisburn, County Down for the next season.

Top goalscorer 1978-79

1) Thomas ARMSTRONG   (Ards FC)   21

No clubs promoted or relegated

IRISH CUP FINAL   (Windsor Park, Belfast – 15,000)

CLIFTONVILLE FC (BELFAST)   3-2   Portadown FC (Portadown)
Platt 32', Adair 46', Bell 89'   *Campbell 02', Alexander 77'*

Cliftonville: Johnston, McGuickan, Largey, Flanagan, M. Quinn, McCurry, T. Bell, McCusker, Mills (O'Connor 66'), Platt, Adair.

Portadown: McCullum, Smyth, Douglas, Wilson, Kilburn, Cleary, Gordon, Magee (J. Bell 66'), Alexander, Campbell, Quinn.

Semi-finals

Larne FC (Larne)	2-2, 0-1	Cliftonville FC (Belfast)
Portadown FC (Portadown)	2-1	Glenavon FC (Lurgan)

Quarter-finals

Ballymena United FC (Ballymena)	0-0, 1-2	Portadown FC (Portadown)
Coleraine FC (Coleraine)	2-3	Cliftonville FC (Belfast)
Glenavon FC (Lurgan)	3-2	Banbridge Town FC (Banbridge)
Royal Ulster Constabulary FC (Belfast)	0-1	Larne FC (Larne)

1979-80

Irish League 1979-80 Season	Ards	Ballymena U.	Bangor	Cliftonville	Coleraine	Crusaders	Distillery	Glenavon	Glentoran	Larne	Linfield	Portadown
Ards FC	■	1-3	1-1	0-2	4-1	2-5	0-1	3-0	1-3	1-1	1-1	4-1
Ballymena United FC	2-0	■	2-0	1-1	5-0	2-1	8-0	0-1	1-1	4-0	5-0	2-1
Bangor FC	3-2	2-3	■	0-2	0-5	2-3	0-1	0-0	1-1	4-2	0-2	1-4
Cliftonville FC	2-0	2-1	3-0	■	1-3	1-0	0-1	2-0	2-2	0-0	0-1	0-0
Coleraine FC	2-0	1-1	2-3	1-5	■	5-2	2-2	3-1	1-3	1-0	1-5	2-2
Crusaders FC	2-0	1-1	0-1	1-0	3-1	■	1-2	0-0	1-0	2-0	0-1	2-0
Distillery FC	1-1	1-3	1-2	1-1	1-5	0-4	■	2-0	0-4	2-1	1-2	0-3
Glenavon FC	2-2	1-1	4-1	0-1	0-2	0-1	1-1	■	1-1	2-1	1-2	1-0
Glentoran FC	2-0	2-0	1-1	1-1	2-4	0-2	2-1	3-1	■	1-0	1-2	1-0
Larne FC	0-3	1-1	1-3	1-0	2-2	2-1	1-0	0-1	1-2	■	2-3	0-2
Linfield FC	1-0	4-1	7-0	1-0	2-0	3-0	6-1	2-1	5-0	2-0	■	6-0
Portadown FC	3-0	2-5	3-2	1-3	4-2	1-0	1-2	2-1	1-1	3-1	2-1	■

Irish League

		Pd	Wn	Dw	Ls	GF	GA	Pts
1.	LINFIELD FC (BELFAST)	22	19	1	2	59	17	39
2.	Ballymena United FC (Ballymena)	22	12	6	4	52	23	30
3.	Glentoran FC (Belfast)	22	10	7	5	34	27	27
4.	Cliftonville FC (Belfast)	22	10	6	6	29	16	26
5.	Crusaders FC (Belfast)	22	11	2	9	32	24	24
6.	Portadown FC (Portadown)	22	10	3	9	36	37	23
7.	Coleraine FC (Coleraine)	22	9	4	9	46	48	22
8.	Distillery FC (Lisburn)	22	7	4	11	22	48	18
9.	Glenavon FC (Lurgan)	22	5	6	11	19	30	16
10.	Bangor FC (Bangor)	22	6	4	12	27	50	16
11.	Ards FC (Newtownards)	22	4	5	13	26	39	13
12.	Larne FC (Larne)	22	3	4	15	17	40	10
		264	106	52	106	399	399	264

Top goalscorer 1979-80

1) James MARTIN   (Glentoran FC)   17

No clubs promoted or relegated

IRISH CUP FINAL (The Oval, Belfast – 26/04/1980 – 10,000)

LINFIELD FC (BELFAST)   2-0   Crusaders FC (Belfast)

McCurdy 12', McKeown 68' pen.

Linfield: Dunlop, Fraser, Hayes, Dornan, Rafferty, McKeown, Nixon (Jameson 74'), McKee, McCurdy, Feeney, Anderson.

Crusaders: McDonald, Thompson, Gorman, Mulhall, Gillespie, McPolin, Kennedy (Patterson 61'), Currie, Byrne, King.

Semi-finals

| Linfield FC (Belfast) | 1-0 | Ballymena United FC (Ballymena) |
| Royal Ulster Constabulary FC (Belfast) | 1-1, 1-2 | Crusaders FC (Belfast) |

Quarter-finals

Ballymena United FC (Ballymena)	3-2	Portadown FC (Portadown)
Glenavon FC (Lurgan)	0-0, 3-0	Crusaders FC (Belfast)
Linfield FC (Belfast)	4-0	Glentoran FC (Belfast)
Royal Ulster Constabulary FC (Belfast)	1-1, 0-0, 1-0	Coleraine FC (Coleraine)

1980-81

Irish League 1980-81 Season	Ards	Ballymena U.	Bangor	Cliftonville	Coleraine	Crusaders	Distillery	Glenavon	Glentoran	Larne	Linfield	Portadown
Ards FC	■	0-1	2-2	0-0	4-2	2-0	2-0	2-2	1-1	2-0	1-1	2-0
Ballymena United FC	3-2	■	5-1	4-3	2-0	1-1	2-0	1-1	1-2	1-0	1-0	2-0
Bangor FC	3-4	3-1	■	6-1	3-5	0-2	3-1	1-1	2-3	0-2	1-3	1-1
Cliftonville FC	3-0	1-1	1-1	■	3-2	0-0	1-0	0-2	2-4	2-4	0-2	0-2
Coleraine FC	0-1	0-0	2-0	0-0	■	0-1	1-1	3-3	1-1	0-0	1-2	2-5
Crusaders FC	8-2	1-0	2-0	1-0	0-1	■	1-0	3-1	1-1	1-2	2-2	1-1
Distillery FC	1-2	1-2	0-2	1-0	2-2	1-1	■	3-4	1-7	0-2	0-6	1-2
Glenavon FC	1-1	2-1	2-2	2-2	1-2	4-0	2-1	■	1-2	2-1	0-3	2-1
Glentoran FC	4-3	2-0	3-2	2-0	1-1	3-1	4-2	3-1	■	1-1	2-1	2-2
Larne FC	0-2	0-3	3-1	2-0	2-0	0-1	2-0	2-2	0-3	■	0-2	1-1
Linfield FC	5-0	1-0	7-0	0-1	4-1	4-0	4-2	2-1	1-1	1-0	■	2-1
Portadown FC	3-0	0-1	3-1	2-0	0-2	1-0	2-0	1-1	1-7	1-2	0-4	■

	Irish League	Pd	Wn	Dw	Ls	GF	GA	Pts
1.	GLENTORAN FC (BELFAST)	22	15	7	-	59	26	37
2.	Linfield FC (Belfast)	22	16	3	3	57	15	35
3.	Ballymena United FC (Ballymena)	22	12	4	6	33	21	28
4.	Crusaders FC (Belfast)	22	9	6	7	28	26	24
5.	Ards FC (Newtownards)	22	9	6	7	35	40	24
6.	Glenavon FC (Lurgan)	22	7	8	7	37	37	22
7.	Larne FC (Larne)	22	9	4	9	26	26	22
8.	Portadown FC (Portadown)	22	8	5	9	30	34	21
9.	Coleraine FC (Coleraine)	22	5	8	9	28	36	18
10.	Cliftonville FC (Belfast)	22	5	5	12	20	37	15
11.	Bangor FC (Bangor)	22	4	5	13	35	54	13
12.	Distillery FC (Lisburn)	22	1	3	18	18	54	5
		264	100	64	100	406	406	264

Top goalscorers 1980-81

1) Des DICKSON   (Coleraine FC)   18
   Paul MALONE   (Ballymena United FC)   18

No clubs promoted or relegated

IRISH CUP FINAL   (Windsor Park, Belfast – 02/05/1981 – 8,000)

BALLYMENA UNITED FC (B'MENA)   1-0   Glenavon FC (Lurgan)

McQuiston

Ballymena: Matthews, Beattie, Worthington, Fox, R. McCullough, Smyth, Neill, Sloan, McQuiston, P. Malone, McCusker.

Glenavon: T. McCullough, Fielding, McGuckin, McGuigan, Stitt, Bowyer, Wilson, M. Malone, McDonald, Tully, Dennison.

Semi-finals

Ballymena United FC (Ballymena)	2-2, 2-0	Glentoran FC (Belfast)
Glenavon FC (Lurgan)	1-0	Linfield FC (Belfast)

Quarter-finals

Ards FC (Newtownards)	1-3	Glentoran FC (Belfast)
Cliftonville FC (Belfast)	1-4	Ballymena United FC (Ballymena)
Glenavon FC (Lurgan)	2-1	Carrick Rangers FC (Carrickfergus)
Linfield FC (Belfast)	4-1	Newry Town FC (Newry)

1981-82

Irish League 1981-82 Season	Ards	Ballymena U.	Bangor	Cliftonville	Coleraine	Crusaders	Distillery	Glenavon	Glentoran	Larne	Linfield	Portadown
Ards FC	■	0-0	2-0	0-1	0-3	0-0	2-0	2-4	1-7	1-0	1-2	0-1
Ballymena United FC	2-1	■	1-2	1-3	4-2	0-0	1-1	0-0	1-0	2-0	1-1	1-3
Bangor FC	0-1	1-3	■	1-1	1-5	2-1	3-3	1-2	2-1	0-4	0-5	0-1
Cliftonville FC	4-0	1-1	1-0	■	2-2	0-1	1-0	2-3	0-1	4-1	0-4	1-0
Coleraine FC	0-1	2-0	3-2	3-1	■	0-2	3-1	4-0	1-2	0-0	3-1	4-2
Crusaders FC	1-0	2-1	5-1	2-1	3-4	■	1-3	2-1	3-0	2-3	1-2	2-1
Distillery FC	1-0	2-3	4-0	2-2	1-0	1-2	■	4-2	0-5	1-0	0-7	3-0
Glenavon FC	2-2	1-1	1-1	2-2	0-3	2-2	3-1	■	1-3	3-3	0-6	0-2
Glentoran FC	2-0	3-1	4-0	1-2	2-2	6-1	6-1	3-1	■	4-1	1-2	3-1
Larne FC	2-3	1-1	2-1	0-2	2-5	0-1	1-0	4-0	0-1	■	2-3	0-3
Linfield FC	5-0	3-0	4-2	1-0	2-1	2-2	1-1	2-1	1-2	2-1	■	2-0
Portadown FC	1-1	1-0	2-0	2-2	2-4	1-0	1-0	2-1	0-4	3-0	0-1	■

	Irish League	Pd	Wn	Dw	Ls	GF	GA	Pts
1.	LINFIELD FC (BELFAST)	22	17	3	2	59	19	37
2.	Glentoran FC (Belfast)	22	16	1	5	61	22	33
3.	Coleraine FC (Coleraine)	22	14	3	5	63	31	31
4.	Crusaders FC (Belfast)	22	11	4	7	36	31	26
5.	Cliftonville FC (Belfast)	22	9	6	7	33	28	24
6.	Portadown FC (Portadown)	22	11	2	9	29	29	24
7.	Ballymena United FC (Ballymena)	22	6	8	8	25	30	20
8.	Distillery FC (Lisburn)	22	7	4	11	30	44	18
9.	Glenavon FC (Lurgan)	22	4	7	11	30	52	15
10.	Ards FC (Newtownards)	22	5	4	13	18	47	14
11.	Larne FC (Larne)	22	5	3	14	27	42	13
12.	Bangor FC (Bangor)	22	3	3	16	20	56	9
		264	108	48	108	431	431	264

Top goalscorer 1981-82

1) Gary BLACKLEDGE   (Glentoran FC)   18

No clubs promoted or relegated

IRISH CUP FINAL (The Oval, Belfast – 24/04/1982 – 12,000)

LINFIELD FC (BELFAST)　　　　　　　　　2-1　　　　　　　　　　Coleraine FC (Coleraine)

McKeown, Murray pen.　　　　　　　　　　　　　　　　　　　　　　　　　　　　*Healey*

Linfield: Dunlop, Mooney, Hayes, Walsh, Gibson, Dornan (Rafferty 61'), McKee, McKeown, McGaughey, Murray, Anderson.

Coleraine: Magee, McDowall, McNutt, O'Kane, Shannon, Mullan, Mahon, Healey, McManus, Dickson, Henry.

Semi-finals

Coleraine FC (Coleraine)	1-0	Cliftonville FC (Belfast)
Linfield FC (Belfast)	2-1	Ards FC (Newtownards)

Quarter-finals

Cliftonville FC (Belfast)	3-2	Royal Ulster Constabulary FC (Belfast)
Distillery FC (Lisburn)	2-2, 0-0, 2-0	Ards FC (Newtownards)
Limavady United FC (Limavady)	0-2	Coleraine FC (Coleraine)
Portadown FC (Portadown)	0-1	Linfield FC (Belfast)

1982-83

Irish League 1982-83 Season	Ards	Ballymena U.	Bangor	Cliftonville	Coleraine	Crusaders	Distillery	Glenavon	Glentoran	Larne	Linfield	Portadown
Ards FC	■	4-0	5-1	2-4	0-3	3-1	1-0	4-2	1-3	1-0	0-1	3-2
Ballymena United FC	4-4	■	1-1	1-0	2-4	0-0	1-2	2-0	1-3	4-2	0-2	0-0
Bangor FC	1-2	0-3	■	0-3	1-3	0-3	0-1	0-0	0-3	1-1	3-6	0-6
Cliftonville FC	0-0	1-0	5-0	■	1-0	1-0	2-0	1-1	1-3	3-2	0-0	0-1
Coleraine FC	2-0	2-4	4-1	3-1	■	5-0	3-3	1-1	3-1	1-0	0-0	1-1
Crusaders FC	0-0	6-0	3-1	2-1	1-3	■	3-1	0-1	2-1	2-1	0-3	2-0
Distillery FC	3-2	2-1	1-2	2-1	2-1	1-6	■	1-0	1-3	1-4	0-4	0-0
Glenavon FC	5-3	1-3	3-1	1-2	0-0	0-3	5-0	■	1-3	0-1	0-3	1-0
Glentoran FC	4-1	1-0	2-1	1-1	0-1	3-0	4-0	4-1	■	5-0	3-0	0-1
Larne FC	2-3	1-2	5-2	0-1	3-2	0-1	2-2	2-1	2-9	■	0-1	2-2
Linfield FC	0-0	4-1	6-0	1-0	2-1	1-0	0-0	3-1	2-2	3-1	■	1-0
Portadown FC	3-1	1-2	2-1	4-1	1-1	0-0	1-0	0-1	1-0	2-0	1-0	■

	Irish League	Pd	Wn	Dw	Ls	GF	GA	Pts
1.	LINFIELD FC (BELFAST)	22	15	5	2	43	13	35
2.	Glentoran FC (Belfast)	22	14	2	6	49	21	30
3.	Coleraine FC (Coleraine)	22	11	6	8	44	25	28
4.	Portadown FC (Portadown)	22	10	6	6	29	17	26
5.	Crusaders FC (Belfast)	22	11	3	8	35	26	25
6.	Cliftonville FC (Belfast)	22	10	4	8	30	24	24
7.	Ards FC (Newtownards)	22	9	4	9	40	41	22
8.	Ballymena United FC (Ballymena)	22	8	4	10	32	41	20
9.	Distillery FC (Lisburn)	22	7	4	11	23	46	18
10.	Glenavon FC (Lurgan)	22	6	4	12	26	37	16
11.	Larne FC (Larne)	22	6	3	13	31	40	15
12.	Bangor FC (Bangor)	22	1	3	18	17	68	5
		264	108	48	108	399	399	264

Top goalscorer 1982-83
1) James CAMPBELL   (Ards FC)   15

Elected: Carrick Rangers FC (Carrickfergus), Newry Town FC (Newry)

The league was extended to 14 clubs for next season

IRISH CUP FINAL   (Windsor Park, Belfast – 30/04/1983 – 10,000)
GLENTORAN FC (BELFAST)   1-1   Linfield FC (Belfast)
Mullan   *McKeown pen.*

Glentoran: Patterson, G. Neill, Keeley, Harrison, Connell, Cleary, Jameson, Bowers (Morrison 80'), Manley, Mullan, D. Neill.

Linfield: Dunlop, Hayes, Crawford, Gibson, McKeown, Walsh (Garrett 84'), McKee, Dornan, Doherty, McGaughey, Anderson.

IRISH CUP FINAL REPLAY   (The Oval, Belfast – 07/05/1983 – 8,000)
GLENTORAN FC (BELFAST)   2-1   Linfield FC (Belfast)
Jameson 2   *McGaughey*

Linfield: Dunlop, Hayes, Crawford, Walsh, Gibson, McKeown, McKee, Doherty (Anderson 58'), McGaughey, Dornan, Murray.

Glentoran: Patterson, G. Neill, Connell, Keeley (Morrison 68'), Harrison, Cleary, Jameson, Strain, Manley, Mullan, D. Neill.

Semi-finals
Ards FC (Newtownards)	1-2	Linfield FC (Belfast)
Glentoran FC (Belfast)	3-0	Ballyclare Comrades FC (Ballyclare)

Quarter-finals
Ards FC (Newtownards)	2-1	Larne FC (Larne)
Ballyclare Comrades FC (Ballyclare)	1-1, 1-0	Cliftonville FC (Belfast)
Coleraine FC (Coleraine)	2-3	Glentoran FC (Belfast)
Linfield FC (Belfast)	3-1	Royal Ulster Constabulary FC (Belfast)

1983-84

Irish League 1983-84 Season	Ards	Ballymena U.	Bangor	Carrick R.	Cliftonville	Coleraine	Crusaders	Distillery	Glenavon	Glentoran	Larne	Linfield	Newry Town	Portadown
Ards FC	■	3-0	1-0	2-1	0-0	0-0	1-1	1-0	0-3	0-0	2-0	0-2	2-0	0-0
Ballymena United FC	2-0	■	1-1	2-2	0-0	1-2	2-1	0-2	2-2	1-4	2-1	1-2	2-0	2-1
Bangor FC	2-2	1-2	■	4-1	1-2	0-1	1-0	0-2	0-5	1-3	1-0	1-4	1-2	2-1
Carrick Rangers FC	0-1	1-0	1-1	■	1-2	0-3	2-3	1-2	3-0	0-2	0-3	0-3	2-2	1-3
Cliftonville FC	1-1	0-3	1-0	1-0	■	0-0	0-1	1-0	2-0	0-1	0-3	0-1	3-1	0-1
Coleraine FC	5-3	0-0	3-1	0-3	2-2	■	1-2	4-1	1-1	0-1	4-0	1-2	4-1	0-0
Crusaders FC	0-0	2-1	3-3	1-0	1-4	3-1	■	2-3	1-1	2-3	3-1	3-1	1-2	1-0
Distillery FC	2-1	0-1	0-0	3-2	0-2	2-1	2-0	■	1-4	0-4	3-0	2-7	2-1	2-2
Glenavon FC	2-1	1-3	1-1	2-1	0-0	3-1	2-3	1-1	■	1-3	1-0	0-1	0-1	3-1
Glentoran FC	3-3	0-0	6-0	6-1	1-2	1-0	1-0	1-1	1-1	■	2-2	4-1	5-0	2-0
Larne FC	1-1	0-1	3-1	2-0	2-0	1-4	2-1	0-2	0-3	0-2	■	1-2	2-1	0-1
Linfield FC	1-1	1-0	4-1	3-1	0-1	6-1	6-1	3-1	2-1	3-0	8-0	■	3-0	3-0
Newry Town FC	0-4	2-2	2-0	4-0	2-3	0-3	1-1	2-1	1-2	0-1	2-0	1-3	■	0-1
Portadown FC	0-2	1-1	5-0	2-0	1-1	0-2	0-1	1-0	2-1	0-0	4-1	1-4	0-2	■

	Irish League	Pd	Wn	Dw	Ls	GF	GA	Pts	
1.	LINFIELD FC (BELFAST)	26	22	1	3	76	23	45	
2.	Glentoran FC (Belfast)	26	18	6	2	65	19	42	
3.	Cliftonville FC (Belfast)	26	12	7	7	28	23	31	
4.	Ards FC (Newtownards)	26	9	11	6	32	26	29	
5.	Coleraine FC (Coleraine)	26	11	6	9	44	34	28	
6.	Ballymena United FC (Ballymena)	26	10	8	8	32	30	28	
7.	Glenavon FC (Lurgan)	26	10	7	9	41	33	27	
8.	Crusaders FC (Belfast)	26	11	5	10	38	41	27	
9.	Distillery FC (Lisburn)	26	11	4	11	35	42	26	
10.	Portadown FC (Portadown)	26	9	6	11	28	31	24	
11.	Newry Town FC (Newry)	26	8	3	15	30	48	19	
12.	Bangor FC (Bangor)	26	4	6	16	24	57	14	
13.	Larne FC (Larne)	26	7	1	18	25	58	13	-2
14.	Carrick Rangers FC (Carrickfergus)	26	3	3	20	24	57	9	
		364	145	74	145	522	522	362	

Note: Larne FC (Larne) had 2 points deducted for fielding an ineligible player against Bangor FC (Bangor).

Top goalscorers 1983-84

1) Trevor ANDERSON (Linfield FC) 15
   Martin McGAUGHEY (Linfield FC) 15

No clubs promoted or relegated

IRISH CUP FINAL   (Windsor Park, Belfast – 05/05/1984 – 5,000)

BALLYMENA UNITED FC (BALLYMENA)   4-1   Carrick Rangers FC (Carrickfergus)

Fox, Crockard, Harrison pen., Speak   *Fellows*

Ballymena: Platt, McCreery, Fox, Harrison, Crockard, Burns, Sloan, Ring, Speak, Guy, Wright.

Carrick: Coburn (Rodgers), Fraser, M. Smyth, Blair, McCullough, Bowyer, Conville, Fellows, Hardy, Thompson, Richardson.

Semi-finals

Ballymena United FC (Ballymena)	2-1	Cliftonville FC (Belfast)
Carrick Rangers FC (Carrickfergus)	2-1	Glentoran FC (Belfast)

Quarter-finals

Ballymena United FC (Ballymena)	2-1	Linfield FC (Belfast)
Cliftonville FC (Belfast)	2-0	P.O.S.C. Belfast (Belfast)
Glentoran FC (Belfast)	1-0	Glenavon FC (Lurgan)
Newry Town FC (Newry)	0-1	Carrick Rangers FC (Carrickfergus)

1984-85

Irish League 1984-85 Season	Ards	Ballymena U.	Bangor	Carrick R.	Cliftonville	Coleraine	Crusaders	Distillery	Glenavon	Glentoran	Larne	Linfield	Newry Town	Portadown
Ards FC	■	1-2	1-0	4-0	0-1	1-2	1-1	0-0	1-3	3-1	2-1	0-0	1-0	4-1
Ballymena United FC	1-3	■	1-3	1-1	2-0	2-2	0-0	3-0	3-1	1-3	3-2	0-3	2-2	2-0
Bangor FC	1-3	1-0	■	2-0	0-3	2-6	1-1	0-0	1-3	0-1	0-2	2-2	2-2	1-1
Carrick Rangers FC	3-2	2-2	1-1	■	1-2	0-2	2-2	1-3	1-3	0-2	2-0	1-4	0-2	2-1
Cliftonville FC	1-0	0-2	0-1	3-3	■	2-2	0-0	1-2	2-1	1-1	1-3	0-4	1-1	2-3
Coleraine FC	1-1	3-0	2-0	3-1	1-2	■	3-0	3-2	1-3	2-2	3-1	0-1	1-1	2-1
Crusaders FC	3-1	0-3	1-1	0-0	3-2	0-5	■	1-0	3-1	1-1	1-4	0-0	1-2	5-0
Distillery FC	2-1	2-1	0-2	3-1	0-0	2-2	3-2	■	3-2	0-2	1-1	1-1	7-2	1-3
Glenavon FC	1-1	2-2	2-1	4-0	1-1	1-2	1-1	3-1	■	0-4	1-0	0-7	0-3	1-2
Glentoran FC	2-0	1-0	1-1	3-0	2-3	2-1	1-3	0-0	5-0	■	6-0	2-3	3-0	1-1
Larne FC	3-0	0-3	2-0	2-1	1-4	0-1	1-2	0-0	5-2	1-2	■	1-4	2-1	1-0
Linfield FC	5-0	0-0	2-0	6-1	1-3	1-2	0-2	5-1	3-4	3-1	3-1	■	2-0	1-0
Newry Town FC	4-1	3-1	1-1	3-0	1-2	3-3	0-1	3-1	0-4	1-4	2-3	0-6	■	1-2
Portadown FC	1-0	1-0	1-0	2-0	0-0	0-0	3-0	1-0	0-1	1-0	2-0	0-3	6-1	■

	Irish League	Pd	Wn	Dw	Ls	GF	GA	Pts
1.	LINFIELD FC (BELFAST)	26	17	5	4	70	22	39
2.	Coleraine FC (Coleraine)	26	14	8	4	56	31	36
3.	Glentoran FC (Belfast)	26	14	6	6	53	26	34
4.	Portadown FC (Portadown)	26	13	4	9	33	29	30
5.	Cliftonville FC (Belfast)	26	10	8	8	37	36	28
6.	Crusaders FC (Belfast)	26	9	10	7	34	37	28
7.	Glenavon FC (Lurgan)	26	11	4	11	45	53	26
8.	Ballymena United FC (Ballymena)	26	9	7	10	37	36	25
9.	Distillery FC (Lisburn)	26	8	8	10	35	41	24
10.	Larne FC (Larne)	26	10	2	14	37	47	22
11.	Ards FC (Newtownards)	26	8	5	13	32	40	21
12.	Newry Town FC (Newry)	26	7	6	13	39	57	20
13.	Bangor FC (Bangor)	26	5	9	12	24	39	19
14.	Carrick Rangers FC (Carrickfergus)	26	3	6	17	24	62	12
		364	138	88	138	556	556	364

Top goalscorer 1984-85

1) Martin McGAUGHEY   (Linfield FC)   34

No clubs promoted or relegated

IRISH CUP FINAL   (Windsor Park, Belfast – 04/05/1985 – 12,000)

GLENTORAN FC (BELFAST)   1-1   Linfield FC (Belfast)
Mullan   *McKeown*

Glentoran: Paterson, Neill, Leeman, Morrison, Dixon, Cleary, Stewart, Bowers, Blackledge, Mullan, Caskey.

Linfield: Dunlop, Mooney, Crawford, Dornan, Gibson, Jeffrey, McKee, Doherty, McClurg, McKeown, Anderson (Murray).

IRISH CUP FINAL REPLAY   (Windsor Park, Belfast – 11/05/1985 – 12,000)

GLENTORAN FC (BELFAST)   1-1, 1-0   Linfield FC (Belfast)
Mooney o.g.

Linfield: Dunlop, Mooney, Crawford, Gibson, Jeffrey, Dornan (Murray), McKee, Doherty, McKeown, McClurg, Anderson.

Glentoran: Paterson, Neill, Leeman, Morrison, Dixon, Cleary, Stewart, Bowers, Blackledge (Jameson), Mullan, Caskey.

Semi-finals

| Ballymena United FC (Ballymena) | 0-3 | Linfield FC (Belfast) |
| Coleraine FC (Coleraine) | 1-2 | Glentoran FC (Belfast) |

Quarter-finals

Ards FC (Newtownards)	0-1	Ballymena United FC (Ballymena)
Distillery FC (Lisburn)	0-3	Glentoran FC (Belfast)
Glenavon FC (Lurgan)	0-4	Coleraine FC (Coleraine)
Portadown FC (Portadown)	1-2	Linfield FC (Belfast)

1985-86

Irish League 1985-86 Season	Ards	Ballymena U.	Bangor	Carrick R.	Cliftonville	Coleraine	Crusaders	Distillery	Glenavon	Glentoran	Larne	Linfield	Newry Town	Portadown
Ards FC		1-0	2-1	4-1	4-0	1-0	1-3	4-0	2-0	0-0	1-1	2-1	0-1	3-0
Ballymena United FC	1-0		2-1	7-1	4-2	1-2	0-0	3-1	3-3	0-1	0-2	1-1	3-1	0-1
Bangor FC	1-1	0-2		2-0	1-0	2-1	0-1	2-2	1-1	0-3	2-0	0-0	1-1	0-1
Carrick Rangers FC	0-3	0-4	1-1		0-1	0-2	0-1	0-0	0-4	0-2	2-2	0-4	3-1	0-1
Cliftonville FC	0-0	1-0	4-3	0-0		2-1	2-1	1-1	1-1	1-1	3-1	0-1	4-0	0-0
Coleraine FC	1-1	2-1	3-1	2-0	3-1		4-3	0-3	2-2	1-5	7-1	0-2	4-1	4-0
Crusaders FC	2-1	0-0	2-0	1-0	2-1	2-1		4-1	1-1	4-2	2-2	1-3	3-0	2-1
Distillery FC	0-2	1-1	2-1	1-1	1-2	1-1	2-1		4-2	0-1	0-6	0-4	2-1	0-3
Glenavon FC	0-0	0-2	2-1	1-1	1-1	0-1	1-2	0-2		1-0	1-1	0-3	2-2	2-0
Glentoran FC	2-1	2-0	1-4	2-0	3-2	0-2	1-0	1-2	0-1		1-0	2-3	4-0	1-0
Larne FC	2-1	0-0	5-0	5-0	1-1	0-2	3-1	0-1	3-0	0-0		1-1	3-0	1-2
Linfield FC	0-2	5-1	2-1	5-0	2-0	0-1	3-0	5-0	1-0	2-1	3-1		2-1	2-0
Newry Town FC	0-0	1-6	5-1	0-1	0-0	1-2	2-2	3-2	2-0	0-5	2-6	1-3		1-0
Portadown FC	2-0	1-1	1-4	2-1	2-1	0-2	2-1	0-1	0-0	2-1	1-2	0-1	0-1	

	Irish League	**Pd**	**Wn**	**Dw**	**Ls**	**GF**	**GA**	**Pts**
1.	LINFIELD FC (BELFAST)	26	20	3	3	59	16	43
2.	Coleraine FC (Coleraine)	26	16	3	7	51	31	35
3.	Ards FC (Newtownards)	26	12	7	7	37	19	31
4.	Glentoran FC (Belfast)	26	14	3	9	42	26	31
5.	Crusaders FC (Belfast)	26	13	5	8	42	34	31
6.	Larne FC (Larne)	26	10	8	8	49	34	28
7.	Ballymena United FC (Ballymena)	26	10	7	9	43	30	27
8.	Cliftonville FC (Belfast)	26	8	9	9	31	34	25
9.	Distillery FC (Lisburn)	26	9	6	11	30	49	24
10.	Portadown FC (Portadown)	26	10	3	13	22	32	23
11.	Glenavon FC (Lurgan)	26	5	11	10	26	36	21
12.	Bangor FC (Bangor)	26	6	6	14	31	45	18
13.	Newry Town FC (Newry)	26	6	5	15	28	59	17
14.	Carrick Rangers FC (Carrickfergus)	26	2	6	18	12	58	10
		364	141	82	141	503	503	364

Top goalscorer 1985-86

1) Trevor ANDERSON   (Linfield FC)   14

No clubs promoted or relegated

IRISH CUP FINAL   (Windsor Park, Belfast – 03/05/1986 – 8,000)

GLENTORAN FC (BELFAST)   2-1   Coleraine FC (Coleraine)

Mullan, Millar   *Healy pen.*

Glentoran: Paterson, Neill, Leeman, Connell, More, Cleary, Jameson, Morrison, Manley (Millar 78'), Mullan, Stewart.

Coleraine: Platt, McDowell, Edgar, McIlhinney, Tabb, Wade (Henry 34'), Healey, McQuiston, Campbell, McCreadie, McCoy.

Semi-finals

Coleraine FC (Coleraine)	2-0	Ards FC (Newtownards)
Glentoran FC (Belfast)	3-0	Brantwood FC (Belfast)

Quarter-finals

Brantwood FC (Belfast)	1-0	Portadown FC (Portadown)
Chimney Corner FC (Antrim)	0-4	Coleraine FC (Coleraine)
Carrick Rangers FC (Carrickfergus)	0-1	Ards FC (Newtownards)
Glentoran FC (Belfast)	1-0	Cliftonville FC (Belfast)

1986-87

Irish League 1986-87 Season	Ards	Ballymena U.	Bangor	Carrick R.	Cliftonville	Coleraine	Crusaders	Distillery	Glenavon	Glentoran	Larne	Linfield	Newry Town	Portadown
Ards FC	■	1-1	0-1	4-4	0-0	1-2	3-0	1-0	1-0	1-1	0-5	2-1	4-3	3-1
Ballymena United FC	2-1	■	4-3	3-0	1-1	2-1	2-3	2-0	1-1	2-0	1-1	0-0	1-2	0-0
Bangor FC	0-4	0-1	■	2-0	1-1	0-3	3-2	4-1	1-0	0-2	0-3	0-1	2-2	3-2
Carrick Rangers FC	0-5	3-2	2-1	■	1-0	2-2	2-4	1-0	1-4	0-1	0-2	0-3	2-5	0-0
Cliftonville FC	0-1	3-1	1-2	2-2	■	0-1	2-1	1-0	3-1	2-2	1-1	0-1	4-0	1-1
Coleraine FC	1-3	2-2	5-1	4-2	4-1	■	6-0	4-1	1-1	1-2	1-0	2-0	5-0	1-1
Crusaders FC	1-3	3-3	1-0	1-0	3-2	1-5	■	2-2	2-2	3-1	1-1	1-0	1-3	1-2
Distillery FC	0-2	3-1	3-1	0-1	1-4	2-8	1-3	■	1-3	1-2	1-2	0-5	0-6	1-2
Glenavon FC	1-0	1-2	2-0	2-0	0-0	0-1	1-0	3-1	■	1-1	1-1	1-2	1-3	4-0
Glentoran FC	2-3	7-2	4-1	2-0	2-2	0-1	3-0	5-0	1-1	■	3-0	3-1	2-0	4-0
Larne FC	1-2	1-2	2-0	1-1	1-0	2-0	1-0	0-0	0-0	4-0	■	1-1	3-0	2-0
Linfield FC	2-0	3-0	4-0	2-1	1-0	2-1	3-1	6-0	1-0	1-0	5-0	■	0-1	2-0
Newry Town FC	0-0	1-5	2-0	1-0	0-1	0-0	2-1	4-1	2-1	1-1	2-1	0-2	■	1-1
Portadown FC	2-2	1-2	0-2	0-2	0-2	0-3	1-1	1-1	1-0	2-3	2-2	1-1	1-1	■

	Irish League	Pd	Wn	Dw	Ls	GF	GA	Pts	
1.	LINFIELD FC (BELFAST)	26	18	3	5	50	15	57	
2.	Coleraine FC (Coleraine)	26	16	5	5	65	26	53	
3.	Ards FC (Newtownards)	26	14	6	6	47	31	48	
4.	Larne FC (Larne)	26	11	9	6	38	24	42	
5.	Newry Town FC (Newry)	26	12	6	8	42	40	42	
6.	Ballymena United FC (Ballymena)	26	11	8	7	45	42	41	
7.	Glentoran FC (Belfast)	26	14	6	6	54	30	40	-8
8.	Cliftonville FC (Belfast)	26	8	9	9	34	29	33	
9.	Glenavon FC (Lurgan)	26	8	8	10	32	27	32	
10.	Bangor FC (Bangor)	26	8	2	16	28	52	26	
11.	Crusaders FC (Belfast)	26	8	5	13	37	54	25	-4
12.	Carrick Rangers FC (Carrickfergus)	26	6	5	13	27	53	23	
13.	Portadown FC (Portadown)	26	3	11	12	22	45	20	
14.	Distillery FC (Lisburn)	26	2	3	21	21	74	9	
		364	139	86	139	542	542	491	

From this season onwards a Win was worth 3 points, a Draw was worth 1 point and a Loss was worth 0 points.

Note: Glentoran FC (Belfast) had 8 points deducted and Crusaders FC (Belfast) had 4 points deducted, both for fielding ineligible players in league matches.

Top goalscorers 1986-87

1)	Gary McCARTNEY	(Glentoran FC)	14
	Ray McCOY	(Coleraine FC)	14
3)	BAXTER	(Ards FC)	12
	Martin McGAUGHEY	(Linfield FC)	12
	O'BOYLE	(Linfield FC)	12

No clubs promoted or relegated

IRISH CUP FINAL   (Windsor Park, Belfast – 02/05/1987 – 8,000)

GLENTORAN FC (BELFAST)　　　　　　1-0　　　　　　　　　　Larne FC (Larne)

Mullan

Glentoran: Paterson, J. Smyth, Stewart, Bowers, Harrison, Cleary, Jameson (Craig 83'), Caskey, Mullan, McCartney, Morrison.

Larne: Magee, McMullan, Huston, Garland, Spiers, Bustard (Campbell 79'), McLoughlin, D. Smyth (Dickey 60'), Guy, Hardy, Sloan.

Semi-finals

Coleraine FC (Coleraine)	1-2	Larne FC (Larne)
Glentoran FC (Belfast)	1-1, 2-1	Newry Town FC (Newry)

Semi-finals

Ards FC (Newtownards)	1-2	Larne FC (Larne)
Bangor FC (Bangor)	1-6	Coleraine FC (Coleraine)
Glentoran FC (Belfast)	3-2	Glenavon FC (Lurgan)
Newry Town FC (Newry)	0-0, 2-0	Cliftonville FC (Belfast)

1987-88

Irish League 1987-88 Season	Ards	Ballymena U.	Bangor	Carrick R.	Cliftonville	Coleraine	Crusaders	Distillery	Glenavon	Glentoran	Larne	Linfield	Newry Town	Portadown
Ards FC	■	0-1	1-1	1-2	1-0	1-1	1-2	1-1	1-1	0-2	2-3	1-2	0-1	2-0
Ballymena United FC	1-1	■	1-0	1-0	1-1	2-1	0-0	2-1	1-1	3-2	0-1	1-4	3-4	2-1
Bangor FC	2-4	1-1	■	2-1	1-3	0-4	1-1	1-6	3-0	0-1	0-2	0-4	1-0	0-0
Carrick Rangers FC	2-1	1-2	0-2	■	0-2	0-3	1-2	2-0	0-0	0-2	2-2	1-0	1-1	0-1
Cliftonville FC	0-0	1-1	1-2	0-2	■	0-2	0-0	2-0	2-3	1-1	0-2	0-5	1-1	1-0
Coleraine FC	4-2	5-5	2-1	3-1	3-0	■	1-1	3-1	1-0	1-2	3-0	1-2	1-3	1-0
Crusaders FC	3-0	0-0	4-1	2-1	2-0	0-1	■	3-0	1-2	2-3	1-4	1-3	0-3	1-2
Distillery FC	1-3	0-5	0-1	1-1	1-2	1-2	2-0	■	0-1	0-3	2-1	0-1	0-2	1-2
Glenavon FC	0-1	1-0	1-0	3-2	4-0	3-2	1-0	4-0	■	1-2	0-1	0-3	0-0	1-2
Glentoran FC	2-2	3-0	3-0	1-1	1-1	2-2	1-0	1-0	1-0	■	4-0	0-1	1-0	1-0
Larne FC	2-0	1-0	1-2	3-1	0-0	0-4	1-2	2-1	1-0	0-3	■	1-2	5-1	0-0
Linfield FC	1-0	3-1	3-1	1-0	4-0	0-1	1-1	2-0	3-0	0-2	3-0	■	1-0	1-1
Newry Town FC	1-0	1-0	1-0	3-1	1-0	1-0	3-0	3-0	0-0	0-2	0-0	1-0	■	3-2
Portadown FC	2-3	0-0	3-1	4-2	0-1	0-1	2-0	3-0	0-1	0-2	2-1	1-1	3-0	■

	Irish League	Pd	Wn	Dw	Ls	GF	GA	Pts
1.	GLENTORAN FC (BELFAST)	26	19	5	2	48	15	62
2.	Linfield FC (Belfast)	26	19	3	4	51	15	60
3.	Coleraine FC (Coleraine)	26	16	4	6	53	28	52
4.	Newry Town FC (Newry)	26	15	5	6	34	22	50
5.	Larne FC (Larne)	26	12	4	10	35	35	40
6.	Glenavon FC (Lurgan)	26	11	5	10	28	27	38
7.	Ballymena United FC (Ballymena)	26	9	9	8	34	34	36
8.	Portadown FC (Portadown)	26	10	5	11	31	27	35
9.	Crusaders FC (Belfast)	26	8	6	12	29	35	30
10.	Cliftonville FC (Belfast)	26	6	8	12	18	38	26
11.	Ards FC (Newtownards)	26	6	7	13	29	38	25
12.	Bangor FC (Bangor)	26	7	4	15	24	47	25
13.	Carrick Rangers FC (Carrickfergus)	26	5	5	16	25	44	20
14.	Distillery FC (Lisburn)	26	3	2	21	19	53	11
		364	146	72	146	458	458	510

On 16/01/1988 the Crusaders FC 1-3 Carrick Rangers FC and Linfield FC 2-1 Glentoran FC matches were both abandoned and replayed at later dates with the results as shown in the above results chart.

Top goalscorers 1987-88

1)	Martin McGAUGHEY	(Linfield FC)	18
2)	David HANNA	(Portadown FC)	10
	Raymond MORRISON	(Glentoran FC)	10
4)	Duncan MacLEOD	(Linfield FC)	9
	Ray McCOY	(Coleraine FC)	9
	Ron MANLEY	(Glentoran FC)	9
	Ricky WADE	(Coleraine FC)	9

No clubs promoted or relegated

IRISH CUP FINAL   (Windsor Park, Belfast – 30/04/1988)

GLENTORAN FC (BELFAST)   1-0   Glenavon FC (Lurgan)

Cleary 89' pen.

Glentoran: Smyth, Neill, Stewart, Devine, Moore (Mathieson 75'), Cleary, Morrison, Caskey, McCartney, Mullan (Manley 56'), Jameson.

Glenavon: Beck, McKeown, Russell, Dennison, Byrne, D. Lowry, Denver, McLoughlin, McGroarty, McBride, McCann.

Semi-finals

Glenavon FC (Lurgan)	2-0	Ballymena United FC (Ballymena)
Glentoran FC (Belfast)	3-2	Portadown FC (Portadown)

Semi-finals

Ballymena United FC (Ballymena)	0-0, 3-0	Distillery FC (Lisburn)
Glenavon FC (Lurgan)	2-1	Ards FC (Newtownards)
Glentoran FC (Belfast)	5-0	Newry Town FC (Newry)
Linfield FC (Belfast)	1-1, 0-2	Portadown FC (Portadown)

1988-89

Irish League 1988-89 Season	Ards	Ballymena U.	Bangor	Carrick R.	Cliftonville	Coleraine	Crusaders	Distillery	Glenavon	Glentoran	Larne	Linfield	Newry Town	Portadown
Ards FC	■	0-0	2-3	0-1	0-4	0-2	2-0	1-1	1-5	1-5	3-1	1-3	4-3	0-0
Ballymena United FC	3-2	■	2-1	1-2	3-3	2-0	1-1	3-0	0-3	1-2	0-0	0-4	2-2	3-1
Bangor FC	2-1	1-1	■	1-1	3-1	3-4	1-0	2-0	1-1	2-1	1-1	1-1	2-0	1-1
Carrick Rangers FC	1-0	0-0	2-3	■	2-1	0-1	0-2	1-0	1-3	0-3	3-1	1-3	1-0	1-2
Cliftonville FC	2-2	4-1	0-1	5-1	■	1-1	1-0	4-0	0-1	0-0	0-0	0-3	1-2	1-1
Coleraine FC	1-1	4-1	2-1	0-1	0-0	■	3-1	2-0	0-1	2-3	2-0	0-2	3-2	2-0
Crusaders FC	0-1	0-0	0-3	0-3	1-2	0-3	■	2-1	1-0	0-3	1-1	1-2	3-1	1-3
Distillery FC	2-0	2-2	1-2	0-2	0-4	0-3	2-2	■	2-1	1-3	1-6	1-5	1-2	0-2
Glenavon FC	3-0	2-1	3-2	2-1	3-2	1-2	3-3	3-2	■	2-3	2-2	0-1	0-0	0-2
Glentoran FC	1-0	3-2	2-1	4-0	2-2	1-1	3-0	8-2	2-3	■	3-1	2-3	2-0	0-1
Larne FC	1-1	1-1	1-1	1-2	0-0	0-2	4-0	7-0	1-3	0-1	■	3-2	1-2	1-0
Linfield FC	2-1	1-0	0-1	4-1	2-0	2-0	3-0	3-0	2-1	1-2	2-2	■	1-0	2-1
Newry Town FC	6-1	2-3	1-1	2-0	1-3	0-2	0-3	3-0	1-0	1-1	1-2	0-3	■	1-1
Portadown FC	2-0	0-0	1-1	1-1	0-1	0-0	1-0	0-1	1-1	2-0	4-0	0-1	2-0	■

	Irish League	Pd	Wn	Dw	Ls	GF	GA	Pts
1.	LINFIELD FC (BELFAST)	26	21	2	3	58	19	65
2.	Glentoran FC (Belfast)	26	17	4	5	60	29	55
3.	Coleraine FC (Coleraine)	26	15	5	6	42	23	50
4.	Bangor FC (Bangor)	26	12	9	5	42	30	45
5.	Glenavon FC (Lurgan)	26	13	5	8	47	34	44
6.	Portadown FC (Portadown)	26	10	9	7	29	19	39
7.	Cliftonville FC (Belfast)	26	9	9	8	42	30	36
8.	Carrick Rangers FC (Carrickfergus)	26	11	3	12	29	40	36
9.	Ballymena United FC (Ballymena)	26	6	11	9	33	41	29
10.	Larne FC (Larne)	26	6	10	10	38	38	28
11.	Newry Town FC (Newry)	26	7	5	14	33	43	26
12.	Crusaders FC (Belfast)	26	5	5	16	22	47	20
13.	Ards FC (Newtownards)	26	4	6	16	25	54	18
14.	Distillery FC (Lisburn)	26	3	3	20	20	73	12
		364	139	86	139	520	520	503

Top goalscorers 1988-89

1) Stephen BAXTER (Linfield FC) 17
2) Gary McCARTNEY (Glentoran FC) 16
3) Martin MAGEE (Portadown FC) 15

No clubs promoted or relegated

IRISH CUP FINAL   (The Oval, Belfast – 06/05/1989 – 5,000)

BALLYMENA UNITED FC (BALLYMENA)   1-0   Larne FC (Larne)
Hardy 73'

Ballymena: Grant, Scott, M. Smyth, Garrett, Heron, Young, McKee, Curry, Pyper, Hardy, Doherty (Simpson 64').
Larne: Magee, McMullan, Huston, Garland, Spiers, Bustard, Murphy, Kernoghan, F. Smith (McDonald 49'), Sloan, D. Smyth (Hannan 76').

Semi-finals

Cliftonville FC (Belfast)   1-1, 1-2   Larne FC (Larne)
Linfield FC (Belfast)   1-1, 1-2   Ballymena United FC (Ballymena)

Quarter-finals

Cliftonville FC (Belfast)   0-0, 2-1   Tobermore United FC (Tobermore)
Crusaders FC (Belfast)   2-3   Ballymena United FC (Ballymena)
Glentoran FC (Belfast)   0-3   Linfield FC (Belfast)
Larne FC (Larne)   0-0, 3-2   Carrick Rangers FC (Carrickfergus)

1989-90

Irish League 1989-90 Season	Ards	Ballymena U.	Bangor	Carrick R.	Cliftonville	Coleraine	Crusaders	Distillery	Glenavon	Glentoran	Larne	Linfield	Newry Town	Portadown
Ards FC	■	0-2	0-2	1-1	3-4	0-4	3-1	5-0	0-1	2-1	0-1	1-2	1-5	0-1
Ballymena United FC	0-0	■	1-0	3-1	1-2	1-1	0-0	2-1	3-1	1-1	0-0	5-1	1-3	2-3
Bangor FC	3-0	0-1	■	2-0	1-2	0-1	3-0	2-0	0-0	0-0	0-0	1-0	2-0	1-0
Carrick Rangers FC	2-0	0-1	1-1	■	3-1	4-0	2-0	2-2	2-2	1-1	4-3	0-3	2-0	1-1
Cliftonville FC	1-2	1-0	1-2	0-2	■	2-0	2-2	2-2	1-1	0-0	2-2	1-0	3-2	1-3
Coleraine FC	4-0	0-2	3-2	1-0	1-1	■	1-2	0-3	0-3	1-1	2-1	1-3	0-2	0-0
Crusaders FC	0-3	0-2	2-0	3-2	1-1	1-1	■	3-3	1-2	0-4	1-2	2-3	2-1	1-2
Distillery FC	2-1	1-1	0-0	1-0	0-3	2-4	2-2	■	0-5	0-3	2-2	0-7	1-1	0-2
Glenavon FC	0-0	2-1	0-1	1-0	2-2	2-1	1-1	6-0	■	2-1	4-1	3-1	2-1	2-0
Glentoran FC	0-0	1-0	1-3	2-0	1-0	5-3	6-0	2-0	2-3	■	2-1	3-2	1-0	2-3
Larne FC	1-0	1-2	3-0	0-2	1-0	2-1	2-2	1-0	0-2	0-0	■	1-4	0-2	2-0
Linfield FC	0-0	1-2	3-0	3-1	1-4	4-3	2-0	3-1	1-3	1-3	2-0	■	4-1	1-1
Newry Town FC	2-2	3-3	2-0	2-0	3-0	1-3	2-0	2-4	3-1	1-0	2-0	1-2	■	0-0
Portadown FC	4-1	1-0	1-0	2-0	3-0	0-0	3-0	2-0	3-1	0-0	2-2	2-0	3-0	■

	Irish League	Pd	Wn	Dw	Ls	GF	GA	Pts
1.	PORTADOWN FC (PORTADOWN)	26	16	7	3	42	17	55
2.	Glenavon FC (Lurgan)	26	16	6	4	52	26	54
3.	Glentoran FC (Belfast)	26	12	8	6	43	24	44
4.	Linfield FC (Belfast)	26	14	2	10	54	40	44
5.	Ballymena United FC (Ballymena)	26	12	7	7	37	25	43
6.	Bangor FC (Bangor)	26	11	5	10	26	22	38
7.	Newry Town FC (Newry)	26	11	4	11	42	37	37
8.	Cliftonville FC (Belfast)	26	9	8	9	37	39	35
9.	Larne FC (Larne)	26	8	7	11	29	38	31
10.	Carrick Rangers FC (Carrickfergus)	26	8	6	12	33	36	30
11.	Coleraine FC (Coleraine)	26	8	6	12	36	44	30
12.	Ards FC (Newtownards)	26	5	6	15	25	44	21
13.	Crusaders FC (Belfast)	26	4	8	14	27	55	20
14.	Distillery FC (Lisburn)	26	4	8	14	27	63	20
		364	138	88	138	510	510	502

Top goalscorers 1989-90

1)	Martin McGAUGHEY	(Linfield FC)	19
2)	Gary McCARTNEY	(Glentoran FC)	17
3)	Oliver RALPH	(Newry Town FC)	14
4)	Gary BLACKLEDGE	(Glenavon FC)	12
	Stephen McBRIDE	(Glenavon FC)	12

Elected: Ballyclare Comrades FC (Ballyclare), Omagh Town FC (Omagh)

The league was extended to 16 clubs for next season

IRISH CUP FINAL (Windsor Park, Belfast – 05/05/1990 – 12,000)

GLENTORAN FC (BELFAST) 3-0 Portadown FC (Portadown)

Neill 60', Douglas 85', Morrison 87'

Glentoran: Smyth, Neill, Moore, Devine, Bowers, McCaffrey, Jameson, Caskey, Campbell (Morrison 49'), McCartney (Totten 46'), Douglas.

Portadown: Keenan, Major, Stewart, Strain, Curliss, Mills (Cunningham 65'), McKeever (Bell 65'), McCreadie, Davidson, Fraser, Cowan.

Semi-finals

Glentoran FC (Belfast)	2-0	Linfield FC (Belfast)
Portadown FC (Portadown)	4-0	Coleraine FC (Coleraine)

Quarter-finals

Banbridge Town FC (Banbridge)	0-1	Coleraine FC (Coleraine)
Larne FC (Larne)	1-2	Linfield FC (Belfast)
Newry Town FC (Newry)	2-3	Glentoran FC (Belfast)
Portadown FC (Portadown)	2-1	Bangor FC (Bangor)

1990-91

Irish League 1990-91 Season	Ards	Ballyclare C.	Ballymena U.	Bangor	Carrick R.	Cliftonville	Coleraine	Crusaders	Distillery	Glenavon	Glentoran	Larne	Linfield	Newry Town	Omagh Town	Portadown
Ards FC	■	4-3	0-0	0-2	2-0	1-1	1-0	0-0	2-1	1-2	2-3	4-1	1-1	1-2	5-1	1-2
Ballyclare Comrades FC	1-0	■	1-5	0-2	1-0	1-3	1-1	2-3	2-0	3-3	0-1	3-3	1-1	0-2	0-3	0-3
Ballymena United FC	4-1	1-1	■	3-0	2-1	1-1	4-0	1-0	1-2	4-3	2-3	4-4	2-2	2-1	2-0	0-2
Bangor FC	1-1	2-0	2-2	■	2-1	4-2	3-1	2-1	2-1	1-2	1-0	2-0	1-0	2-0	3-0	0-1
Carrick Rangers FC	2-5	1-2	2-1	1-3	■	1-3	1-0	2-2	0-2	1-2	2-3	1-1	1-2	0-0	0-3	1-4
Cliftonville FC	2-0	4-0	1-3	2-0	0-2	■	2-0	3-1	2-1	0-2	2-1	4-0	2-2	6-0	3-2	1-2
Coleraine FC	0-1	2-1	0-1	0-4	1-1	2-2	■	1-1	3-4	1-1	1-2	1-0	0-2	2-4	1-4	1-3
Crusaders FC	0-2	1-2	0-0	3-2	3-3	1-1	4-1	■	4-1	1-3	2-0	5-0	2-2	2-1	4-1	2-3
Distillery FC	2-2	4-1	2-0	1-3	2-1	2-2	2-0	1-3	■	3-2	2-3	1-3	2-1	1-3	0-1	0-0
Glenavon FC	1-2	4-0	3-1	2-3	2-0	1-2	5-3	2-2	2-1	■	1-1	2-0	2-1	1-1	3-0	2-1
Glentoran FC	1-1	2-1	2-0	0-1	2-1	3-2	4-0	2-0	3-1	2-0	■	1-0	1-0	2-2	4-1	1-1
Larne FC	0-2	1-1	1-2	0-1	1-0	4-1	2-0	2-2	0-4	0-4	0-1	■	0-1	4-1	3-3	1-3
Linfield FC	1-0	3-1	3-0	2-1	1-0	0-4	2-1	2-0	2-2	0-0	1-1	4-2	■	1-2	0-0	0-1
Newry Town FC	3-1	3-2	3-0	1-1	2-0	0-0	3-1	1-2	3-0	1-0	2-0	1-2	3-1	■	2-1	1-3
Omagh Town FC	2-4	2-1	1-1	0-0	3-4	2-1	2-1	0-1	5-1	2-5	3-1	0-5	0-1	2-1	■	2-5
Portadown FC	1-0	3-1	4-0	2-0	1-0	2-0	3-0	3-1	1-1	0-1	0-0	0-1	1-1	2-1	4-2	■

Irish League

		Pd	Wn	Dw	Ls	GF	GA	Pts
1.	PORTADOWN FC (PORTADOWN)	30	22	5	3	61	22	71
2.	Bangor FC (Bangor)	30	19	4	7	52	29	61
3.	Glentoran FC (Belfast)	30	18	6	6	50	32	60
4.	Glenavon FC (Lurgan)	30	17	6	7	63	38	57
5.	Newry Town FC (Newry)	30	15	5	10	50	42	50
6.	Cliftonville FC (Belfast)	30	14	7	9	59	41	49
7.	Linfield FC (Belfast)	30	12	10	8	40	34	46
8.	Ballymena United FC (Ballymena)	30	12	8	10	49	46	44
9.	Ards FC (Newtownards)	30	12	7	11	47	40	43
10.	Crusaders FC (Belfast)	30	11	9	10	53	46	42
11.	Distillery FC (Lisburn)	30	10	5	15	47	57	35
12.	Omagh Town FC (Omagh)	30	10	4	16	48	66	34
13.	Larne FC (Larne)	30	8	6	16	41	59	30
14.	Ballyclare Comrades FC (Ballyclare)	30	5	6	19	33	68	21
15.	Carrick Rangers FC (Carrickfergus)	30	4	5	21	30	58	17
16.	Coleraine FC (Coleraine)	30	2	5	23	25	70	11
		480	191	98	191	748	748	671

Note: Cliftonville FC 1-2 Portadown FC match was abandoned after 67 minutes due to crowd trouble but the result was allowed to stand and the points were awarded to Portadown FC.

Top goalscorers 1990-91

1)	Stephen McBRIDE	(Glenavon FC)	22
2)	William HAMILTON	(Distillery FC)	19
3)	Steven COWAN	(Portadown FC)	18
	Gary McCARTNEY	(Glentoran FC)	18
5)	Glenn HUNTER	(Crusaders FC)	17

No clubs promoted or relegated

IRISH CUP FINAL (Windsor Park, Belfast – 04/05/1991 – 15,000)

PORTADOWN FC (PORTADOWN)   2-1   Glenavon FC (Lurgan)
Cowan 06', 44'   *Ferguson 46'*

Portadown: Keenan, Major, Strain, Stewart, Curliss, Doolin, Rafferty, Cunningham, Davidson, Cowan, Fraser
Glenavon: Beck, McKeown, McCullough, Byrne, Scrappaticci, McDermott (Davies 69'), Conville, Russell (McCann 80'), McCoy, Ferguson, McBride.

Semi-finals

Ards FC (Newtownards)	1-2	Portadown FC (Portadown)
Glenavon FC (Lurgan)	3-1	Glentoran FC (Belfast)

Quarter-finals

Ards FC (Newtownards)	3-2	Linfield FC (Belfast)
Crusaders FC (Belfast)	2-4	Portadown FC (Portadown)
Glenavon FC (Lurgan)	4-0	Ballyclare Comrades FC (Ballyclare)
Larne FC (Larne)	1-1, 1-4	Glentoran FC (Belfast)

1991-92

Irish League 1991-92 Season	Ards	Ballyclare C.	Ballymena U.	Bangor	Carrick R.	Cliftonville	Coleraine	Crusaders	Distillery	Glenavon	Glentoran	Larne	Linfield	Newry Town	Omagh Town	Portadown
Ards FC	■	0-0	6-1	1-4	1-0	3-0	0-1	1-1	4-4	2-3	1-1	1-1	2-2	2-2	2-0	2-1
Ballyclare Comrades FC	2-1	■	2-5	1-5	2-2	1-1	4-3	2-1	2-1	1-8	0-2	0-5	0-0	6-1	2-2	1-0
Ballymena United FC	1-2	2-0	■	2-2	3-3	1-1	1-1	1-3	0-0	1-2	2-1	1-1	2-2	0-2	1-1	0-6
Bangor FC	1-4	2-2	2-0	■	3-0	0-0	0-2	1-1	4-2	1-0	1-2	0-4	0-2	5-1	1-3	0-2
Carrick Rangers FC	1-1	0-1	1-1	1-1	■	0-3	2-2	1-3	0-3	1-3	0-3	0-3	0-1	1-1	1-2	1-4
Cliftonville FC	0-0	1-2	0-0	2-0	2-0	■	1-1	2-2	0-1	1-2	0-0	1-1	0-1	1-0	1-2	0-0
Coleraine FC	1-4	1-0	0-1	3-0	0-2	2-0	■	0-2	2-0	2-2	1-4	0-0	1-3	0-1	1-1	0-2
Crusaders FC	2-1	2-0	1-2	0-1	6-0	5-1	5-1	■	0-1	3-1	2-3	2-1	0-2	2-0	3-3	0-2
Distillery FC	1-1	1-1	0-0	0-1	2-2	2-0	1-2	1-3	■	1-2	0-2	1-2	0-4	1-2	2-1	1-3
Glenavon FC	3-0	2-1	2-0	0-0	2-0	0-2	3-0	2-1	4-0	■	0-2	0-1	2-1	0-0	4-0	1-2
Glentoran FC	1-1	4-2	4-0	3-1	7-0	1-0	6-1	1-0	3-0	5-1	■	2-0	3-3	2-1	4-2	1-0
Larne FC	1-0	4-1	3-1	3-1	5-0	1-0	2-2	0-1	2-2	3-2	2-3	■	2-1	1-0	3-0	0-4
Linfield FC	5-2	0-0	1-0	5-1	4-0	1-0	2-0	0-1	3-2	1-1	0-0	0-0	■	3-0	2-1	1-2
Newry Town FC	1-2	2-1	1-4	4-3	0-3	1-5	2-2	1-0	2-1	0-2	1-0	0-1		■	0-2	0-1
Omagh Town FC	3-0	3-0	0-2	2-3	6-2	1-2	4-3	2-2	3-0	1-0	3-4	1-2	1-7	1-1	■	0-1
Portadown FC	2-3	3-0	0-2	0-1	3-0	3-0	2-0	3-1	1-0	3-0	1-2	3-1	0-0	3-0	2-1	■

	Irish League	Pd	Wn	Dw	Ls	GF	GA	Pts	
1.	GLENTORAN FC (BELFAST)	30	24	5	1	78	26	77	
2.	Portadown FC (Portadown)	30	21	2	7	59	19	65	
3.	Linfield FC (Belfast)	30	17	9	4	58	23	60	
4.	Larne FC (Larne)	30	16	7	7	54	31	55	
5.	Glenavon FC (Lurgan)	30	16	4	10	54	36	52	
6.	Crusaders FC (Belfast)	30	14	5	11	55	37	47	
7.	Ards FC (Newtownards)	30	10	11	9	50	46	41	
8.	Omagh Town FC (Omagh)	30	10	6	14	52	58	36	
9.	Bangor FC (Bangor)	30	11	6	13	45	52	36	-3
10.	Ballymena United FC (Ballymena)	30	8	11	11	37	50	35	
11.	Ballyclare Comrades FC (Ballyclare)	30	8	8	14	37	64	32	
12.	Cliftonville FC (Belfast)	30	7	10	13	27	34	31	
13.	Coleraine FC (Coleraine)	30	7	8	15	35	57	29	
14.	Newry Town FC (Newry)	30	8	5	17	28	57	29	
15.	Distillery FC (Lisburn)	30	5	7	18	31	56	22	
16.	Carrick Rangers FC (Carrickfergus)	30	2	8	20	24	78	14	
		480	184	112	184	724	724	661	

Note: Bangor FC (Bangor) had 3 points deducted as a result of irregularities in the signing of 19 year-old Paul Byrne from Oxford United FC (Oxford) in England.

Top goalscorers 1991-92

1) Stephen McBRIDE   (Glenavon FC)   18
   Harold McCOURT   (Omagh Town/Ards FC)   18   (15/3)

3)	Justin McBRIDE	(Glentoran FC)	15
4)	Stephen BARNES	(Larne FC)	14
	Robert CAMPBELL	(Ards FC)	14
	Steven COWAN	(Portadown FC)	14
	Martin McGAUGHEY	(Linfield FC)	14

No clubs promoted or relegated

IRISH CUP FINAL   (The Oval, Belfast – 02/05/1992 – 14,000)

GLENAVON FC (LURGAN)   2-1   Linfield FC (Belfast)
Ferris 42', McMahon 56'   *McHaughey 13'*

Glenavon: Beck, McCullough, Scrappaticci, Quigley, Byrne, Crawford, McConville, McCoy, McMahon, Ferris (Crowe), Kennedy.

Linfield: Patterson, Dornan, Easton, McConnell, Spiers, Beattie (Hunter), Curry, Doherty (Allen), McGaughey, Baxter, Baillie.

Semi-finals

| Glenavon FC (Lurgan) | 3-1 | Ballymena United FC (Ballymena) |
| Linfield FC (Belfast) | 2-0 | Crusaders FC (Belfast) |

Quarter-finals

Ballymena United FC (Ballymena)	4-0	Oxford United Stars FC
Glenavon FC (Lurgan)	3-0	Ards FC (Newtownards)
Linfield FC (Belfast)	1-0	Cliftonville FC (Belfast)
Portadown FC (Portadown)	0-1	Crusaders FC (Belfast)

1992-93

Irish League 1992-93 Season	Ards	Ballyclare C.	Ballymena U.	Bangor	Carrick R.	Cliftonville	Coleraine	Crusaders	Distillery	Glenavon	Glentoran	Larne	Linfield	Newry Town	Omagh Town	Portadown
Ards FC	■	1-1	0-0	1-4	2-0	1-0	3-1	2-0	1-1	1-2	0-3	0-0	0-2	1-0	2-2	2-2
Ballyclare Comrades FC	0-1	■	2-3	0-2	0-1	1-1	3-4	1-3	0-2	0-2	2-5	3-2	1-3	2-4	2-2	0-0
Ballymena United FC	3-4	2-2	■	0-1	2-1	0-1	1-1	1-0	4-1	0-5	2-8	2-1	1-2	3-2	0-1	0-2
Bangor FC	4-3	4-1	3-2	■	4-0	3-1	3-1	2-1	1-3	1-3	2-1	5-1	1-0	0-0	1-0	2-2
Carrick Rangers FC	3-2	4-1	3-3	2-4	■	1-2	3-0	0-3	1-5	3-1	1-1	3-1	0-4	0-2	3-1	1-6
Cliftonville FC	1-2	1-0	1-1	0-1	2-3	■	4-0	1-2	1-2	0-2	2-3	3-1	0-4	5-1	3-1	2-0
Coleraine FC	1-3	3-0	1-3	0-2	1-2	1-1	■	1-4	1-2	2-0	2-1	1-4	0-1	1-2	1-2	0-3
Crusaders FC	1-1	1-1	1-0	1-0	2-0	1-2	3-1	■	2-0	3-2	2-1	3-2	1-0	3-0	2-0	0-3
Distillery FC	2-1	4-0	1-0	3-2	3-2	2-1	2-0	0-2	■	1-2	0-3	2-1	1-0	5-0	2-0	3-0
Glenavon FC	0-0	2-1	0-2	1-1	4-1	2-0	0-1	0-2	2-1	■	2-2	1-0	1-2	4-0	3-2	0-3
Glentoran FC	1-1	5-0	1-4	0-2	1-2	3-0	2-2	1-2	1-1	0-0	■	4-0	1-2	6-1	3-0	3-2
Larne FC	1-3	3-1	1-0	0-1	4-1	2-0	1-0	0-1	1-4	1-3	2-4	■	0-0	4-2	4-2	0-1
Linfield FC	1-0	4-0	1-1	0-0	3-0	3-0	2-0	1-0	2-1	1-0	2-0	5-2	■	0-0	1-0	0-3
Newry Town FC	2-3	0-2	0-1	2-1	2-4	1-5	2-0	1-3	2-5	1-1	1-1	0-1	0-2	■	0-1	1-1
Omagh Town FC	1-4	2-1	2-0	0-4	1-3	2-1	2-0	1-2	1-2	3-2	0-4	1-1	1-1	4-0	■	2-2
Portadown FC	6-0	4-0	2-0	3-0	6-2	2-1	2-1	2-2	2-0	1-1	1-1	3-0	0-0	3-1	3-1	■

	Irish League	Pd	Wn	Dw	Ls	GF	GA	Pts
1.	LINFIELD FC (BELFAST)	30	20	6	4	49	15	66
2.	Crusaders FC (Belfast)	30	21	3	6	53	27	66
3.	Bangor FC (Bangor)	30	20	4	6	61	32	64
4.	Portadown FC (Portadown)	30	18	9	3	70	26	63
5.	Distillery FC (Lisburn)	30	20	2	8	61	36	62
6.	Glenavon FC (Lurgan)	30	14	6	10	48	36	48
7.	Glentoran FC (Belfast)	30	13	8	9	70	40	47
8.	Ards FC (Newtownards)	30	12	9	9	45	45	45
9.	Carrick Rangers FC (Carrickfergus)	30	12	2	16	50	73	38
10.	Ballymena United FC (Ballymena)	30	10	6	14	41	51	36
11.	Cliftonville FC (Belfast)	30	10	3	17	42	48	33
12.	Omagh Town FC (Omagh)	30	9	5	16	38	57	32
13.	Larne FC (Larne)	30	9	3	18	41	59	30
14.	Newry Town FC (Newry)	30	5	5	20	30	72	20
15.	Coleraine FC (Coleraine)	30	5	3	22	28	63	18
16.	Ballyclare Comrades FC (Ballyclare)	30	2	6	22	28	75	12
		480	200	80	200	756	756	680

Note: Ballyclare Comrades FC 3-4 Coleraine FC on 14/11/1992 was abandoned after 87 minutes due to a power failure but the result was allowed to stand.

Top goalscorers 1992-93

1)	Steven COWAN	(Portadown FC)	27
2)	David McCALLAN	(Bangor FC)	21
3)	Darren ERSKINE	(Ards FC)	20
4)	Tom CLELLAND	(Distillery FC)	16
	Liam COYLE	(Omagh Town FC)	16
	Sandy FRASER	(Portadown FC)	16
	Gary McCARTNEY	(Glentoran FC)	16
	Tom McCOURT	(Larne FC)	16

No clubs promoted or relegated

IRISH CUP FINAL   (Windsor Park, Belfast – 01/05/1993 – 8,500)

BANGOR FC (BANGOR)   1-1   Ards FC (Newtownards)
Glendinning 88'   *McCourt 86'*

Bangor: Eachus, Canning, Glendinning, Muldoon (Surgeon), Brown, O'Connor, Hill, Magee (McCreadie), McCallan, Byrne, McEvoy.

Ards: Vance, McDonald, Leeman, Mitchell, Jeffrey, Bustard, Beattie, Connell, Erskine, McCourt, Davies.

IRISH CUP FINAL REPLAY   (Windsor Park, Belfast – 08/05/1993 – 6,000)

BANGOR FC (BANGOR)   1-1 (aet)   Ards FC (Newtownards)
Glendinning 35'   *Erskine 02'*

Ards: Vance, McDonald, Leeman, Mitchell, Jeffrey, Bustard, Beattie (Kavanagh), Connell, Erskine, McCourt, Davies (Campbell).

Bangor: Eachus, Canning, Glendinning, Hill, Brown, O'Connor, Surgeon, McCreadie (Magee), McCallan, Byrne, McEvoy (Muldoon).

IRISH CUP FINAL 2ND REPLAY (Windsor Park, Belfast – 11/05/1993 – 5,000)

BANGOR FC (BANGOR)　　　　　　　　1-0　　　　　　　　Ards FC (Newtownards)

Byrne 89'

Bangor: Eachus, Canning, Glendinning, Muldoon, Brown, O'Connor, Hill, McCreadie, McCallan (Magee), Byrne, McEvoy.

Ards: Vance, McDonald, Leeman, Mitchell, Jeffrey, Bustard, Beattie (Kavanagh), Connell, Erskine, McCourt, Davies (Campbell).

Semi-finals

Ards FC (Newtownards)	3-2	Cliftonville FC (Belfast)
Bangor FC (Bangor)	3-1	Glentoran FC (Belfast)

Quarter-finals

Distillery FC (Lisburn)	0-0, 1-4	Ards FC (Newtownards)
Dundela FC (Belfast)	1-2	Glentoran FC (Belfast)
Larne FC (Larne)	1-1, 0-2	Cliftonville FC (Belfast)
Linfield FC (Belfast)	1-2	Bangor FC (Bangor)

1993-94

Irish League 1993-94 Season	Ards	Ballyclare C.	Ballymena U.	Bangor	Carrick R.	Cliftonville	Coleraine	Crusaders	Distillery	Glenavon	Glentoran	Larne	Linfield	Newry Town	Omagh Town	Portadown
Ards FC	■	2-0	1-2	5-3	3-3	1-2	3-2	2-4	1-0	4-1	1-0	4-0	0-3	9-0	3-3	1-2
Ballyclare Comrades FC	1-0	■	1-1	3-0	0-3	0-0	0-1	0-0	2-2	1-1	2-1	1-0	1-2	1-2	4-1	2-0
Ballymena United FC	0-2	2-3	■	1-2	0-2	2-1	1-0	0-0	1-1	1-3	3-2	2-0	0-1	0-0	1-3	1-1
Bangor FC	0-2	4-2	1-0	■	5-1	2-1	2-0	2-1	1-2	1-0	0-3	2-1	0-1	3-1	4-2	1-1
Carrick Rangers FC	1-2	2-4	2-5	3-2	■	1-0	1-1	3-2	2-2	1-5	1-2	2-1	1-2	0-3	0-0	1-6
Cliftonville FC	6-2	0-2	0-2	1-0	3-1	■	1-2	2-1	1-1	0-1	1-1	0-1	2-2	1-1	1-1	1-1
Coleraine FC	4-0	3-2	5-2	3-1	3-2	0-0	■	0-2	0-2	1-1	2-1	2-2	1-1	2-0	0-1	
Crusaders FC	3-1	4-0	1-0	4-0	3-0	1-1	2-0	■	2-2	2-4	3-2	3-1	1-1	2-1	3-0	1-1
Distillery FC	3-2	4-0	4-1	1-2	2-0	1-2	1-2	1-2	■	1-1	0-2	0-1	2-2	1-0	1-1	1-6
Glenavon FC	1-0	5-2	3-2	3-1	8-0	0-1	2-1	2-0	1-0	■	2-1	6-1	3-2	5-0	1-0	2-2
Glentoran FC	2-0	3-0	1-1	2-2	3-1	1-4	5-3	0-1	0-2	0-1	■	0-0	0-2	4-0	3-1	1-3
Larne FC	4-1	1-1	5-1	1-1	1-1	0-3	3-3	1-1	1-2	0-2	2-2	■	0-2	0-3	4-2	0-5
Linfield FC	2-1	5-0	2-1	1-0	2-1	3-1	5-0	0-1	3-0	0-0	2-0	3-0	■	1-0	4-1	2-2
Newry Town FC	1-3	2-0	1-2	1-2	2-2	0-3	0-0	0-2	0-1	1-1	1-1	2-0	1-1	■	1-2	0-2
Omagh Town FC	1-2	2-0	1-2	0-1	3-3	0-1	1-0	0-1	0-1	1-2	2-3	1-0	1-3	1-0	■	1-2
Portadown FC	1-0	4-0	5-0	2-0	6-1	1-1	4-0	3-0	1-0	3-1	1-0	4-0	0-2	1-1	5-0	■

	Irish League	Pd	Wn	Dw	Ls	GF	GA	Pts	
1.	LINFIELD FC (BELFAST)	30	21	7	2	63	22	70	
2.	Portadown FC (Portadown)	30	20	8	2	76	21	68	
3.	Glenavon FC (Lurgan)	30	21	5	4	69	29	68	
4.	Crusaders FC (Belfast)	30	17	7	6	53	30	58	
5.	Bangor FC (Bangor)	30	14	3	13	45	49	45	
6.	Ards FC (Newtownards)	30	13	2	15	59	55	41	
7.	Distillery FC (Lisburn)	30	11	8	11	41	40	41	
8.	Cliftonville FC (Belfast)	30	11	10	9	41	32	40	-3
9.	Glentoran FC (Belfast)	30	10	7	13	46	43	37	
10.	Coleraine FC (Coleraine)	30	10	7	13	41	50	37	
11.	Ballymena United FC (Ballymena)	30	9	6	15	37	55	33	
12.	Ballyclare Comrades FC (Ballyclare)	30	9	6	15	35	57	33	
13.	Carrick Rangers FC (Carrickfergus)	30	6	7	17	42	81	25	
14.	Newry Town FC (Newry)	30	5	9	16	26	52	24	
15.	Omagh Town FC (Omagh)	30	6	5	19	32	58	23	
16.	Larne FC (Larne)	30	5	7	18	30	62	22	
		480	188	104	188	736	736	668	

Note: Cliftonville FC (Belfast) had 3 points deducted for fielding an unregistered player in a league match.

Top goalscorers 1993-94

1)	Darren ERSKINE	(Ards FC)	22
	Stephen McBRIDE	(Glenavon FC)	22
3)	Garry HAYLOCK	(Linfield FC)	21
4)	Trevor SMITH	(Portadown FC)	19
5)	Brian ROBSON	(Carrick Rangers FC)	15

Promotion/relegation was introduced from season 1995-96 when the league was re-structured to a Premier Division and a Division 1 each comprising 8 teams. The top 8 clubs over the 1993-94 and 1994-95 seasons formed the new Premier Division with the remaining 8 clubs forming the new Division 1.

IRISH CUP FINAL   (The Oval, Belfast – 07/05/1994 – 10,000)

LINFIELD FC (BELFAST)	2-0	Bangor FC (Bangor)

Peebles 45', Fenton 90'

Linfield: Lamont, A. Dornan, Easton, Peebles, J. Spiers (Doherty), Beatty, Campbell, Gorman, Haylock, Fenlon, Baillie.

Bangor: Dalton, Canning, Glendinning, E.Spiers, Brown, O'Connor, Hill. McCaffrey, McCallan, Magee (Surgeon), McEvoy.

Semi-finals

Bangor FC (Bangor)	2-0	Portadown FC (Portadown)
Glenavon FC (Lurgan)	0-3	Linfield FC (Belfast)

Quarter-finals

Distillery FC (Lisburn)	2-4	Glenavon FC (Lurgan)
Glentoran FC (Belfast)	0-2	Bangor FC (Bangor)
Linfield FC (Belfast)	0-0, 1-0	Cliftonville FC (Belfast)
Omagh Town FC (Omagh)	1-2	Portadown FC (Portadown)

1994-95

Irish League 1994-95 Season	Ards	Ballyclare C.	Ballymena U.	Bangor	Carrick R.	Cliftonville	Coleraine	Crusaders	Distillery	Glenavon	Glentoran	Larne	Linfield	Newry Town	Omagh Town	Portadown
Ards FC	■	3-0	4-1	2-0	2-0	1-2	1-2	0-0	2-1	2-2	2-3	3-1	3-1	4-0	1-1	1-4
Ballyclare Comrades FC	1-4	■	1-3	2-0	1-3	0-2	1-2	1-2	0-4	0-3	0-4	3-0	2-1	2-3	7-2	0-1
Ballymena United FC	1-2	2-2	■	0-3	2-2	0-1	1-1	0-2	2-3	0-1	3-3	0-0	2-1	1-1	0-2	3-2
Bangor FC	3-1	2-2	2-3	■	0-0	0-0	3-3	1-1	2-2	1-0	1-3	1-1	0-0	2-2	2-1	0-2
Carrick Rangers FC	4-1	2-1	2-1	0-3	■	2-1	2-2	2-6	1-3	0-5	2-3	1-2	0-1	2-0	0-4	1-2
Cliftonville FC	1-0	2-2	1-0	1-1	6-1	■	0-0	2-2	0-3	3-1	1-0	2-0	1-2	2-2	0-1	1-2
Coleraine FC	2-2	1-1	0-0	3-3	3-3	1-2	■	0-1	0-1	2-1	1-0	4-0	2-1	3-0	1-1	3-1
Crusaders FC	1-2	3-0	2-1	1-0	1-0	1-0	3-3	■	2-1	1-3	1-2	4-1	1-0	4-0	1-1	2-1
Distillery FC	0-3	2-0	2-1	1-2	2-1	1-1	0-2	0-3	■	1-3	3-2	2-4	1-1	2-2	1-1	1-4
Glenavon FC	3-0	4-2	3-1	2-2	4-4	2-2	1-4	0-0	3-0	■	3-1	5-1	4-0	4-0	1-1	1-0
Glentoran FC	4-1	3-1	2-0	1-0	2-2	2-3	1-1	0-2	1-0	1-3	■	3-1	2-2	2-1	0-0	1-6
Larne FC	0-1	0-0	2-3	0-1	1-2	1-2	0-2	1-3	0-1	0-5	0-4	■	0-4	1-1	0-2	0-1
Linfield FC	1-1	2-1	3-0	0-5	1-1	0-0	1-2	1-1	0-0	4-0	1-1	6-0	■	2-0	1-1	2-2
Newry Town FC	1-3	1-3	0-8	1-1	6-1	1-1	4-1	2-5	0-3	2-3	0-0	1-0	0-4	■	0-2	1-1
Omagh Town FC	1-3	4-2	1-2	0-0	4-1	0-0	1-1	0-1	2-3	3-2	0-0	2-0	0-3	3-2	■	1-1
Portadown FC	1-0	1-1	2-2	3-1	5-4	3-4	3-0	0-1	2-1	2-4	0-2	0-1	1-2	4-0	2-0	■

	Irish League	Pd	Wn	Dw	Ls	GF	GA	Pts
1.	CRUSADERS FC (BELFAST)	30	20	7	3	58	25	67
2.	Glenavon FC (Lurgan)	30	18	6	6	76	40	60
3.	Portadown FC (Portadown)	30	15	5	10	59	41	50
4.	Ards FC (Newtownards)	30	15	5	10	55	42	50
5.	Glentoran FC (Belfast)	30	14	8	8	53	41	50
6.	Cliftonville FC (Belfast)	30	13	11	6	44	32	50
7.	Coleraine FC (Coleraine)	30	12	13	5	52	39	49
8.	Linfield FC (Belfast)	30	11	11	8	48	34	44
9.	Omagh Town FC (Omagh)	30	10	12	8	42	38	42
10.	Distillery FC (Lisburn	30	12	6	12	45	47	42
11.	Bangor FC (Bangor)	30	8	14	8	42	38	38
12.	Ballymena United FC (Ballymena)	30	7	8	15	43	53	29
13.	Carrick Rangers FC (Carrickfergus)	30	7	7	16	46	75	28
14.	Ballyclare Comrades FC (Ballyclare)	30	5	6	19	39	66	21
15.	Newry Town FC (Newry)	30	4	9	17	34	74	21
16.	Larne FC (Larne)	30	3	4	23	18	69	13
		480	174	132	174	754	754	654

Top goalscorers 1994-95

1)	Glenn FERGUSON	(Glenavon FC)	27
2)	Glenn HUNTER	(Crusaders FC)	19
3)	Darren ERSKINE	(Ards FC)	17
	Stephen McBRIDE	(Glenavon FC)	17
5)	Garry HAYLOCK	(Linfield FC)	15
	Trevor SMITH	(Glentoran FC)	15

The League was split into a Premier Division and Division 1 (8 clubs each) from the next season with automatic promotion and relegation between the divisions to be introduced.

Qualification for the new Premier Division was decided on the top 8 clubs combined "position total" over the 1993-1994 and 1994-95 seasons and not on the actual "points" total.

	Team	1993-94	1994-95	Total	Pts	
1.	Glenavon FC (Lurgan)	3	2	5	128	
2.	Crusaders FC (Belfast)	4	1	5	125	
3.	Portadown FC (Portadown)	2	3	5	118	
4.	Linfield FC (Belfast)	1	8	9	114	
5.	Ards FC (Newtownards)	6	4	10	91	
6.	Cliftonville FC (Belfast)	8	6	14	90	
7.	Glentoran FC (Belfast)	9	5	14	87	
8.	Bangor FC (Bangor)	5	11	16	83	
9.	Coleraine FC (Coleraine)	10	7	17	86	
10.	Distillery FC (Lisburn)	7	10	17	83	
11.	Ballymena United FC (Ballymena)	11	12	23	62	
12.	Omagh Town FC (Omagh)	16	9	25	65	
13.	Ballyclare Comrades FC (Ballyclare)	12	14	26	54	
14.	Carrick Rangers FC (Carrickfergus)	13	13	26	53	
15.	Newry Town FC (Newry)	14	15	29	45	
16.	Larne FC (Larne)	15	16	31	35	
		136	136	272	1319	

As a result of this system Bangor FC finished above Coleraine FC who had actually won more points (86 to 83) and Ballymena United FC finished above Omagh Town FC who had won more actual points (65 to 62).

	Actual Playing Record	Pd	Wn	Dw	Ls	GF	GA	Pts	
1.	Glenavon FC (Lurgan)	60	39	11	10	145	69	128	
2.	Crusaders FC (Belfast)	60	37	14	9	111	55	125	
3.	Portadown FC (Portadown)	60	35	13	12	135	62	118	
4.	Linfield FC (Belfast)	60	32	18	10	111	56	114	
5.	Ards FC (Newtownards)	60	28	7	25	114	97	91	
6.	Cliftonville FC (Belfast)	60	24	21	15	85	64	90	-3
7.	Glentoran FC (Belfast)	60	24	15	21	99	84	87	
8.	Coleraine FC (Coleraine)	60	22	20	18	93	89	86	
9.	Bangor FC (Bangor)	60	22	17	21	87	87	83	
10.	Distillery FC (Lisburn)	60	23	14	23	86	87	83	
11.	Omagh Town FC (Omagh)	60	16	17	27	74	96	65	
12.	Ballymena United FC (Ballymena)	60	16	14	30	80	108	62	
13.	Ballyclare Comrades FC (Ballyclare)	60	14	12	34	74	123	54	
14.	Carrick Rangers FC (Carrickfergus)	60	13	14	33	88	156	53	
15.	Newry Town FC (Newry)	60	9	18	33	60	126	45	
16.	Larne FC (Larne)	60	8	11	41	48	131	35	
		960	362	236	362	1490	1490	1319	

IRISH CUP FINAL   (The Oval, Belfast – 07/05/1995 – 6,000)

LINFIELD FC (BELFAST)   3-1   Carrick Rangers FC (Carrickfergus)
Haylock 18', 56', McCoosh 85'   *Gilmore 40'*

Linfield: Lamont, Dornan, Easton, Peebles (McCoosh 81'), Spiers, Beatty, Campbell, Gorman, Haylock, Fenlon, Baillie.

Carrick: Miskelly, Wilson, Gilmore, Muldoon, Gordon, Coulter, Kirk, McDermott, Donaghey (Doherty 79'), Ferris, MacAuley (Crawford 73').

Semi-finals

Ards FC (Newtownards)	0-0, 1-2	Linfield FC (Belfast)
Carrick Rangers FC (Carrickfergus)	1-0	Portadown FC (Portadown)

Quarter-finals

Ards FC (Newtownards)	3-2	Glenavon FC (Lurgan)
Carrick Rangers FC (Carrickfergus)	2-1	Bangor FC (Bangor)
Linfield FC (Belfast)	1-1, 1-0	Loughgall FC (Loughgall)
Portadown FC (Portadown)	1-1, 1-0	Cliftonville FC (Belfast)

1995-96

Irish Premier League 1995-96 Season	Ards	Bangor	Cliftonville	Crusaders	Glenavon	Glentoran	Linfield	Portadown
Ards FC		2-1	2-2	0-1	1-2	0-2	1-2	0-1
		3-0	3-0	0-0	1-1	1-4	2-3	1-1
Bangor FC	0-1		2-3	0-2	1-2	1-1	0-2	0-0
	2-1		3-2	1-2	0-1	1-6	1-2	0-3
Cliftonville FC	1-0	1-1		2-1	0-1	1-0	0-0	0-4
	0-0	2-1		1-4	22	0-0	1-1	0-3
Crusaders FC	2-0	1-0	1-1		1-0	1-3	4-2	3-3
	1-2	2-0	1-0		1-2	2-1	3-0	3-1
Glenavon FC	3-1	0-1	1-1	1-1		1-3	2-2	7-0
	3-0	1-0	1-2	4-0		2-3	0-3	0-1
Glentoran FC	3-1	3-0	2-1	2-2	1-2		3-0	3-3
	3-2	1-1	1-1	3-1	0-2		0-3	1-1
Linfield FC	0-0	2-1	3-1	0-1	2-1	2-0		0-1
	0-0	0-0	0-0	1-2	0-3	0-4		1-0
Portadown FC	1-3	4-3	4-1	1-1	2-1	3-2	1-1	
	3-1	4-2	6-1	1-1	2-1	3-1	3-2	

	Premier Division	Pd	Wn	Dw	Ls	GF	GA	Pts	
1.	PORTADOWN FC (PORTADOWN)	28	16	8	4	61	40	56	
2.	Crusaders FC (Belfast)	28	15	7	6	45	32	52	
3.	Glentoran FC (Belfast)	28	13	7	8	56	38	46	
4.	Glenavon FC (Lurgan)	28	13	5	10	47	32	44	
5.	Linfield FC (Belfast)	28	11	8	9	34	35	41	
6.	Cliftonville FC (Belfast)	28	6	11	11	27	48	29	
7.	Ards FC (Newtownards)	28	6	7	15	29	43	25	
8.	Bangor FC (Bangor)	28	3	5	20	23	54	14	R
		224	83	58	83	322	322	307	

The Premier Division was to be extended to 10 clubs from the 1996-97 season, so the next season (1995-96) the bottom club of the Premier Division automatically entered a play-off against the 3rd placed team in Division 1 for a place in the Premier Division. The top 2 teams of Division 1 were promoted automatically.

Top goalscorers 1995-96

1)	Garry HAYLOCK	(Portadown FC)	19
2)	Stephen BAXTER	(Crusaders FC)	10
	Peter KENNEDY	(Portadown FC)	10
4)	Glenn FERGUSON	(Glenavon FC)	9
	Glenn HUNTER	(Crusaders FC)	9
	Glen LITTLE	(Glentoran FC)	9
	Stephen McBRIDE	(Glenavon FC)	9

Irish League First Division 1995-96 Season

	Ballyclare C.	Ballymena U.	Carrick R.	Coleraine	Distillery	Larne	Newry Town	Omagh Town
Ballyclare Comrades FC	■	0-1	3-2	0-2	0-3	1-1	1-2	0-5
	■	1-3	2-1	1-0	0-2	2-3	1-1	3-2
Ballymena United FC	2-1	■	1-2	4-3	1-1	2-2	3-0	2-0
	0-0	■	3-1	1-2	0-1	0-0	0-0	2-0
Carrick Rangers FC	0-3	0-2	■	2-5	0-0	1-0	1-0	2-0
	3-0	1-1	■	0-3	0-0	1-0	3-1	2-3
Coleraine FC	1-3	4-0	5-1	■	4-2	3-2	5-0	2-1
	2-0	1-1	6-0	■	2-1	1-0	8-0	5-2
Distillery FC	0-1	1-3	2-1	1-1	■	0-1	1-1	0-1
	1-2	0-1	3-1	1-1	■	1-0	2-1	3-2
Larne FC	0-1	0-1	3-1	1-2	3-1	■	1-1	1-3
	2-0	0-0	0-1	0-2	2-0	■	1-2	2-2
Newry Town FC	3-0	1-0	1-0	1-2	0-2	2-0	■	2-2
	2-0	1-2	2-3	1-4	2-5	3-2	■	1-2
Omagh Town FC	3-0	2-2	6-2	0-4	0-0	1-1	4-0	■
	1-3	0-0	1-0	2-2	3-1	1-3	1-0	■

	Division 1	Pd	Wn	Dw	Ls	GF	GA	Pts	
1.	Coleraine FC (Coleraine)	28	21	4	3	82	28	67	P
2.	Ballymena United FC (Ballymena)	28	13	10	5	38	25	49	
3.	Omagh Town FC (Omagh)	28	12	7	9	50	43	43	
4.	Distillery FC (Lisburn)	28	10	7	11	35	34	37	
5.	Ballyclare Comrades FC (Ballyclare)	28	10	3	15	29	48	33	
6.	Carrick Rangers FC (Carrickfergus)	28	9	3	16	32	56	30	
7.	Larne FC (Larne)	28	7	7	14	31	36	28	
8.	Newry Town FC (Newry)	28	7	5	16	31	58	26	
		224	89	46	89	330	330	313	

IRISH CUP FINAL (Windsor Park, Belfast – 04/05/1996 – 10,000)

GLENTORAN FC (BELFAST)   1-0   Glenavon FC (Lurgan)

Little 85'

Glentoran: D. Devine, Nixon, Finlay, Walker, J. Devine, Parker, T. Smith, Little, Coyle, Batey, J. McBride.

Glenavon: Straney, J. Smyth, Glendinning, Murphy, Gould, G. Smyth, Johnston, Shepherd, Ferguson, McBride (McCoy 77'), Shipp.

Semi-finals

Glenavon FC (Lurgan)	1-1, 4-1	Portadown FC (Portadown)
Glentoran FC (Belfast)	2-2, 2-1	Crusaders FC (Belfast)

Quarter-finals

Crusaders FC (Belfast)	2-0	Linfield FC (Belfast)
Glenavon FC (Lurgan)	3-1	Carrick Rangers FC (Carrickfergus)
Glentoran FC (Belfast)	0-0, 4-2	Ballymena United FC (Ballymena)
Portadown FC (Portadown)	2-1	Ards FC (Newtownards)

1996-97

Irish Premier League 1996-97 Season	Ards	Cliftonville	Coleraine	Crusaders	Glenavon	Glentoran	Linfield	Portadown
Ards FC	■	0-1	3-3	1-5	2-2	3-0	4-1	2-2
	■	0-2	1-4	0-0	0-0	4-3	2-3	2-3
Cliftonville FC	2-1	■	1-1	0-2	2-0	1-0	0-3	0-0
	0-1	■	0-1	1-1	0-0	0-2	2-4	1-1
Coleraine FC	0-0	1-1	■	3-1	1-1	0-0	1-1	0-2
	1-0	0-1	■	1-0	1-1	3-2	1-3	1-1
Crusaders FC	2-2	3-0	0-0	■	1-0	1-1	3-0	2-1
	3-1	2-1	1-1	■	2-2	2-3	0-1	2-0
Glenavon FC	1-1	1-0	1-1	1-2	■	1-2	3-1	1-2
	2-1	4-0	2-3	0-0	■	2-1	2-1	1-0
Glentoran FC	2-0	1-1	1-0	4-0	2-1	■	0-2	2-0
	0-0	1-1	1-0	1-1	2-2	■	1-1	2-3
Linfield FC	3-1	2-3	0-1	0-0	0-2	0-0	■	0-2
	0-0	1-1	2-3	0-1	3-0	0-0	■	1-0
Portadown FC	5-0	1-0	2-3	1-0	1-1	0-1	0-2	■
	0-1	4-1	2-2	0-2	2-1	1-1	0-0	■

	Premier Division	**Pd**	**Wn**	**Dw**	**Ls**	**GF**	**GA**	**Pts**	
1.	CRUSADERS FC (BELFAST)	28	12	10	6	39	26	46	
2.	Coleraine FC (Coleraine)	28	10	13	5	37	31	43	
3.	Glentoran FC (Belfast)	28	10	11	7	36	30	41	
4.	Portadown FC (Portadown)	28	10	8	10	36	32	38	
5.	Linfield FC (Belfast)	28	10	8	10	35	33	38	
6.	Glenavon FC (Lurgan)	28	8	11	9	35	34	35	
7.	Cliftonville FC (Belfast)	28	7	9	12	23	38	30	
8.	Ards FC (Newtownards)	28	5	10	13	33	50	25	PO
		224	72	80	72	274	274	296	

Top goalscorers 1996-97

1) Garry HAYLOCK   (Portadown FC)   16
2) Glenn FERGUSON   (Glenavon FC)   12
   Glenn HUNTER   (Crusaders FC)   12
4) Stephen BAXTER   (Crusaders FC)   11
5) David McCALLAN   (Coleraine FC)   10

Promotion/Relegation Play-off

Bangor FC (Bangor)   0-1, 0-1   Ards FC (Newtownards)

The Premier Division was extended to 10 clubs for the next season

Irish League First Division 1996-97 Season	Ballyclare C.	Ballymena U.	Bangor	Carrick R.	Distillery	Larne	Newry Town	Omagh Town
Ballyclare Comrades FC		2-2	0-2	2-0	2-2	4-0	0-2	4-0
		0-1	0-1	1-2	1-0	3-1	0-2	3-1
Ballymena United FC	3-0		0-0	2-1	1-0	1-0	3-1	0-1
	4-1		2-1	1-0	0-1	4-2	2-0	3-1
Bangor FC	3-1	2-1		1-0	0-1	2-0	1-2	3-0
	3-0	0-3		1-0	2-1	1-2	2-2	3-4
Carrick Rangers FC	0-4	0-2	2-1		0-1	2-3	0-2	1-1
	4-2	1-2	0-2		2-4	3-1	1-2	2-5
Distillery FC	0-1	0-1	1-4	1-0		0-0	0-1	0-1
	0-3	1-1	0-1	2-0		1-3	1-2	1-2
Larne FC	1-1	0-1	3-1	0-0	4-4		1-0	1-0
	1-3	1-3	0-1	1-0	2-4		2-1	0-1
Newry Town FC	3-2	1-0	0-1	1-2	1-0	2-2		0-1
	1-2	0-1	1-1	1-1	0-1	1-3		1-2
Omagh Town FC	0-2	0-4	1-0	2-1	1-1	2-0	2-2	
	1-0	0-1	2-2	3-1	2-3	0-1	1-0	

	Division 1	Pd	Wn	Dw	Ls	GF	GA	Pts	
1.	Ballymena United FC (Ballymena)	28	21	2	5	49	17	65	P
2.	Omagh Town FC (Omagh)	28	15	5	8	40	39	50	P
3.	Bangor FC (Bangor)	28	15	4	9	42	29	49	PO
4.	Ballyclare Comrades FC (Ballyclare)	28	11	4	13	44	42	37	
5.	Newry Town FC (Newry)	28	10	5	13	32	35	35	
6.	Distillery FC (Lisburn)	28	10	4	14	31	37	34	
7.	Larne FC (Larne)	28	9	5	14	34	48	32	
8.	Carrick Rangers FC (Carrickfergus)	28	5	3	20	26	51	18	
		224	96	32	96	298	298	320	

Promoted: Dungannon Swifts FC (Dungannon), Limavady United FC (Limavady)

IRISH CUP FINAL   (Windsor Park, Belfast – 03/05/1997 – 18,222 – restricted on police advice)

GLENAVON FC (LURGAN)   1-0   Cliftonville FC (Belfast)

Grant 23'

Glenavon: O'Neill, Caffrey, Glendinning, Doherty, Byrne, Smyth, Johnston, McCoy (Murphy 66'), Ferguson, Grant, Gregg (Williamson 78').

Cliftonville: Reece, Hill (Strang 64'), Flynn, Tabb, Davey, O'Neill, McCann, Collins, Small (Toland 78') Stokes, Donnelly.

Semi-finals

Cliftonville FC (Belfast)	3-1	Loughgall FC (Loughgall)
Glenavon FC (Lurgan)	5-0	Omagh Town FC (Omagh)

Quarter-finals

Cliftonville FC (Belfast)	3-1	Crusaders FC (Belfast)
Glenavon FC (Lurgan)	4-0	Coagh United FC (Coagh)
Loughgall FC (Loughgall)	1-1, 1-0	Coleraine FC (Coleraine)
Omagh Town FC (Omagh)	2-2, 1-0	Limavady United FC (Limavady)

1997-98

Irish Premier League 1997-98 Season	Ards	Ballymena	Cliftonville	Coleraine	Crusaders	Glenavon	Glentoran	Linfield	Omagh	Portadown
Ards FC	■	0-2	1-1	1-0	0-1	1-1	0-2	1-5	1-2	0-1
	■	2-1	2-3	0-0	1-1	3-4	1-1	0-1	2-2	1-1
Ballymena United FC	1-1	■	4-0	2-2	1-0	2-1	1-2	0-2	2-1	1-2
	3-1	■	2-0	1-0	2-3	0-0	0-2	1-1	4-2	1-2
Cliftonville FC	2-2	5-2	■	1-0	0-1	1-0	1-1	0-3	1-0	1-0
	1-0	0-2	■	3-1	2-2	1-1	0-2	2-1	4-0	3-1
Coleraine FC	2-2	0-0	0-2	■	0-0	0-1	1-5	0-0	1-1	2-0
	2-1	0-1	5-1	■	4-0	1-2	2-1	1-0	4-3	0-1
Crusaders FC	1-0	3-4	0-2	3-0	■	4-1	0-3	1-2	2-2	2-1
	4-0	4-2	2-2	1-3	■	3-2	0-2	1-0	1-0	1-3
Glenavon FC	0-0	3-3	0-0	4-0	2-2	■	1-0	2-4	2-4	3-0
	1-2	1-2	0-0	1-1	2-0	■	1-0	2-3	2-2	1-5
Glentoran FC	2-0	2-2	1-0	3-0	1-1	1-0	■	1-1	2-0	2-1
	3-0	1-2	0-2	1-0	1-1	0-1	■	0-3	1-0	1-1
Linfield FC	2-0	1-0	0-1	1-0	0-0	2-0	3-0	■	0-0	1-1
	4-0	0-0	0-1	1-1	0-0	1-1	2-0	■	1-1	0-0
Omagh Town FC	2-1	3-0	0-1	1-3	1-2	2-1	0-5	0-3	■	0-2
	2-4	3-2	0-1	1-3	1-1	2-2	1-1	1-0	■	1-2
Portadown FC	1-0	4-0	1-2	1-1	3-2	2-0	2-0	0-0	1-1	■
	1-0	1-1	0-2	0-1	1-1	2-1	3-2	0-2	3-1	■

	Premier Division	**Pd**	**Wn**	**Dw**	**Ls**	**GF**	**GA**	**Pts**	
1.	CLIFTONVILLE FC (BELFAST)	36	20	8	8	49	37	68	
2.	Linfield FC (Belfast)	36	17	13	6	50	19	64	
3.	Portadown FC (Portadown)	36	17	9	10	50	38	60	
4.	Glentoran FC (Belfast)	36	17	8	11	52	34	59	
5.	Crusaders FC (Belfast)	36	13	12	11	51	51	51	
6.	Ballymena United FC (Ballymena)	36	14	9	13	54	55	51	
7.	Coleraine FC (Coleraine)	36	11	10	15	41	47	43	
8.	Glenavon FC (Lurgan)	36	9	12	15	47	56	39	
9.	Omagh Town FC (Omagh)	36	7	10	19	43	68	31	PO
10.	Ards FC (Newtownards)	36	4	11	21	31	63	23	R
		360	129	102	129	468	468	489	

Cliftonville FC 1-1 Glenavon FC on 03/01/1998 was abandoned and replayed on 28/01/1998 with a 1-0 scoreline.
Coleraine FC 1-0 Linfield FC on 29/11/1997 was abandoned after 83minutes but the result was allowed to stand.
Coleraine FC 3-3 Glenavon FC on 17/01/1998 was awarded 0-1 as Coleraine fielded an ineligible player.

Top goalscorers 1997-98

1)	Vinny ARKINS	(Portadown FC)	22	
2)	Tony GRANT	(Glenavon FC)	15	
	Justin McBRIDE	(Glentoran FC)	15	
4)	Glenn FERGUSON	(Glenavon FC/Linfield FC)	14	(6/8)
	Michael McHUGH	(Omagh Town FC)	14	
	Barry O'CONNOR	(Cliftonville FC)	14	
	Barry PATTON	(Ballymena United FC)	14	

Promotion/Relegation Play-off

Bangor FC (Bangor)   0-5, 0-1   Omagh Town FC (Omagh)

Irish League First Division 1997-98 Season	Ballyclare C.	Bangor	Carrick R.	Distillery	Dungannon	Larne	Limavady	Newry Town
Ballyclare Comrades FC	■	2-1	2-0	2-4	3-2	2-0	0-1	2-2
	■	0-1	1-1	0-3	0-1	3-1	3-2	0-2
Bangor FC	2-1	■	2-1	2-2	3-0	1-0	4-0	1-2
	1-2	■	3-2	3-0	1-2	2-0	0-0	1-0
Carrick Rangers FC	2-3	1-2	■	1-2	1-3	2-1	0-3	0-5
	0-1	0-2	■	1-2	0-0	0-1	3-1	1-4
Distillery FC	1-5	1-2	1-0	■	1-2	3-0	0-0	1-0
	2-1	2-1	1-0	■	2-2	0-2	3-0	2-2
Dungannon Swifts FC	3-1	3-4	4-1	0-2	■	4-3	2-1	1-1
	4-5	3-3	2-1	2-2	■	4-2	9-0	0-4
Larne FC	3-2	0-3	1-2	0-1	2-2	■	1-0	0-1
	1-1	1-2	1-0	3-2	1-2	■	3-2	0-2
Limavady United FC	0-2	0-1	1-1	0-1	1-3	1-2	■	1-3
	1-2	0-3	4-0	0-5	1-2	5-1	■	2-0
Newry Town FC	1-0	1-0	3-0	1-1	1-0	6-0	3-1	■
	3-1	0-0	3-0	2-1	2-1	3-0	4-1	■

	Division 1	Pd	Wn	Dw	Ls	GF	GA	Pts	
1.	Newry Town FC (Newry)	28	20	5	3	61	18	65	P
2.	Bangor FC (Bangor)	28	18	4	6	51	26	58	PO
3.	Distillery FC (Lisburn)	28	15	6	7	48	34	51	
4.	Dungannon Swifts FC (Dungannon)	28	14	6	8	63	49	48	
5.	Ballyclare Comrades FC (Ballyclare)	28	13	3	12	47	45	42	
6.	Larne FC (Larne)	28	8	2	18	30	58	26	
7.	Limavady United FC (Limavady)	28	6	2	20	29	61	20	
8.	Carrick Rangers FC (Carrickfergus)	28	3	2	23	21	59	11	
		224	97	30	97	349	349	321	

IRISH CUP FINAL (Windsor Park, Belfast – 02/05/1998 – 8,250)

GLENTORAN FC (BELFAST)   1-0 (aet)   Glenavon FC (Lurgan)

Kennedy 97'

Glentoran: Russell, Nixon, Kennedy, Walker, Devine, Leeman (Livingstone 97'), Mitchell, Finlay, Kirk, Batey, Hamill.

Glenavon: O'Neill (Welch 108'), Wright (O'Flaherty 102'), Glendinning, Quigley, Cash (Murphy 80'), Smyth, McCoy, Byrne, Shepherd, Grant, Caffrey.

Semi-finals

Crusaders FC (Belfast)	1-3	Glenavon FC (Lurgan)
Glentoran FC (Belfast)	2-1	Linfield FC (Belfast)

Quarter-finals

Crusaders FC (Belfast)	4-0	Institute FC (Londonderry)
Distillery FC (Belfast)	0-2	Glenavon FC (Lurgan)
Glentoran FC (Belfast)	3-1	Armagh City FC (Armagh)
Linfield FC (Belfast)	3-0	Portadown FC (Portadown)

1998-99

Irish Premier League 1998-99 Season	Ballymena	Cliftonville	Coleraine	Crusaders	Glenavon	Glentoran	Linfield	Newry Town	Omagh	Portadown
Ballymena United FC		2-2	0-1	1-2	0-1	3-6	4-2	0-0	1-2	2-2
		1-2	1-0	2-0	1-0	1-1	1-0	1-1	0-0	1-0
Cliftonville FC	1-0		0-0	1-1	0-0	0-0	0-1	0-2	2-1	0-0
	0-1		1-1	2-3	2-2	2-4	1-1	1-4	2-1	0-2
Coleraine FC	0-1	3-1		0-2	0-0	0-1	2-1	3-0	1-0	0-2
	2-1	1-1		0-2	1-3	1-3	0-0	2-2	2-1	1-0
Crusaders FC	1-0	1-0	2-0		1-1	0-3	3-2	3-2	2-0	0-0
	2-0	2-1	0-1		1-0	0-0	1-4	2-0	5-0	1-1
Glenavon FC	1-0	0-0	3-1	2-0		0-1	2-2	1-1	6-1	2-2
	0-0	0-1	3-1	3-0		0-1	1-1	1-2	2-0	1-0
Glentoran FC	1-0	1-1	5-0	2-1	1-0		1-2	5-1	2-0	3-1
	2-1	0-1	5-4	1-4	5-2		0-1	1-3	2-0	1-0
Linfield FC	4-1	2-1	1-1	4-2	3-1	1-1		2-1	3-0	3-1
	1-0	1-0	2-1	2-1	2-0	1-1		2-2	2-0	2-2
Newry Town FC	1-0	1-0	1-0	3-0	0-2	1-0	2-1		1-1	1-2
	0-0	2-1	1-1	0-0	1-0	1-2	2-1		0-2	3-2
Omagh Town FC	0-5	1-1	1-1	1-2	0-3	1-4	1-5	2-3		1-0
	1-4	2-2	2-0	0-0	0-3	0-2	1-3	1-3		1-0
Portadown FC	2-1	3-0	1-2	0-0	2-2	1-3	1-1	2-1	3-0	
	1-3	0-1	3-0	0-1	1-1	0-3	0-2	2-3	2-0	

	Premier Division	Pd	Wn	Dw	Ls	GF	GA	Pts	
1.	GLENTORAN FC (BELFAST)	36	24	6	6	74	35	78	
2.	Linfield FC (Belfast)	36	20	10	6	68	39	70	
3.	Crusaders FC (Belfast)	36	18	8	10	48	39	62	
4.	Newry Town FC (Newry)	36	17	9	10	52	46	60	
5.	Glenavon FC (Lurgan)	36	13	12	11	49	35	51	
6.	Ballymena United FC (Ballymena)	36	11	8	17	40	42	41	
7.	Coleraine FC (Coleraine)	36	10	9	17	34	53	39	
8.	Portadown FC (Portadown)	36	9	10	17	41	47	37	
9.	Cliftonville FC (Belfast)	36	7	14	15	31	47	35	PO
10.	Omagh Town FC (Omagh)	36	5	6	25	25	79	21	R
		360	134	92	134	462	462	494	

Note: Glenavon FC 1-0 Portadown FC on 26/12/1998 was abandoned after 60 minutes due to storm. It was replayed on 26/01/1999 and finished with a 2-2 scoreline.

Top goalscorers 1998-99

1)	Vinny ARKINS	(Portadown FC)	19
2)	Des GORMAN	(Newry Town FC)	17
3)	Stephen BAXTER	(Glenavon FC)	16
4)	Glenn FERGUSON	(Linfield FC)	15
5)	Rory HAMILL	(Glentoran FC)	13
	David LARMOUR	(Linfield FC)	13

Promotion/Relegation Play-off

Ards FC (Newtownards)   0-1, 2-4   Cliftonville FC (Belfast)

** Distillery FC (Lisburn) changed their club name to Lisburn Distillery FC (Lisburn) for the next season.

Irish League First Division 1998-99 Season	Ards	Ballyclare C.	Bangor	Carrick R.	Distillery	Dungannon	Larne	Limavady
Ards FC		0-2	1-2	2-4	0-2	1-0	5-1	1-2
		2-1	2-0	1-0	2-0	2-1	1-0	3-0
Ballyclare Comrades FC	2-0		0-1	1-1	3-1	6-0	0-1	4-4
	2-5		3-0	2-1	0-1	1-2	2-0	5-1
Bangor FC	0-0	1-4		2-2	1-0	3-1	1-0	3-4
	1-0	3-2		0-1	2-0	2-1	0-1	0-0
Carrick Rangers FC	1-0	0-2	0-1		2-3	0-1	1-1	4-0
	4-1	3-2	1-2		0-1	3-2	1-0	2-3
Distillery FC	4-3	1-0	2-0	3-2		3-1	0-0	1-0
	0-2	3-3	0-3	0-0		1-1	1-0	3-1
Dungannon Swifts FC	1-2	1-1	1-3	2-0	2-1		1-0	1-2
	2-1	1-0	3-2	2-1	1-5		1-1	2-0
Larne FC	0-2	5-3	2-0	3-2	0-1	0-1		0-0
	0-2	4-1	0-1	1-0	0-1	1-0		4-0
Limavady United FC	0-3	2-2	1-3	2-3	0-1	3-3	1-0	
	2-3	0-1	3-0	1-2	1-5	1-1	3-3	

	Division 1	Pd	Wn	Dw	Ls	GF	GA	Pts	
1.	Distillery FC (Lisburn)	28	17	4	7	44	30	55	P **
2.	Ards FC (Newtownards)	28	16	1	11	47	34	49	PO
3.	Bangor FC (Bangor)	28	15	3	10	37	35	48	
4.	Ballyclare Comrades FC (Ballyclare)	28	11	5	12	55	44	38	
5.	Dungannon Swifts FC (Dungannon)	28	11	5	12	36	46	38	
6.	Carrick Rangers FC (Carrickfergus)	28	10	4	14	41	41	34	
7.	Larne FC (Larne)	28	9	5	14	28	32	32	
8.	Limavady United FC (Limavady)	28	6	7	15	37	63	25	
		224	95	34	95	325	325	319	

Promoted: Armagh City FC (Armagh), Institute FC (Londonderry)

Division 1 was extended to 10 clubs for the next season

IRISH CUP FINAL (not played)

PORTADOWN FC (PORTADOWN)   w/o   Cliftonville FC (Belfast)

The final was not played as Cliftonville FC had fielded Simon Gribben as a substitute in the semi-final match against Linfield FC. Gribben was ineligible to appear as he had played in the competition for an amateur club Kilmore Recreation FC in an earlier round before being signed by Cliftonville FC. Cliftonville were expelled from the competition and the cup was awarded by default to Portadown FC.

Semi-finals

Cliftonville FC (Belfast)	1-1, 1-0	Linfield FC (Belfast)
Portadown FC (Portadown)	2-0	Ballymena United FC (Ballymena)

Quarter-finals

Carrick Rangers FC (Carrickfergus)	1-2	Cliftonville FC (Belfast)
Coleraine FC (Coleraine)	1-2	Portadown FC (Portadown)
Distillery FC (Lisburn)	1-1, 1-2	Ballymena United FC (Ballymena)
Linfield FC (Belfast)	0-0, 2-1	Glenavon FC (Lurgan)

1999-2000

Irish Premier League 1999-2000 Season	Ballymena	Cliftonville	Coleraine	Crusaders	Glenavon	Glentoran	Linfield	Lisburn Dis.	Newry Town	Portadown
Ballymena United FC	■	2-2	2-2	2-2	2-0	2-1	0-1	2-1	0-0	2-4
	■	2-1	0-0	1-1	0-3	0-0	1-3	1-1	2-2	1-1
Cliftonville FC	3-2	■	0-0	1-1	1-1	2-0	2-3	2-0	0-2	2-0
	1-1	■	1-4	1-1	1-2	1-2	0-1	0-0	3-2	1-2
Coleraine FC	1-0	0-1	■	4-2	2-0	1-2	2-1	3-0	4-1	4-0
	1-1	1-1	■	1-2	1-1	1-2	0-1	3-0	2-0	4-1
Crusaders FC	2-2	1-1	0-2	■	0-4	2-2	0-4	2-0	1-0	0-1
	3-0	1-1	1-3	■	3-1	1-0	1-1	1-2	1-0	2-4
Glenavon FC	2-0	4-0	0-0	1-0	■	3-3	3-0	1-2	3-0	1-1
	0-0	0-1	0-1	2-1	■	3-3	0-0	2-0	2-1	3-1
Glentoran FC	3-2	3-0	2-0	1-2	2-1	■	1-1	2-0	2-1	1-0
	3-1	1-1	3-2	2-0	1-2	■	1-0	3-1	0-3	5-3
Linfield FC	3-2	1-2	3-0	0-0	1-1	1-2	■	1-0	3-2	2-1
	3-0	3-1	3-1	0-0	1-0	2-0	■	3-2	3-1	3-1
Lisburn Distillery FC	2-1	1-0	1-2	0-1	1-2	1-0	1-4	■	2-3	2-1
	3-4	0-1	1-3	2-2	1-1	2-0	1-2	■	0-1	2-1
Newry Town FC	2-2	3-2	0-1	2-0	0-2	3-4	0-3	1-1	■	0-1
	3-1	3-1	3-0	1-1	0-1	1-0	0-3	2-1	■	1-1
Portadown FC	0-2	3-0	3-2	4-2	2-0	4-0	0-2	3-2	5-0	■
	2-2	2-2	3-6	2-1	1-3	1-0	1-1	4-1	0-0	■

	Premier Division	Pd	Wn	Dw	Ls	GF	GA	Pts	
1.	LINFIELD FC (BELFAST)	36	24	7	5	67	30	79	
2.	Coleraine FC (Coleraine)	36	18	7	11	64	42	61	
3.	Glenavon FC (Lurgan)	36	17	10	9	55	34	61	
4.	Glentoran FC (Belfast)	36	18	7	11	59	51	61	
5.	Portadown FC (Portadown)	36	15	7	14	64	62	52	
6.	Newry Town FC (Newry)	36	11	7	18	44	58	40	
7.	Crusaders FC (Belfast)	36	9	13	14	41	55	40	
8.	Ballymena United FC (Ballymena)	36	6	16	14	45	62	34	
9.	Cliftonville FC (Belfast)	36	7	13	16	38	59	34	PO
10.	Lisburn Distillery FC (Lisburn)	36	9	5	22	39	63	32	R
		360	134	92	134	516	516	494	

Top goalscorers 1999-2000

1) Vinny ARKINS   (Portadown FC)   29
2) Tony GRANT   (Glenavon FC)   20
   Glenn HUNTER   (Ballymena United FC) 20
4) Stuart ELLIOTT   (Glentoran FC)   16
5) Darren LARMOUR   (Linfield FC)   15

Promotion/Relegation Play-offs

Ards FC (Newtownards)   0-2, 0-1   Cliftonville FC (Belfast)

Irish League First Division 1999-2000 Season	Ards	Armagh	Ballyclare C.	Bangor	Carrick R.	Dungannon	Institute	Larne	Limavady	Omagh Town
Ards FC		1-1	2-1	1-1	3-0	2-2	4-2	1-0	1-2	1-1
		4-1	4-0	1-1	2-1	0-0	3-1	1-1	2-0	0-1
Armagh City FC	1-2		3-4	0-1	0-2	1-2	3-1	1-0	0-0	2-2
	0-4		5-0	2-0	0-0	3-3	3-3	6-2	2-0	0-1
Ballyclare Comrades FC	2-2	1-2		2-1	0-1	2-1	1-2	1-5	0-1	0-3
	2-2	2-0		1-2	3-1	1-2	0-2	0-1	1-3	0-3
Bangor FC	1-1	2-0	2-0		2-1	1-0	2-1	0-2	2-0	2-2
	2-2	2-0	3-3		1-1	2-0	1-2	3-0	0-3	1-2
Carrick Rangers FC	1-4	4-0	3-0	2-4		3-1	2-4	1-2	0-1	1-3
	0-0	0-0	0-2	1-4		2-2	0-3	2-1	6-3	0-0
Dungannon Swifts FC	2-2	2-1	1-3	0-1	1-0		1-3	1-0	0-3	0-2
	3-1	1-3	1-3	3-4	2-3		0-0	3-1	1-2	2-0
Institute FC	0-2	7-0	2-1	0-3	2-0	2-1		2-3	3-2	0-0
	0-0	0-1	4-1	3-3	1-1	0-2		1-2	2-0	0-0
Larne FC	2-2	1-0	2-2	3-1	2-2	2-0	2-2		2-2	0-2
	0-2	1-1	4-0	2-1	3-0	1-1	1-0		0-0	3-2
Limavady United FC	1-0	1-1	1-0	2-0	2-2	0-0	3-1	1-2		1-2
	1-1	3-2	2-0	3-2	1-1	2-1	0-1	4-1		2-3
Omagh Town FC	1-2	0-3	1-0	1-1	3-1	2-0	1-1	3-2	0-2	
	1-3	2-2	7-0	2-1	2-0	4-1	4-1	2-0	0-0	

	Division 1	Pd	Wn	Dw	Ls	GF	GA	Pts	
1.	Omagh Town FC (Omagh)	36	20	10	6	65	35	70	P
2.	Ards FC (Newtownards)	36	16	16	4	65	36	64	PO
3.	Limavady United FC (Limavady)	36	17	9	10	54	42	60	
4.	Bangor FC (Bangor)	36	16	9	11	60	49	57	
5.	Larne FC (Larne)	36	15	9	12	56	53	54	
6.	Institute FC (Londonderry)	36	14	9	13	59	53	51	
7.	Armagh City FC (Armagh)	36	10	10	16	50	61	40	
8.	Dungannon Swifts FC (Dungannon)	36	9	8	19	43	62	35	
9.	Carrick Rangers FC (Carrickfergus)	36	8	10	18	45	64	34	
10.	Ballyclare Comrades FC (Ballyclare)	36	8	4	24	39	81	28	
		360	133	94	133	535	535	493	

IRISH CUP FINAL (Windsor Park, Belfast – 06/05/2000 – 8,355)

GLENTORAN FC (BELFAST)　　　　　　1-0　　　　　　　　　　Portadown FC (Portadown)

Gilzean 59'

Glentoran: Gough, Nixon, Kennedy, Dickson, McCombe, Young, McCann, Hamill, Russell (Gilzean 54'), Batey, Elliott.

Portadown: Dalton, Brown, O'Hara, Byrne, Strain, Major, Larkin, Clarke, Sheridan, Arkins, Hill (Davidson 65').

Semi-finals

Coleraine FC (Coleraine)	0-0, 0-1	Portadown FC (Portadown)
Glentoran FC (Belfast)	3-2	Linfield FC (Belfast)

Quarter-finals

Coleraine FC (Coleraine)	1-0	Ballymena United FC (Ballymena)
Linfield FC (Belfast)	2-2, 2-1 (aet)	Dungannon Swifts FC (Dungannon)
Lisburn Distillery FC (Lisburn)	0-2	Portadown FC (Portadown)
Newry Town FC (Newry)	1-3	Glentoran FC (Belfast)

2000-2001

Irish Premier League 2000-01 Season	Ballymena	Cliftonville	Coleraine	Crusaders	Glenavon	Glentoran	Linfield	Newry Town	Omagh Town	Portadown
Ballymena United FC	■	2-1	0-1	0-1	1-0	1-3	1-1	0-1	2-1	3-3
	■	2-2	0-1	2-1	1-2	0-3	1-5	1-0	1-2	1-1
Cliftonville FC	3-1	■	1-0	0-3	2-1	1-1	1-4	1-0	1-2	0-0
	2-2	■	1-1	1-1	4-2	1-0	1-3	2-2	2-2	5-3
Coleraine FC	1-0	2-2	■	1-2	0-2	1-1	1-1	5-2	1-3	1-0
	0-2	3-1	■	2-2	0-1	5-2	1-0	2-1	0-0	3-3
Crusaders FC	3-1	1-2	2-3	■	0-2	0-1	1-3	2-2	0-0	2-1
	2-3	0-4	1-1	■	4-3	1-1	0-2	1-3	2-1	0-1
Glenavon FC	4-0	1-0	2-1	1-0	■	0-0	0-4	1-0	3-0	3-3
	2-1	1-0	1-1	1-1	■	3-0	0-1	0-1	3-0	1-2
Glentoran FC	2-1	1-0	0-1	2-0	2-2	■	2-0	0-0	1-2	4-1
	1-1	4-0	1-1	1-1	1-1	■	0-1	1-0	2-0	3-1
Linfield FC	2-2	3-0	3-1	3-1	3-0	2-0	■	1-3	3-2	0-0
	4-1	4-2	0-3	0-0	4-2	1-1	■	2-0	1-1	4-1
Newry Town FC	0-2	2-1	0-0	2-0	1-4	0-0	0-0	■	1-0	0-0
	5-2	0-3	2-0	3-2	1-2	1-3	0-2	■	0-2	4-3
Omagh Town FC	0-1	2-2	3-1	0-2	1-2	1-3	0-0	2-3	■	2-1
	4-0	0-1	1-2	2-2	1-1	2-1	1-5	2-2	■	0-0
Portadown FC	3-2	1-1	1-0	3-2	1-2	4-1	1-0	4-0	1-4	■
	1-0	0-2	0-1	1-1	0-0	0-3	0-3	2-0	1-2	■

	Premier Division	**Pd**	**Wn**	**Dw**	**Ls**	**GF**	**GA**	**Pts**	
1.	LINFIELD FC (BELFAST)	36	22	9	5	75	31	75	
2.	Glenavon FC (Lurgan)	36	18	8	10	56	42	62	
3.	Glentoran FC (Belfast)	36	15	12	9	52	37	57	
4.	Coleraine FC (Coleraine)	36	14	11	11	48	44	53	
5.	Cliftonville FC (Belfast)	36	12	11	13	53	57	47	
6.	Newry Town FC (Newry)	36	12	8	16	42	55	44	
7.	Omagh Town FC (Omagh)	36	11	10	15	48	54	43	
8.	Portadown FC (Portadown)	36	10	11	15	48	60	41	
9.	Crusaders FC (Belfast)	36	8	11	17	44	59	35	PO
10.	Ballymena United FC (Ballymena)	36	9	7	20	41	68	34	R
		360	131	98	131	507	507	491	

Note: Glenavon FC 0-0 Linfield FC on 12/08/2000 was later awarded 0-1 to Linfield FC as Glenavon FC had fielded Gerard McMahon who was ineligible to play at the time.

Top goalscorers 2000-01

1)	David LARMOUR	(Linfield FC)	17
2)	Glenn FERGUSON	(Linfield FC)	16
	Garry HAYLOCK	(Glenavon FC)	16
4)	Jody TOLAN	(Coleraine FC)	15
5)	Barry CURRAN	(Omagh Town FC)	14
	Tom McCALLION	(Cliftonville FC)	14

Promotion/Relegation Play-off

Lisburn Distillery FC (Lisburn)   2-1, 1-3   Crusaders FC (Belfast)

Irish League First Division 2000-01 Season	Ards	Armagh	Ballyclare C.	Bangor	Carrick R.	Dungannon	Institute	Larne	Limavady	Lisburn Dis.
Ards FC		2-2	3-1	0-0	3-0	1-0	1-1	0-2	3-0	2-3
		2-2	1-0	1-1	2-0	3-1	2-0	1-1	0-0	3-3
Armagh City FC	2-1		2-2	2-1	2-1	1-3	1-1	2-0	2-0	0-3
	4-0		4-2	1-1	3-0	1-1	3-0	2-2	3-2	1-1
Ballyclare Comrades FC	0-4	1-4		1-1	4-3	1-2	1-0	1-1	0-1	0-3
	1-3	1-2		1-1	2-1	1-1	0-1	1-1	1-2	1-2
Bangor FC	0-2	2-1	2-0		6-1	1-0	2-1	2-0	2-0	0-0
	0-2	3-1	1-0		5-0	3-1	1-4	3-2	1-2	2-1
Carrick Rangers FC	0-3	2-3	2-1	0-3		0-1	2-1	1-0	2-0	0-1
	0-5	0-3	2-2	2-0		1-1	2-3	2-5	2-2	0-1
Dungannon Swifts FC	1-2	3-5	1-0	0-2	1-1		1-2	3-2	0-0	2-3
	1-1	1-2	3-0	1-2	4-1		1-1	0-1	1-1	1-1
Institute FC	0-2	3-1	3-1	1-2	3-2	0-1		1-2	0-0	2-1
	3-1	3-3	3-1	3-1	1-0	1-1		1-2	2-0	1-2
Larne FC	0-3	1-1	2-0	0-1	4-0	2-1	1-2		1-4	2-8
	0-3	2-3	3-2	1-1	3-0	1-3	1-1		1-1	2-4
Limavady United FC	2-2	0-2	0-1	2-2	1-4	1-2	1-6	2-0		1-1
	0-2	1-2	1-2	4-0	1-0	1-0	3-0	0-1		0-0
Lisburn Distillery FC	0-0	2-1	2-2	1-1	3-0	1-0	0-2	1-1	2-1	
	1-3	2-1	1-0	3-0	4-0	1-1	2-1	1-3	1-0	

	Division 1	Pd	Wn	Dw	Ls	GF	GA	Pts	
1.	Ards FC (Newtownards)	36	21	10	5	69	31	73	P
2.	Lisburn Distillery FC (Lisburn)	36	20	11	5	66	37	71	PO
3.	Armagh City FC (Armagh)	36	19	9	8	74	52	66	
4.	Bangor FC (Bangor)	36	18	9	9	56	42	63	
5.	Institute FC (Londonderry)	36	16	7	13	58	48	55	
6.	Larne FC (Larne)	36	12	9	15	53	62	45	
7.	Dungannon Swifts FC (Dungannon)	36	10	11	15	45	48	41	
8.	Limavady United FC (Limavady)	36	9	10	17	37	51	37	
9.	Ballyclare Comrades FC (Ballyclare)	36	5	6	23	35	69	23	
10.	Carrick Rangers FC (Carrickfergus)	36	6	4	26	34	87	22	
		360	136	88	136	527	527	496	

IRISH CUP FINAL (Windsor Park, Belfast – 05/05/2001 – 14,000)

GLENTORAN FC (BELFAST)   1-0 (aet)   Linfield FC (Belfast)

Halliday 99'

Glentoran: Gough, Nixon, Ferguson, Young, Leeman, Smyth, McCann, Halliday, Fitzgerald, Batey, Lockhart (McBride 62').

Linfield: Robinson, McDonald (Collier 88'), Easton (Morgan 91'), Marks, Murphy, Arthur, Larmour, Scates, Ferguson, Kelly (Beatty 75'), Baillie.

Semi-finals

Glenavon FC (Lurgan)	1-3	Linfield FC (Belfast)
Lisburn Distillery FC (Lisburn)	1-2	Glentoran FC (Belfast)

Quarter-finals

Glenavon FC (Lurgan)	2-1	Ballyclare Comrades FC (Ballyclare)
Institute FC (Londonderry)	1-2	Glentoran FC (Belfast)
Linfield FC (Belfast)	1-0	Bangor FC (Bangor)
Portadown FC (Portadown)	0-1	Lisburn Distillery FC (Lisburn)

2001-2002

Irish Premier League 2001-02 Season	Ards	Cliftonville	Coleraine	Crusaders	Glenavon	Glentoran	Linfield	Newry Town	Omagh Town	Portadown
Ards FC	■	0-0	1-4	2-1	1-2	0-4	2-2	4-2	0-2	0-2
	■	2-1	1-2	0-0	0-0	0-0	2-4	1-4	1-3	1-4
Cliftonville FC	1-0	■	2-3	3-0	0-1	1-2	3-1	0-2	1-0	0-0
	2-0	■	2-4	1-1	1-0	0-4	1-2	2-2	0-2	0-0
Coleraine FC	5-0	3-2	■	1-2	4-0	1-0	0-2	1-2	2-1	1-3
	1-2	0-0	■	1-0	2-1	2-0	1-0	1-0	2-1	2-4
Crusaders FC	1-1	1-3	2-1	■	2-0	0-1	1-3	4-3	7-2	1-2
	3-0	0-2	0-2	■	3-4	0-2	0-2	1-1	1-2	0-1
Glenavon FC	0-1	2-1	1-2	0-1	■	1-1	2-0	0-1	3-4	2-3
	2-1	1-3	1-0	0-2	■	0-0	0-2	1-1	5-1	1-4
Glentoran FC	1-1	0-0	2-1	6-0	5-1	■	3-3	2-2	2-0	1-0
	4-0	2-0	1-0	1-0	1-0	■	1-0	3-0	4-1	2-2
Linfield FC	2-1	2-0	0-0	0-0	0-0	2-2	■	4-0	3-2	1-1
	4-0	2-2	3-1	4-0	1-3	0-0	■	1-1	0-1	0-1
Newry Town FC	1-1	1-4	7-1	0-1	1-1	0-1	0-2	■	0-1	1-1
	0-1	1-0	3-1	2-2	1-1	0-1	0-2	■	1-1	2-2
Omagh Town FC	1-1	1-1	3-2	3-0	2-0	2-1	1-1	0-1	■	1-2
	1-0	0-0	2-2	2-2	1-1	2-2	1-0	4-2	■	3-0
Portadown FC	3-1	3-1	3-0	3-1	0-0	1-0	0-0	6-1	3-1	■
	2-1	1-1	3-4	4-1	4-0	0-1	1-2	4-0	2-0	■

	Premier Division	Pd	Wn	Dw	Ls	GF	GA	Pts
1.	PORTADOWN FC (PORTADOWN)	36	22	9	5	75	34	75
2.	Glentoran FC (Belfast)	36	21	11	4	63	23	74
3.	Linfield FC (Belfast)	36	17	11	8	64	35	62
4.	Coleraine FC (Coleraine)	36	19	2	15	64	58	59
5.	Omagh Town FC (Omagh)	36	15	9	12	55	55	54
6.	Cliftonville FC (Belfast)	36	9	11	16	37	46	38
7.	Glenavon FC (Lurgan)	36	9	9	18	37	57	36
8.	Newry Town FC (Newry)	36	8	12	16	40	62	36
9.	Crusaders FC (Belfast)	36	9	7	20	41	65	34
10.	Ards FC (Newtownards)	36	6	9	21	30	71	27
		360	135	90	135	506	506	495

Top goalscorers 2001-02

1) Vinny ARKINS   (Portadown FC)   30
2) Chris MORGAN   (Linfield FC)   17
3) Gary HAMILTON   (Portadown FC)   15
4) Andrew CRAWFORD   (Omagh Town FC)   12
   Gerard McMAHON   (Glenavon FC)   12

The Premier Division was extended to 12 clubs and Division 1 was reduced to 8 clubs for the next season.

Irish League First Division 2001-02 Season	Armagh	Ballyclare C.	Ballymena	Bangor	Carrick R.	Dungannon	Institute	Larne	Limavady	Lisburn Dis.
Armagh City FC		2-2	0-2	1-1	3-0	0-3	0-3	0-4	0-5	1-4
		3-4	0-0	0-0	1-3	0-2	2-1	0-3	4-0	0-2
Ballyclare Comrades FC	1-0		3-3	1-3	1-1	2-3	0-0	0-3	0-2	0-4
	0-4		2-2	3-2	1-0	4-3	0-1	2-2	0-1	0-1
Ballymena United FC	3-1	2-2		1-0	3-2	0-1	2-0	4-4	4-3	1-2
	2-1	2-0		3-2	3-1	1-1	2-5	2-1	1-2	0-1
Bangor FC	0-0	1-1	1-1		2-1	0-1	0-2	0-0	3-0	0-0
	1-1	1-1	1-3		1-1	1-0	0-1	1-3	2-0	0-3
Carrick Rangers FC	1-0	1-0	0-2	2-2		0-1	0-3	1-0	2-1	0-1
	2-0	0-0	0-2	0-1		1-3	1-1	0-1	1-0	1-5
Dungannon Swifts FC	4-2	3-0	3-1	0-0	0-1		1-2	4-2	2-2	3-1
	0-2	4-0	2-2	2-1	1-1		1-3	0-1	0-0	0-1
Institute FC	4-1	7-0	2-1	3-1	2-1	1-2		2-1	3-0	2-4
	0-1	2-1	1-1	5-1	4-4	3-1		3-0	0-0	1-2
Larne FC	2-1	3-1	1-1	0-3	1-0	0-0	1-2		7-1	0-1
	1-1	1-1	1-1	1-0	0-0	1-1	1-1		0-3	0-1
Limavady United FC	1-3	0-0	1-0	3-1	3-1	0-1	1-4	0-1		1-1
	3-3	3-5	2-1	0-3	5-2	1-2	1-1	1-2		1-2
Lisburn Distillery FC	2-0	0-1	3-0	0-1	0-1	2-0	0-1	1-2	3-1	
	1-2	3-1	4-0	1-2	1-1	3-0	0-0	2-1	2-1	

	Division 1	**Pd**	**Wn**	**Dw**	**Ls**	**GF**	**GA**	**Pts**	
1.	Lisburn Distillery FC (Lisburn)	36	24	4	8	64	26	76	P
2.	Institute FC (Londonderry)	36	22	8	6	76	35	74	P
3.	Dungannon Swifts FC (Dungannon)	36	17	8	11	55	42	59	
4.	Larne FC (Larne)	36	14	11	11	52	42	53	
5.	Ballymena United FC (Ballymena)	36	14	11	11	59	56	53	
6.	Bangor FC (Bangor)	36	10	12	14	40	45	42	
7.	Limavady United FC (Limavady)	36	10	7	19	49	68	37	
8.	Carrick Rangers FC (Carrickfergus)	36	9	9	18	34	55	36	
9.	Ballyclare Comrades FC (Ballyclare)	36	7	12	17	40	73	33	
10.	Armagh City FC (Armagh)	36	8	8	20	40	67	32	
		360	135	90	135	509	509	495	

IRISH CUP FINAL (Windsor Park, Belfast – 11/05/2002 – 11,129)

LINFIELD FC (BELFAST)　　　　2-1　　　　Portadown FC (Portadown)

Morgan 15', 21'　　　　　　　　　　　　　　　　　　　　　　　　　　　*Neill 06'*

Linfield: Mannus, Collier, McShane (N. Kelly 80'), Hunter, King (D. Murphy 67'), R. Kelly, Morgan (McBride 56'), Gorman, Ferguson, Marks, Baillie.

Portadown: Keenan, Douglas, O'Hara, McCann, Feeney (Ogden 26'), Major, Clarke (A. Hamilton 63'), Collins, G.Hamilton, Arkins, Neill.

Semi-finals

Linfield FC (Belfast)	4-0	Killyleagh Y.C. (Killyleagh)
Portadown FC (Portadown)	2-0	Coleraine FC (Coleraine)

Quarter-finals

Coleraine FC (Coleraine)	2-0	Dungannon Swifts FC (Dungannon)
Glentoran FC (Belfast)	1-1, 3-4	Portadown FC (Portadown)
Killyleagh Y.C. (Killyleagh)	1-0	Ballyclare Comrades FC (Ballyclare)
Linfield FC (Belfast)	3-0	Glenavon FC (Lurgan)

2002-2003

Irish Premier League 2002-03 Season	Ards	Cliftonville	Coleraine	Crusaders	Glenavon	Glentoran	Institute	Linfield	Lisburn D.	Newry T.	Omagh T.	Portadown
Ards FC	■	0-0	---	0-0	1-0	0-2	1-0	---	1-0	1-0	---	0-3
	■	1-0	0-1	2-2	1-1	1-2	3-0	1-2	1-0	2-1	0-0	0-2
Cliftonville FC	1-0	■	---	0-1	2-0	0-2	1-3	---	1-0	1-0	---	---
	0-0	■	1-1	0-1	3-1	0-1	2-0	2-2	0-2	1-0	2-1	0-3
Coleraine FC	3-1	4-3	■	---	4-1	2-2	2-1	3-1	2-1	---	0-1	1-1
	2-0	1-1	■	3-3	3-2	0-0	3-0	3-1	1-4	3-0	0-1	1-0
Crusaders FC	0-0	1-0	0-2	■	2-0	---	---	0-5	1-1	0-2	2-0	0-5
	0-2	0-0	0-0	■	0-2	2-4	1-0	1-3	0-2	0-0	0-3	0-4
Glenavon FC	3-0	1-1	---	2-0	■	0-1	0-2	2-2	0-2	3-2	---	---
	1-1	2-1	2-2	1-1	■	0-3	3-1	0-0	1-2	3-2	1-3	0-5
Glentoran FC	---	---	1-0	0-1	---	■	6-1	0-0	---	2-1	0-0	1-0
	3-0	3-0	2-0	4-0	2-0	■	4-1	3-2	2-0	3-1	2-0	0-1
Institute FC	---	---	0-1	2-1	---	0-4	■	2-0	---	0-1	3-1	1-0
	2-0	1-1	1-3	2-0	0-0	1-5	■	1-0	0-1	3-2	0-0	3-3
Linfield FC	1-0	0-0	2-0	---	---	1-1	7-0	■	---	4-0	1-0	3-2
	3-1	2-2	2-0	2-0	1-1	1-1	2-3	■	1-4	3-0	3-1	0-1
Lisburn Distillery FC	0-1	1-1	---	0-1	0-0	1-3	1-1	1-2	■	1-2	---	---
	1-0	0-3	1-1	2-1	0-2	0-1	1-2	0-2	■	2-1	1-2	2-4
Newry Town FC	1-0	1-1	0-0	3-0	2-2	---	---	---	0-1	■	0-1	0-3
	1-3	0-3	0-2	0-3	2-2	0-2	1-0	0-6	1-0	■	1-4	0-0
Omagh Town FC	0-1	2-1	0-2	---	2-0	0-4	4-1	1-1	0-3	---	■	3-5
	0-1	2-1	0-3	2-1	3-1	0-2	3-2	1-1	3-0	0-2	■	1-1
Portadown FC	---	2-1	1-5	---	2-1	3-0	3-3	0-0	1-1	---	5-1	■
	1-1	1-0	1-2	1-0	6-0	2-0	4-1	3-1	3-0	4-2	3-1	■

Premier Division (Championship Group)

		Pd	Wn	Dw	Ls	GF	GA	Pts	
1.	GLENTORAN FC (BELFAST)	38	28	6	4	78	22	90	
2.	Portadown FC (Portadown)	38	24	8	6	89	36	80	
3.	Coleraine FC (Coleraine)	38	21	10	7	66	38	73	
4.	Linfield FC (Belfast)	38	17	12	9	70	41	63	
5.	Omagh Town FC (Omagh)	38	15	6	17	47	57	51	
6.	Institute FC (Londonderry)	38	12	6	20	44	75	42	
7.	Ards FC (Newtownards)	38	12	10	16	27	39	46	
8.	Lisburn Distillery FC (Lisburn)	38	12	6	20	39	49	42	
9.	Cliftonville FC (Belfast)	38	9	14	15	37	43	41	
10.	Glenavon FC (Lurgan)	38	8	12	18	41	67	36	
11.	Crusaders FC (Belfast)	38	9	9	20	26	61	36	
12.	Newry Town FC (Newry)	38	8	7	23	33	69	31	PO
		456	175	106	175	597	597	631	

Premier Division (Phase 1)

		Pd	Wn	Dw	Ls	GF	GA	Pts
1.	Glentoran FC (Belfast)	33	27	3	3	71	16	84
2.	Portadown FC (Portadown)	33	22	5	6	77	29	71
3.	Coleraine FC (Coleraine)	33	18	8	7	56	33	62
4.	Linfield FC (Belfast)	33	15	10	8	60	37	55
5.	Omagh Town FC (Omagh)	33	14	5	14	40	48	47
6.	Institute FC (Londonderry)	33	12	5	16	39	55	41
7.	Lisburn Distillery FC (Lisburn)	33	12	4	17	37	44	40
8.	Ards FC (Newtownards)	33	10	8	15	25	38	38
9.	Cliftonville FC (Belfast)	33	7	12	14	33	41	33
10.	Crusaders FC (Belfast)	33	8	7	18	24	55	31
11.	Glenavon FC (Lurgan)	33	6	11	16	36	62	29
12.	Newry Town FC (Newry)	33	5	6	22	24	64	21
		396	156	84	156	522	522	552

After 33 matches in the Premier Division the league was split with the top 6 teams playing-off for the championship and the remaining 6 teams playing-off against the promotion/relegation play-off.

Note: Glentoran FC 4-0 Crusaders FC, Glentoran FC 3-1 Newry FC, Glentoran FC 4-1 Institute FC and Cliftonville FC 0-1 Glentoran FC were initially awarded 1-0 to Glentoran FC's opponents as Glentoran had fielded the ineligible player Andrew Kilmartin during these games. This decision was revoked on appeal and the original results were allowed to stand.

Top goalscorers 2002-03

1)	Vinny ARKINS	(Portadown FC)	29
2)	Gary HAMILTON	(Portadown FC)	23
3)	Andrew SMITH	(Glentoran FC)	22
4)	Glenn FERGUSON	(Linfield FC)	18
5)	Mark HOLLAND	(Lisburn Distillery FC)	15

Irish League First Division 2002-03 Season	Armagh	Ballyclare C.	Ballymena	Bangor	Carrick R.	Dungannon	Larne	Limavady
Armagh City FC		3-2	2-2	1-3	0-0	1-2	1-1	1-1
		2-1	2-3	1-3	1-2	0-1	1-2	1-2
Ballyclare Comrades FC	2-0		2-4	2-1	2-5	1-1	1-3	4-4
	3-6		0-3	2-3	3-2	1-1	0-4	3-2
Ballymena United FC	2-3	3-0		1-1	3-2	2-0	1-0	1-3
	2-2	3-0		2-3	6-1	5-2	3-2	4-1
Bangor FC	1-0	2-1	1-1		2-1	1-2	1-1	3-0
	2-0	1-0	0-2		3-3	1-0	0-2	1-1
Carrick Rangers FC	5-3	0-0	1-4	1-0		1-1	1-3	5-6
	4-2	3-2	1-4	0-2		0-4	0-3	0-1
Dungannon Swifts FC	1-0	3-0	2-1	2-1	1-2		2-1	1-0
	3-3	1-0	2-2	4-3	12-1		1-0	2-0
Larne FC	1-0	1-0	2-1	1-0	0-1	1-1		0-1
	2-1	0-1	1-3	0-3	1-0	1-4		1-0
Limavady United FC	3-0	3-1	2-1	2-0	3-1	1-2	1-0	
	2-0	1-2	1-1	3-1	4-1	1-2	1-1	

Division 1		Pd	Wn	Dw	Ls	GF	GA	Pts	
1.	Dungannon Swifts FC (Dungannon)	28	18	6	4	61	32	60	P
2.	Ballymena United FC (Ballymena)	28	16	6	6	71	40	54	P
3.	Limavady United FC (Limavady)	28	15	5	8	53	37	50	P
4.	Larne FC (Larne)	28	13	4	11	35	30	43	P
5.	Bangor FC (Bangor)	28	12	5	11	40	39	41	
6.	Carrick Rangers FC (Carrickfergus)	28	8	4	16	44	76	28	
7.	Ballyclare Comrades FC (Ballyclare)	28	6	4	18	36	65	22	
8.	Armagh City FC (Armagh)	28	4	6	18	37	58	18	
		224	92	40	92	377	377	316	

Promotion/Relegation Play-off

Bangor FC (Bangor)　　　　　　　　　0-0, 1-2　　　　　　　　　Newry Town FC (Newry)

Promoted: Ballinamallard United FC (Ballinamallard), Ballymoney United FC (Ballymoney), Brantwood FC (Belfast), Donegal Celtic FC (Belfast), Harland & Wolff Welders FC (Belfast), Loughgall FC (Loughgall), Lurgan Celtic FC (Lurgan), Moyola Park FC (Castledawson)

The Premier Division was extended to 16 clubs and Division 1 was extended to 12 clubs for the next season

IRISH CUP FINAL (Windsor Park, Belfast – 03/05/2003 – 10,000)

COLERAINE FC (COLERAINE)　　　　1-0　　　　　　　　　Glentoran FC (Belfast)

Tolan 11'

Coleraine: O'Hare, Clanachan, Flynn, Gaston, McAuley, Beatty, McCoosh, Hamill, Tolan, P. McAllister (Armstrong 87'), Gorman.

Glentoran: Morris, Nixon, Glendinning, Leeman, Young, Smyth, T. McCann, Lockhart (O'Neill 46'), Smith, Armour (Halliday 65'), T.M. McCann (Walker 73').

Semi-finals

Coleraine FC (Coleraine)	5-2	Omagh Town FC (Omagh)
Portadown FC (Portadown)	1-6	Glentoran FC (Belfast)

Quarter-finals

Ards FC (Newtownards)	0-1	Glentoran FC (Belfast)
Coleraine FC (Coleraine)	2-0	Crusaders FC (Belfast)
Omagh Town FC (Omagh)	1-0	Linfield FC (Belfast)
Portadown FC (Portadown)	5-0	Glenavon FC (Lurgan)

2003-2004

Irish Premier League 2003-04 Season	Ards	Ballymena	Cliftonville	Coleraine	Crusaders	Dungannon	Glenavon	Glentoran	Institute	Larne	Limavady	Linfield	Lisburn D.	Newry T.	Omagh T.	Portadown
Ards FC	■	1-1	0-0	2-2	2-0	0-2	2-4	2-1	2-2	1-1	0-0	0-4	1-1	4-0	2-1	2-1
Ballymena United FC	1-0	■	0-1	3-1	1-1	1-0	4-0	0-0	2-1	1-1	0-3	0-0	1-4	4-0	3-1	1-4
Cliftonville FC	2-1	0-3	■	2-0	0-1	1-0	0-1	1-1	1-2	0-0	3-2	1-4	0-0	1-2	1-2	0-1
Coleraine FC	4-1	4-0	1-0	■	0-1	3-1	2-1	0-1	4-2	0-4	2-1	2-0	0-0	4-3	1-1	3-1
Crusaders FC	0-0	0-0	0-0	0-1	■	0-1	0-4	0-1	3-1	3-2	2-0	1-3	0-1	2-2	4-1	1-2
Dungannon Swifts FC	2-2	0-0	2-2	3-2	2-1	■	3-1	1-4	1-1	2-5	1-2	0-4	2-0	3-0	1-0	1-2
Glenavon FC	1-2	0-3	1-1	0-0	2-1	2-2	■	1-2	0-2	0-4	2-3	0-2	2-2	0-2	0-3	0-3
Glentoran FC	3-0	3-1	1-1	0-1	0-1	1-0	4-0	■	1-0	1-0	2-1	1-3	0-1	4-0	4-0	1-2
Institute FC	0-1	0-4	2-1	2-2	1-3	1-0	1-0	3-1	■	4-1	0-4	0-0	0-2	1-1	1-1	0-3
Larne FC	5-1	1-2	2-1	0-2	0-0	0-2	1-0	1-4	2-4	■	2-1	0-3	0-2	3-3	1-2	2-4
Limavady United FC	0-1	0-1	3-1	3-3	2-3	3-1	2-0	1-0	2-0	0-0	■	0-2	0-3	1-0	3-2	0-6
Linfield FC	2-2	4-1	1-0	0-0	1-0	2-0	3-1	2-1	6-0	1-0	3-2	■	3-0	5-0	2-0	0-0
Lisburn Distillery FC	1-0	2-1	2-1	1-1	2-1	2-0	5-0	1-1	3-2	1-0	0-1	1-1	■	3-2	1-2	1-0
Newry Town FC	0-0	1-1	3-1	0-1	2-1	0-0	4-0	0-0	2-1	3-3	1-1	1-2	1-0	■	1-0	1-2
Omagh Town FC	1-4	2-0	2-3	1-1	0-3	1-3	1-2	1-4	0-3	0-0	2-0	1-3	3-2	3-0	■	2-5
Portadown FC	4-0	0-1	5-1	2-1	4-0	5-0	2-0	2-1	0-0	3-1	0-1	1-1	4-1	2-0	1-0	■

	Premier Division	**Pd**	**Wn**	**Dw**	**Ls**	**GF**	**GA**	**Pts**	
1.	LINFIELD FC (BELFAST)	30	22	7	1	67	16	73	
2.	Portadown FC (Portadown)	30	22	4	4	71	22	70	
3.	Lisburn Distillery FC (Lisburn)	30	16	7	7	45	30	55	
4.	Coleraine FC (Coleraine)	30	14	9	7	48	36	51	
5.	Glentoran FC (Belfast)	30	15	5	10	48	27	50	
6.	Ballymena United FC (Ballymena)	30	13	8	9	41	35	47	
7.	Limavady United FC (Limavady)	30	12	5	13	41	43	41	
8.	Ards FC (Newtownards)	30	9	11	10	36	46	38	
9.	Crusaders FC (Belfast)	30	10	6	14	33	38	36	
10.	Dungannon Swifts FC (Dungannon)	30	10	6	14	36	48	36	
11.	Institute FC (Londonderry)	30	9	7	14	37	53	34	
12.	Newry Town FC (Newry)	30	8	9	13	35	53	33	
13.	Omagh Town FC (Omagh)	30	9	4	17	37	58	31	
14.	Larne FC (Larne)	30	7	8	15	42	51	29	
15.	Cliftonville FC (Belfast)	30	6	8	16	27	45	26	PO
16.	Glenavon FC (Lurgan)	30	4	4	22	24	67	16	R
		480	186	108	186	668	668	666	

Note: Glentoran FC 0-0 Crusaders FC, Limavady FC 0-1 Glentoran FC, Glentoran FC 0-0 Lisburn Distillery FC matches were all awarded as 1-0 wins to Glentoran FC's opponents as Glentoran had fielded the ineligible player Gary Smyth in each match.

Newry FC 1-1 Limavady FC on 17/04/2004 was abandoned after 63 minutes due to a waterlogged pitch but the result stood.

Cliftonville FC vs Glenavon FC on 17/04/2004 was abandoned at half-time due to a waterlogged pitch. The match was replayed on 22/04/2004.

Top goalscorers 2003-04

1) Glenn FERGUSON   (Linfield FC)   25
2) Gary HAMILTON   (Portadown FC)   23
3) Vinny ARKINS   (Portadown FC)   18
4) Stephen PARKHOUSE   (Institute FC)   15
5) Chris MORGAN   (Linfield FC)   12

Promotion/Relegation Play-off

Armagh City FC (Armagh)   0-3, 1-1   Cliftonville FC (Belfast)

Irish League First Division 2003-04 Season	Armagh	Ballinamallard	Ballyclare C.	Ballymoney	Bangor	Brantwood	Carrick R.	Donegal Celtic	H & W Welders	Loughgall	Lurgan Celtic	Moyola Park
Armagh City FC		1-0	0-1	1-0	1-1	3-0	4-1	0-0	2-1	2-0	3-1	1-0
Ballinamallard United FC	2-3		1-2	0-1	1-1	1-0	0-1	0-0	1-0	0-1	0-2	3-2
Ballyclare Comrades FC	1-0	0-1		0-0	0-2	0-1	0-1	0-0	2-1	1-2	1-0	2-1
Ballymoney United FC	0-0	1-0	1-3		0-0	0-0	1-0	0-0	2-1	1-4	5-1	1-1
Bangor FC	1-0	4-0	1-3	0-0		2-0	1-2	0-0	1-3	4-0	1-0	1-0
Brantwood FC	0-2	2-2	2-4	1-2	0-4		2-1	2-2	0-1	0-1	1-1	2-1
Carrick Rangers FC	2-0	1-1	1-1	3-3	2-0	2-3		2-2	0-3	0-1	2-3	1-2
Donegal Celtic FC	0-2	2-1	0-2	2-3	1-2	3-0	0-2		1-2	1-2	6-1	2-0
Harland & Wolff Welders FC	0-1	0-0	2-3	2-0	0-4	1-1	2-2	2-1		0-0	1-1	2-1
Loughgall FC	2-1	4-0	1-1	2-1	6-1	1-0	2-2	1-0	0-0		0-0	4-4
Lurgan Celtic FC	0-1	2-2	2-5	2-0	0-3	1-1	1-1	1-1	0-3	0-2		3-3
Moyola Park FC	2-2	1-3	1-2	3-0	1-1	3-0	3-1	2-5	1-2	0-1	2-2	

Division 1		**Pd**	**Wn**	**Dw**	**Ls**	**GF**	**GA**	**Pts**
1.	Loughgall FC (Loughgall)	22	14	6	2	37	20	48	P
2.	Armagh City FC (Armagh)	22	13	4	5	30	15	43	PO
3.	Ballyclare Comrades FC (Ballyclare)	22	13	4	5	34	21	43
4.	Bangor FC (Bangor)	22	11	6	5	35	20	39
5.	Harland & Wolff Welders FC (Belfast)	22	9	6	7	29	24	33
6.	Ballymoney United FC (Ballymoney)	22	7	8	7	22	26	29
7.	Carrick Rangers FC (Carrickfergus)	22	6	7	9	30	35	25
8.	Donegal Celtic FC (Belfast)	22	5	8	9	29	27	23
9.	Ballinamallard United FC (Ballinamallard)	22	5	6	11	20	31	21
10.	Moyola Park FC (Castledawson)	22	4	6	12	34	41	18
11.	Lurgan Celtic FC (Lurgan)	22	3	9	10	24	44	18	R
12.	Brantwood FC (Belfast)	22	4	6	12	18	38	18	R
		264	94	76	94	342	342	358

Note: Carrick Rangers FC vs Brantwood FC on 10/04/2004 was abandoned and replayed on 11/05/2004 with a final scoreline of 2-3.

Lurgan FC vs Ballymoney FC on 20/04/2004 was abandoned after 20 minutes with a 0-0 scoreline after the referee was injured. The match was replayed on 12/05/2004 with a final scoreline of 2-0.

Promoted: Coagh United FC (Coagh), Dundela FC (Belfast)

IRISH CUP FINAL   (Windsor Park, Belfast – 01/05/2004 – 8,300)

GLENTORAN FC (BELFAST)   1-0   Coleraine FC (Coleraine)

M. Halliday 21'

Glentoran: Morris, Nixon, Glendinning, Melaugh, Leeman, G. Smyth, McCann (Kilmartin), Lockhart, Smith, Halliday (Armour), Keegan (McCallion).

Coleraine: O'Hare, Clanachan, Flynn, Gaston, McAuley (Johnson), Beatty, Curran (Armstrong), Hamill, Tolan, Haveron, Gorman.

Semi-finals

Coleraine FC (Coleraine)	3-1	Limavady United FC (Limavady)
Glentoran FC (Belfast)	4-1	Omagh Town FC (Omagh)

Quarter-finals

Ards FC (Newtownards)	1-2	Omagh Town FC (Omagh)
Limavady United FC (Limavady)	2-0	Glenavon FC (Lurgan)
Linfield FC (Belfast)	0-1	Glentoran FC (Belfast)
Newry Town FC (Newry)	1-1, 1-3	Coleraine FC (Coleraine)

2004-2005

Irish Premier League 2004-05 Season	Ards	Ballymena	Cliftonville	Coleraine	Crusaders	Dungannon	Glentoran	Institute	Larne	Limavady	Linfield	Lisburn D.	Loughgall	Newry City	Omagh T.	Portadown
Ards FC		1-1	3-0	1-2	2-2	1-3	0-3	1-2	0-3	0-1	2-2	0-1	0-0	5-1	2-0	0-1
Ballymena United FC	2-2		1-1	2-2	1-1	1-2	0-3	1-1	0-0	2-1	3-4	2-1	2-1	2-1	1-1	2-0
Cliftonville FC	3-1	0-0		1-4	1-0	1-1	0-1	1-0	2-0	0-2	0-0	1-0	1-3	0-1	2-1	0-2
Coleraine FC	3-0	0-2	3-1		1-1	4-2	0-1	2-4	3-0	1-2	0-4	1-3	2-0	6-1	3-4	2-2
Crusaders FC	0-2	2-3	0-2	1-1		0-3	0-2	1-0	1-1	1-0	1-2	0-0	3-2	0-1	3-1	0-1
Dungannon Swifts FC	7-0	1-2	3-1	0-1	0-0		2-0	3-0	3-1	1-1	1-1	1-1	1-0	1-0	2-0	1-3
Glentoran FC	2-0	4-2	4-0	1-0	4-1	5-0		2-0	3-0	2-0	3-2	1-0	2-0	3-1	3-0	1-2
Institute FC	1-1	1-1	1-2	3-1	2-0	3-2	0-1		3-0	0-3	0-1	1-3	3-0	2-1	0-1	2-1
Larne FC	2-2	0-0	0-0	1-5	5-2	3-2	0-5	2-0		0-4	0-2	0-0	2-3	0-1	2-0	2-3
Limavady United FC	0-1	2-1	0-0	0-3	1-1	3-2	2-2	5-1	6-0		0-1	2-2	1-1	3-2	2-0	0-2
Linfield FC	3-0	0-1	3-1	4-1	2-1	2-1	1-1	3-1	1-1	4-1		5-2	3-0	2-0	6-1	0-0
Lisburn Distillery FC	1-1	0-2	3-1	2-2	3-2	2-0	2-1	3-2	2-1	1-1	0-4		3-1	1-3	6-1	2-0
Loughgall FC	3-1	1-0	0-0	1-5	2-0	1-2	1-3	0-1	0-2	1-1	0-4	2-1		1-1	1-3	0-2
Newry City FC	1-0	1-1	4-2	0-1	2-0	0-4	0-4	4-1	1-3	2-2	0-3	0-0	2-5		2-1	0-6
Omagh Town FC	2-1	0-2	0-5	1-3	1-3	1-4	2-3	0-1	3-0	2-5	1-8	2-3	0-2	2-2		1-2
Portadown FC	2-3	-0	3-0	2-0	0-0	1-2	4-3	4-0	3-0	0-1	0-1	2-1	2-2	2-3	9-0	

	Premier Division	Pd	Wn	Dw	Ls	GF	GA	Pts	
1.	GLENTORAN FC (BELFAST)	30	24	2	4	73	22	74	
2.	Linfield FC (Belfast)	30	22	6	2	78	23	72	
3.	Portadown FC (Portadown)	30	18	4	8	64	29	58	
4.	Dungannon Swifts FC (Dungannon)	30	15	5	10	57	39	50	
5.	Limavady United FC (Limavady)	30	13	9	8	52	36	48	
6.	Coleraine FC (Coleraine)	30	14	5	11	62	47	47	
7.	Lisburn Distillery FC (Lisburn)	30	13	8	9	49	42	47	
8.	Ballymena United FC (Ballymena)	30	11	12	7	40	37	45	
9.	Institute FC (Londonderry)	30	11	3	16	36	50	36	
10.	Newry City FC (Newry)	30	10	5	15	38	63	35	**
11.	Cliftonville FC (Belfast)	30	9	7	14	29	44	34	
12.	Loughgall FC (Loughgall)	30	8	6	16	34	53	30	
13.	Larne FC (Larne)	30	7	7	16	31	60	28	
14.	Ards FC (Newtownards)	30	6	8	16	33	54	26	
15.	Crusaders FC (Belfast)	30	5	9	16	27	48	24	POR
16.	Omagh Town FC (Omagh)	30	5	2	23	32	88	17	R
		480	191	98	191	735	735	671	

** Newry Town FC (Newry) changed their name in the summer of 2004 to Newry City FC after the town was granted city status.

Top goalscorers 2004-05

1) Chris MORGAN (Glentoran FC) 19
2) Kevin RAMSAY (Limavady United FC) 18
3) Jody TOLAN (Coleraine FC) 16
4) Vinny ARKINS (Portadown FC) 15
   Michael HALLIDAY (Glentoran FC) 15

Promotion/Relegation Play-off

Glenavon FC (Lurgan) 1-1, 2-1 (aet) Crusaders FC (Belfast)

Irish League First Division 2004-05 Season	Armagh	Ballinamallard	Ballyclare C.	Ballymoney	Bangor	Carrick R.	Coagh United	Donegal Celtic	Dundela	Glenavon	H & W Welders	Moyola Park
Armagh City FC	■	3-0	1-0	1-0	3-2	3-0	1-1	2-1	1-1	3-1	1-0	2-0
Ballinamallard United FC	0-2	■	2-0	4-3	1-2	2-0	2-5	0-0	0-3	1-1	0-1	0-0
Ballyclare Comrades FC	1-1	1-0	■	1-1	0-0	0-0	2-1	0-3	1-1	0-1	2-4	2-0
Ballymoney United FC	0-1	1-0	0-4	■	0-2	4-3	4-3	2-1	3-1	0-1	0-1	0-1
Bangor FC	1-1	2-0	0-0	4-0	■	0-2	3-2	0-2	0-1	1-1	1-3	1-0
Carrick Rangers FC	0-0	2-0	1-2	3-1	2-0	■	0-2	1-2	2-3	4-2	1-1	0-1
Coagh United FC	1-2	3-0	1-1	0-3	1-3	2-0	■	1-1	1-1	0-3	2-4	2-0
Donegal Celtic FC	0-0	0-0	1-0	3-1	3-0	5-0	1-3	■	1-2	0-2	3-0	0-0
Dundela FC	1-3	2-0	1-2	3-2	1-4	0-1	2-2	1-2	■	0-3	1-1	0-0
Glenavon FC	0-2	4-0	1-0	4-1	1-2	3-0	6-1	1-1	2-0	■	1-0	3-0
Harland & Wolff Welders FC	1-1	3-2	3-1	3-3	3-3	1-1	2-3	1-0	1-0	0-1	■	1-0
Moyola Park FC	0-1	2-0	1-2	1-0	2-2	3-2	1-2	2-4	1-3	1-1	2-1	■

Division 1		Pd	Wn	Dw	Ls	GF	GA	Pts	
1.	Armagh City FC (Armagh)	22	15	7	-	35	11	52	P
2.	Glenavon FC (Lurgan)	22	14	4	4	43	17	46	POP
3.	Donegal Celtic FC (Belfast)	22	10	6	6	34	19	36	
4.	Harland & Wolff Welders FC (Belfast)	22	10	6	6	35	29	36	
5.	Bangor FC (Bangor)	22	9	6	7	33	29	33	
6.	Coagh United FC (Coagh)	22	8	5	9	39	42	29	
7.	Ballyclare Comrades FC (Ballyclare)	22	7	7	8	22	24	28	
8.	Dundela FC (Belfast)	22	7	6	9	28	33	27	
9.	Moyola Park FC (Castledawson)	22	6	5	11	18	29	23	
10.	Carrick Rangers FC (Carrickfergus)	22	6	4	12	25	37	22	
11.	Ballymoney United FC (Ballymoney)	22	6	2	14	29	45	20	R
12.	Ballinamallard United FC (Ballinamallard)	22	3	4	15	14	40	13	R
		264	101	62	101	355	355	365	

Promoted: Banbridge Town FC (Banbridge) and Tobermore United FC (Tobermore)

IRISH CUP FINAL (Windsor Park, Belfast – 07/05/2005)

PORTADOWN FC (PORTADOWN) 5-1 Larne FC (Larne)

Arkins 15', 59', Convery 34', McCann 36', Kelly 48' *Ogden 03'*

Portadown: Murphy, Feeney, Convery, Kelly, O'Hara, Boyle, Collins, Clarke, Neill, McCann (Hamilton 47'), Arkins.

Larne: Spackman, Small, Murphy, Curran, Hughes, Rodgers, Weir, Ogden, Hamlin, Dickson, Bonner.

Semi-finals

Ballymena United FC (Ballymena)	0-1	Larne FC (Larne)
Portadown FC (Portadown)	0-0, 1-0	Glentoran FC (Belfast)

Quarter-finals

Ards FC (Newtownards)	0-1	Portadown FC (Portadown)
Ballymena United FC (Ballymena)	0-0, 4-0	Harland & Wolff Welders FC (Belfast)
Coleraine FC (Coleraine)	1-2	Glentoran FC (Belfast)
Loughgall FC (Loughgall)	1-1, 0-3	Larne FC (Larne)